ALL ABOUT STOCKS

FROM THE INSIDE OUT

Esmé Faerber

PROBUS
PUBLISHING
Chicago, Illinois
Cambridge, England

ISBN 1-55738-806-7

Printed in the United States of America

IPC

CTV/LH

1 2 3 4 5 6 7 8 9 0

Contents

Preface

Writing *All About Stocks* has been a pleasurable experience due in part to the exciting nature of the stock markets. Stock prices and stock markets are constantly changing. There are stocks that have increased in value by several hundred percent in short periods of time, and, at the other extreme, stocks that have faded into oblivion. Moreover, the stock market has achieved new highs throughout the past two decades as well as experiencing one of the largest crashes on October 19, 1987.

Investing in the stock market can have a substantial effect on your financial wealth. This book is written to provide a practical guide for existing and potential stock investors. By understanding the basics of investing, the economic and financial conditions of companies and the nature of stock markets, investors will be better able to assess investment opportunities. Investing your own money in stocks is difficult for most investors, particularly beginning investors, but by knowing what to expect, investors will be able to use strategies to manage their portfolios more effectively.

There are many myths concerning investing in the stock market, and this book does not fall into a category of offering a method to get rich quickly. In fact, many sophisticated investors in the stock market know just how difficult it is to outperform the stock market averages consistently over long periods of time. Investors should also be aware that suggested methods or techniques of beating the stock market may not live up to their expectations.

The first chapter begins with discussion of the fundamentals of investing, what stocks are and the advantages of investing in them.

The second chapter compares the risks and returns of stocks with other financial investments. Within the context of the risk-return trade-off, the selection of investments is introduced.

The third chapter includes an overview of the economic influences which have a bearing on the valuation of stocks. Understanding the relationships between the economy and the stock and bond markets is of great significance for stock investors. The next part of the chapter includes tables on how to read the stock quotations listed in the financial newspapers.

The fourth chapter discusses how and where securities are traded. The first part of the chapter has an overview of the types of brokerage firms and what to look for in the selection of a broker. This is followed by a presentation of the costs and mechanics of trading stocks. An understanding of the types of orders and how the stock markets work can only benefit stock investors, which can lead to reductions in the costs of trading.

Chapter Five examines the use of fundamental analysis as a means of identifying stocks which are undervalued or present buying opportunities. The next chapter provides an overview of technical analysis, as a method for selecting stocks.

Chapter Seven evaluates the different investment theories presented, and introduces the efficient market hypothesis and capital asset pricing theory. An understanding of these theories will assist individual investors in the choice of their investment strategies, namely, whether to be active or passive (buy and hold) investors. The chapter concludes with a discussion of formula buying plans.

Chapters Eight and Nine include information on mutual funds and closed-end funds. Investments in these funds are analyzed as to how they work, their risks, how to buy and sell them, their disadvantages, caveats and whether these investments are suitable for you.

Chapter Ten discusses stock derivative investments. Options, rights and warrants are introduced, with a brief discussion on their uses, risks and potential returns.

Chapter Eleven discusses foreign stocks and the various ways that investors can invest in foreign stock markets.

Chapter Twelve discusses portfolio management.

Investing money in the stock market is not easy, and the aim of this book is to make the task a little less difficult. By understanding the risk-return tradeoff, and how stock markets work, will make investors more comfortable with their stock selections.

Esmé Faerber

Acknowledgments

The preparation of this book was greatly facilitated by the people at Probus Publishing Company. I am grateful for their efforts. I would like to thank Ray White of Bryn Mawr Investments Group, Inc., for his assistance.

A special note of thanks to my husband, Eric, and our children Jennifer and Michael for their patience and continued support.

Chapter 1

Why Invest in
Common Stocks?*

Key Concepts

- Stock Market versus Bond Market
- Investment Plan
- What Are Common Stocks?
- Characteristics of Common Stocks
- Classes of Common Stock
- What Is Preferred Stock?

When investors save money, they experience a real sense of satisfaction. However, in order to generate future purchasing power that will keep ahead of inflation, these savings need to be invested wisely. In certain economic climates, a sense of financial security can change quickly to a sense of frustration when the rates of return earned on savings are meager. This feeling of frustration is further exacerbated when interest rates paid on savings accounts barely cover the rate of inflation or when the after-tax rate of return received on these savings is less than the rate of inflation. In other words, investors are earning negative rates of return and are losing purchasing power on their investments.

Despite the vast array of investment alternatives, many investors continue to choose the same few. After buying a house, the bulk of the average investor's savings goes into bank savings accounts, money market funds and certificates of deposit. Investing the bulk of savings

---

* Some of the material in this chapter has been previously published by Esmé Faerber in *All About Bonds*, published by Probus Publishing, 1993.

in low-yielding accounts translates into lower rates of return, higher income taxes and loss of capital appreciation (price growth). Bank accounts and money market funds tend to pay interest at the low end of the yield scale without providing the tax advantages and capital appreciation opportunities of some of the other investment alternatives.

Many investors with money in low-yielding accounts find the complexities of other investments such as common stocks and bonds overwhelming. They also worry that, with the increased volatility of the stock and bond markets, a downturn in either market could erase much of their savings. Thus, these investors are paralyzed with fear into keeping their status quo, low-yielding investments.

Table 1–1 shows the interest rates that investors currently earn on different money market investments. Returns on bank savings accounts earn 2.3 percent, and six-month certificates of deposit are paying 2.81 percent. A 1 year certificate of deposit averages just 3 percent. These miserly returns are hardly enough to keep pace with the rate of inflation, let alone build future purchasing dollars to retire on.

Table 1–1	Current Interest Rates
Six-month Certificate of Deposit	2.81%
Money Market Fund	2.67%
Tax-Exempt Money Market Fund	1.97%
S&P 500 Dividend Yield	2.72%

Source: The New York Times, November 20, 1993 p.34.

Why are these investors attracted to these low-yielding alternatives? The answer lies in the fact that bank savings account and certificate of deposit investors tend to be conservative in their outlook, and they are reassured by the federal deposit insurance on bank accounts that they will not lose any of their principal. However, this riskless, pay-less type of investment strategy does not help these investors keep up with rising costs and growing anxieties about retirement.

This is a puzzling time for all investors, not only for conservative ones. With interest rates currently at a 20-year low, the bond and stock markets are at their record high levels. Consequently, many investors are reluctant to plunge into the stock and bond markets at this stage only to see an erosion of their savings in the event of a stock or bond market crash. Yet over long periods of time, common stocks have outperformed all other investments. This is confirmed by the study done by Ibbotson and Sinquefield (1991), which reported the following average yearly returns for investments in the different portfolios of securities:

	Nominal Average Return	Standard Deviation of Returns	Real Average Returns
Common stocks of large companies	12.1%	20.8%	9%
Common stocks of small firms	17.1%	35.4%	14%
Long-term corporate bonds	5.5%	8.4%	2.4%
Long-term government bonds	4.9%	8.5%	1.8%
Intermediate-term government bonds	5.1%	5.5%	2.0%
U.S. Treasury bills	3.7%	3.4%	0.6%

Common stocks of large companies had nominal average yearly returns of 12.1 percent over the 64-year period from 1926–1990 and were only surpassed by the returns earned by the common stocks of small firms, which averaged 17.1 percent per year. The real average yearly rate of return, which is the nominal rate minus the rate of inflation, is 9 percent for common stocks of large companies and 14 percent for the common stocks of small companies. This surpasses by far the returns earned on corporate bonds (2.4 percent), government bonds (1.8 percent) and Treasury bills (0.6 percent). The astute reader will ask, Why bother with other investments when you can get higher rates of return from investing in common stocks?

The answer concerns the variability of the returns. The standard deviation of the returns measures the riskiness of the portfolios. As expected, Treasury bills have the least risk due to their relatively short maturities and the fact that there is almost no chance of the U.S. government defaulting on them. Risk increases for long-term government bonds, which surprisingly have the same risk as long-term corporate bonds. Corporate bonds generally have increased risks of default over government bonds. This anomaly is primarily due to the sharp increases in interest rates in the late 1970s and early 1980s, which had a negative effect on bond prices. Finally, the greatest risks are those experienced by portfolios of large common stocks (20.8 percent) and small common stocks (35.4 percent).

What this means is that common stock prices are historically more volatile than the other types of investments, as demonstrated by the sizeable risks that the common stockholder is exposed to (20.8 percent for large stocks resembling the Standard and Poor's average and 35.4 percent for a portfolio of small common stocks). Investing in common stocks will produce higher real rates of return (after adjusting for inflation) than most other investments, but common stocks require a longer time horizon so that the variability of the returns can be averaged out. This is confirmed by the Ibbotson study during the time frame of 1926–1990, where common stocks produced negative returns in 18 of the 65 years as compared with only 1 negative year in 65 for Treasury bills (Petty, 118).

Ken Gregory, a money manager in San Francisco, estimates that the risk of losing money on an investment in a basket of common stocks resembling the Standard & Poor's (S&P) Index diminishes over time: 30 percent over a 1-year period versus 15 percent over a 3-year period, and 3–4% over a 10-year period (Gottschalk and Donnelly).

∎ Stock Market versus Bond Market

Comparing stocks to alternative investments in the bond markets will give the investor a clearer picture of the differences in the rates of return and the risks.

Bond investments offer less variability in returns than common stocks (8.4 percent for long-term corporate bonds versus 20.8 percent for common stocks in the Ibbotson study [1991]). However, if there is a long investment period, the higher variability risks for common stocks can be averaged, resulting in higher returns for stocks.

Bonds have a maturity date, at which time the bond is redeemed at the par value ($1,000 per bond). The longer the maturity, the greater the risks for certain types of bonds. For example, 30-year corporate bonds carry a greater risk than 30-year U.S. Treasury bonds because the redemption payments for the Treasury bonds are backed by the U.S. Treasury. Anything could happen within a 30-year period to force a corporation into bankruptcy before the bonds are redeemed. However, in the event of a default, the corporate bondholder still has a priority claim over the common stockholder. In other words, the bondholders' claims would have to be paid before any proceeds are paid to the common stockholders.

Besides the possibility of capital appreciation (an increase in the selling price of the bond/stock over the purchase price), investors invest in bonds to earn interest income. Bond investors can count on a steady stream of interest income, whereas common stockholders are not guaranteed dividend income. Dividends on common stocks are declared at the discretion of the company's board of directors. If the board decides to use the money for alternative purposes or if earnings go down, dividends may be reduced or may not be declared at all.

Thus, investors who are reliant on a steady stream of income and who cannot tolerate the risks of reduced income should not invest in common stocks. Similarly, if the investment horizon is not long, bond investments would be more suitable than common stocks.

However, for long periods, investing in common stocks offer the following advantages over bonds:

■ The potential for greater average rates of return.

■ The ability to reduce federal, state and local income taxes. Capital gains on common stocks are only taxed when the stocks are sold, whereas interest income from bonds (and dividends from common stocks) are taxed when they are earned.

■ The potential for keeping ahead of the rate of inflation.

Investment Plan

Before making investment decisions, investors should assess their financial situations and devise an investment plan.

The first step in any investment plan is to keep enough cash for living expenses and for any emergencies in liquid investments, such as bank money market accounts, money market mutual funds, savings accounts and Treasury bills. The amount to keep in these liquid investments will vary according to individual circumstances. An examination of your personal assets will determine how much to keep. A conservative rule of thumb is to keep three to six months' worth of expenses in liquid investments.

Included in your monthly expenses should be premiums on life, health and disability insurance. It is especially important for families for the breadwinner to have adequate life and disability insurance. Health insurance is important for all members of the family. Similarly, auto and home insurance premiums should be included in your monthly expenses.

Once the emergency fund has been created, an investment program should be started for the medium- to long-term future. Even on a modest starting salary, setting aside small, consistent savings can make a difference to an investment program over time.

The second step in the investment plan is to consider your medium- to long-term objectives. Listing your objectives is a good place to start because they will determine the types of investments to make. For example, the following objectives have a time frame:

■ Buy a car in 2 years.

■ Save for a down payment on a house in 5 years.

▎ Fund a college education in 10 years.

▎ Accumulate a retirement fund in 30 years.

The types of investments can then be geared to the maturities of the objectives. The first two objectives will encompass short- to medium-term investments, such as 2-year and 5-year U.S. Treasury notes, or similar maturity government agency or corporate bonds, and/or mutual funds. Investment options to fund a college education in 10 years are greater and could include a mixture of common stocks and bonds. With a 30-year investment horizon, the mix of investments should be weighted more heavily towards stocks than bonds. This is because stocks have outperformed bonds and most other investments over time, which means that if the past is a reflection of the future, you could expect average yearly returns of 10 percent for stocks versus 4–5 percent for bonds. Investors who are nervous about stock market corrections or crashes might consider investing some of their retirement savings in 30-year U.S. Treasury bonds. However, bonds are not immune from risks, and the degree and type of risk will vary depending on the quality of the bonds and the issuer. Before investing in bonds, you should be aware of the risks and nuances affecting them.

▎ What Are Common Stocks?

Common stocks represent ownership in a corporation. For example, if a company has 100,000 shares of common stock outstanding and you buy 10,000 shares, you are a 10 percent owner of that company. A corporation could have one shareholder/owner or numerous shareholders, as in the case of IBM Corporation. However, owning common stocks of a large corporation does not have the same ownership rights as owning a house, for example. Shareholders of IBM corporation cannot tell IBM management how to run their company or what types of computers they should be producing. This is because shareholders' rights are limited.

The relationship of shareholders to management and the board of directors is illustrated in Figure 1–1.

Shareholders are the true owners of a corporation in that they are the only group with a claim to the company's profits; bondholders and preferred stockholders are viewed as creditors of the corporation and do not share in the company's profits.

When a new company is formed, common stock is sold to the shareholders to raise money for the company. Similarly, when companies need additional funds to expand, they will often sell more com-

Figure 1–1   Responsibilities of Shareholders

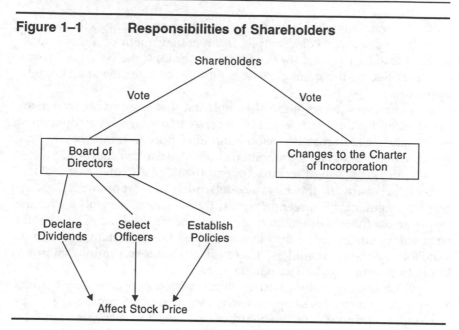

mon stock. Companies can also sell bonds to raise funds. Shareholders invest in the common stock of companies to earn a return on their money. However, before discussing the returns to common shareholders, an examination of the characteristics of common stock will give a better perspective on the variability of the returns to shareholders.

▮ Characteristics of Common Stocks

Ownership of common stock is evidenced by a stock certificate. On the front is the name of the issuing company, the name of the owner of the shares, the number of shares representing the certificate, the identifying serial number, the name of the register and the par value of the stock. The back of the stock certificate normally includes an assignment statement, which must be signed by the holder of the stocks when the holder decides to transfer ownership of the shares.

Voting Rights

A characteristic of common stock is that the shareholders can vote on important issues facing a corporation as well as on members to the board of directors, as illustrated in Figure 1–1. The board of directors, in turn, selects officers to run the corporation.

Common shareholders must approve of any changes to the charter of incorporation. For example, if the management of a corporation wanted to take over another corporation through the issuance of new common shares, the management would have to get the shareholders' approval.

Instead of attending the shareholders' meeting to vote in person, many shareholders use a proxy vote. A *proxy* is a legal document which gives a designated person temporary power of attorney to vote for an absentee, signee shareholder, at the shareholder meeting.

With this setup, it would appear, theoretically, that shareholders choose the board of directors and determine the important issues facing management. However, in reality, the system often works with the opposite bent. Most often, management chooses the slate of candidates to stand for the board of directors as well as the important issues to be voted on by the shareholders. These choices are then sent out on proxy cards to be voted on by shareholders.

Occasionally, proxy battles occur which provide shareholders with a real choice. This happens when there are two opposing groups (an outside group versus the board of directors and management) who solicit the shareholders' proxy votes. Dissident shareholders have used their strength to bring about changes in top management. In late 1993, when Borden Inc.'s shareholders saw their dividends cut and the stock price fall to new lows, they brought pressure on the board of directors to remove the chief executive.

In theory, it is the duty of management and the board of directors to seek the best deal for their shareholders, but in reality there are cases where this has not happened. This agency-ownership conflict is illustrated in the Time-Paramount offer. Time's directors rejected Paramount's all-cash offer for Time stock in favor of the Time-Warner merger in 1989. With the benefit of hindsight, the Paramount offer would have been more lucrative for Time's shareholders. The cash price offered is greater than the existing stock price of Time-Warner shares.

Corporations use either the majority voting procedure (also known as the statutory method) or the cumulative voting procedure. Under the majority voting procedure, the number of votes a shareholder has equals the number of shares he or she holds. The majority of votes cast determines the issue or the director elected. With cumulative voting, shareholders are entitled to a total number of votes equal to the total number of shares owned multiplied by the number of directors being elected. Shareholders can cast all of their votes for a single candidate or split them up as they see fit. Cumulative voting gives increased weight to minority shareholders, enabling them to elect at least one director.

A simple example will illustrate the difference between majority voting and cumulative voting. Assume that the following company has 1,000 shares outstanding and that there are 2 candidates to be elected to the board of directors.

Under majority voting, the minority shareholder with 300 shares will be able to cast 300 votes for each of the 2 candidates. However, under cumulative voting, a minority shareholder with 300 shares in an election for 2 candidates could vote all 600 (300 × 2) votes for 1 candidate. This method is advantageous for minority shareholders, who can get together and place all their votes for 1 candidate who may be more sympathetic to their cause.

Claim on Income

As owners of the corporation, common shareholders have a right to share in the net income, after bondholders and preferred stockholders have been paid. This net income may either be retained by the corporation (and reinvested by the corporation) or paid out in dividends to shareholders. The corporation that retains income increases the value of the firm, which leads to an increase in the value of the stock. This benefit to the shareholders is in the form of capital gains (when shareholders sell their common stock at prices that are higher than the purchase price). Shareholders benefit directly when the corporation pays out its earnings in dividends.

Dividends. When the board of directors of a corporation decides to pay out its earnings or part of its earnings in dividends, all the common shareholders have a right to receive them. If the board of directors decides not to declare a dividend, the shareholders will receive nothing. Companies are not legally required to pay dividends even if they are profitable and they have paid them in the past. However, in contrast, companies are legally required to pay interest to their bondholders on their debt. This is an important distinction for investors who rely on regular inflows from their investments.

Declaration of Dividends. Four dates are important in the declaration of dividends:

The first is the _date of announcement_, which is when the board of directors announces the dividends.

The second is the _date of record_, which determines which shareholders are entitled to receive the dividends. Only those shareholders who own the shares of that company on the date of record are entitled to receive the dividends. If shares are purchased after the record date, the owners will not be entitled to receive the dividends.

The third date, known as the *ex-dividend date*, is important because stock traded on the ex-dividend date does not include the dividend. The ex-dividend date is four business days prior to the date of record. When common stock is bought, it takes five business days for the settlement to go through. However, the settlement period will change to three days beginning on June 1, 1995. Thus, if the record date for a company's dividend is Friday, January 14, 1994, the ex-dividend date is Tuesday, January 11, 1994. Investors who buy these shares on Monday, January 10, 1994 (the day before the ex dividend date) will receive the dividends because the transaction will be recorded in the ownership books for that company in five working days, which would be January 14, 1994.

The fourth date is the *payment date*, which is the date the company pays the dividends.

Dividend payments are important to shareholders, and so companies often make their dividend policies known to investors. Rightly or wrongly, investors use dividend payments as a yardstick or mirror of the company's expected earnings, and so any changes to dividend payments may have a greater effect on the stock price than a change in earnings. This explains the reluctance of management to cut dividends when earnings decline. Similarly, there is a lag in increasing dividends when earnings increase. Management wants to be sure they can maintain the increased dividends from increased earnings.

Shareholders who rely on income from their investments will purchase the stock of companies that have a history of paying regular dividends out of their earnings. These companies tend to be older and well established; their stocks are referred to as *income stocks* or *blue-chip stocks*.

Young companies that are expanding generally retain their earnings; their stocks are referred to as *growth stocks*. Growth stocks appeal to investors who are more interested in capital appreciation.

Dividends can be paid in various forms: cash, stock, property or a combination of these. In order to pay *cash dividends*, companies need to have not only the earnings but also enough cash. A company showing a large amount in retained earnings in the balance sheet is not enough to ensure cash dividends. The amount of cash that a company has is independent of retained earnings. A company can be cash poor and still be very profitable.

Most American companies pay their regular cash dividends on a quarterly basis, while some companies pay their dividends semiannually or annually. In addition to regular dividends, a company may declare *extra dividends*. Instead of battling to maintain a higher amount of regular dividends, companies with fluctuating earnings will pay out additional dividends when their earnings warrant it.

Some companies choose to conserve their cash, and they declare stock dividends. By paying stock dividends, companies recapitalize their earnings and issue new shares. This does not affect the companies' assets and liabilities. See Table 1–2 for an example of a company's balance sheet before and after a 10 percent stock dividend.

Amounts from retained earnings are transferred to the common stock and additional paid in capital accounts. This does not affect the amount in the total equity section of the balance sheet. The amount transferred depends on the market value of the common stock and the number of new shares issued through the stock dividend. In this example, there are 10,000 additional shares at a market price of $5 per share. The retained earnings account is debited for $50,000 ($5 × 10,000

Table 1–2   The Effects of a Stock Dividend on a Balance Sheet

Before Stock Dividend

XYZ Company Balance Sheet

Current Assets	$100,000	Current Liabilities	$ 50,000
Fixed Assets	200,000	Long-Term Liabilities	50,000
		Equity: Common Stock $1 Par 100,000 Shares Outstanding	100,000
		Additional Paid in Capital	30,000
		Retained Earnings	70,000
		Total Equity	200,000
Total Assets	$ 300,000	Total Liabilities & Equity	$300,000

After 10 percent Stock Dividend (Market Price $5 per Share)

Current Assets	$100,000	Current Liabilities	$ 50,000
Fixed Assets	200,000	Long-Term Liabilities	50,000
		Equity: Common Stock $1 Par 110,000 Shares Outstanding	110,000
		Additional Paid in Capital	70,000
		Retained Earnings	20,000

shares), and $10,000 (10,000 shares × $1 par value) is added to the equity account. The other $40,000 ($4 premium over par value × 10,000 shares) is added to the additional paid in capital account.

The astute investor will realize that a stock dividend does not increase the shareholder's wealth. With a stock dividend, shareholders will receive more shares of that company's stock, but because the company's assets and liabilities remain the same, the price of the stock will decline to account for the dilution. For the shareholder, this can be likened to a slice of cake. The slice can be divided into two, three or four pieces. No matter how many ways you slice the piece of cake, the overall size remains the same. After a stock dividend the shareholders receive more shares, but their proportionate ownership interest in the company remains the same.

Stock dividends are usually expressed as a percentage of the number of shares outstanding. For example, if a company announces a 10 percent stock dividend and it has 100,000 shares outstanding, the total shares outstanding will be increased to 110,000 shares after the stock dividend.

Stock Split. A stock split is like a stock dividend in that there is an increase in the number of shares issued on a pro rata basis while the assets, liabilities, equity and earnings remain the same. The only difference between a stock split and a stock dividend is technical in nature.

From an accounting point of view, a stock dividend of greater than 20–25 percent is recorded as a stock split. A 100 percent stock dividend is the same as a 2-for-1 stock split. A small medical imaging company, Adac Labs, split its shares 2 for 1 because the company felt that the price of the stock was too high and that with a lower price the shares would become more marketable. The stock was trading in the $50 range and so an investor owning 100 shares before the split (with a value of $5,000) would own 200 shares after the split with a value of approximately $25 per share (50/2).

Occasionally, companies announce *reverse splits,* which reduce the number of shares and increase the share price. When a company's stock has fallen in price, a reverse split will raise the price of the stock to a respectable level. For example, a stock that is trading in the cats and dogs range of $1 would trade at $10 with a 1-for-10 reverse split. Of course, the number of shares outstanding would be reduced by 10 times after the split.

The Advantages of Stock Dividends and Stock Splits

If shareholder wealth is not increased by stock dividends and stock splits, why do companies distribute them?

The first advantage from the company's point of view is a conservation of cash. By substituting a stock dividend for a cash dividend, a company can conserve its cash or use it for other attractive investment opportunities. It is for this latter reason that the company's earning power will be increased and the stock price may be bid up, thus benefitting the shareholders. However, if this is the case, shareholders will be better off without stock dividends because the costs associated with them are borne by the shareholders. The costs of issuing new shares, transfer fees, and revising the company's record of shareholders is paid by shareholders (from the company's earnings).

Advocates of stock dividends and stock splits believe that the stock price never falls in exact proportion to the increase in shares. For example, in a 2-for-1 stock split, the stock price might fall less than 50 percent, which means that shareholders will be left with a higher total value. This conclusion has not been verified by most academic studies (Hausman).

Stock dividends and stock splits do not increase the wealth of the stockholder, whereas cash dividends increase the shareholder's monetary wealth.

Property dividends are occasionally declared by corporations, whereby shareholders receive securities or assets of the corporation. For example, when a corporation spins off a subsidiary, shareholders could receive assets or shares of that subsidiary. Distributing the stocks or assets of the subsidiary rather than cash allows the shareholders to benefit directly from the market value of the dividends received.

While it is obvious that the shareholders benefit from receiving cash and property dividends, they also benefit when earnings are not paid out but are reinvested in the company. This increases the value of the company and hence the value of its stock. Thus, the claim on income is an important characteristic for common stockholders.

Claim on Assets

In the event of the liquidation of a company, the common shareholders have a residual claim on the assets of the company. However, this is only after the claims of the debtholders have been satisfied. In other words, common shareholders' claims on assets are third in line behind those of the debtholders and the preferred stockholders. If there are insufficient assets to fulfill the claims of the debtholders and preferred stockholders, the common shareholders will come away receiving nothing, as is often the case during bankruptcy. Thus, when companies are doing well, common shareholders may experience large returns; but on the downside, common shareholders may also be exposed to large risks, as there is often nothing left to satisfy their claims in bankruptcy.

Limited Liability

The limited liability feature of a corporation limits the amount of the loss of common shareholders in the event of bankruptcy. The most that common shareholders can lose is the amount of their investment in the common stock.

Preemptive Rights

For those corporations that include preemptive rights in their charters, stockholders are allowed to maintain their proportionate share of ownership. This means that when the company issues new shares, they must first be offered to the existing shareholders. For example, if a shareholder owns 10 percent of the company's stock, that shareholder is entitled to purchase 10 percent of the new shares. Thus, existing shareholders have the first right of refusal on purchasing the new shares.

Certificates called *rights* are issued to the shareholders, giving them the option to purchase a stated number of new shares at a specific price during a specific period. These rights may be exercised (which allows the purchase of new common stock at a lower price than the market price), sold or allowed to expire. Rights will be discussed in greater detail in Chapter 10.

In recent years, the importance of preemptive rights has diminished and the number of rights offerings has declined.

▌ Classes of Common Stock

Some corporations issue different classes of common stock, which may have different characteristics. For example, Ford Motor Company has two classes of common stock, Class A and Class B. Class B shares are owned by the Ford family and some board members. The key characteristic of this class of shares is that it controls 40 percent of the total voting rights of Ford Motor Company. Class A Ford shares have limited voting rights (Hall 42).

In other companies with more than one class of common stock, there may be different dividend rates. For example, Food Lion Inc. pays its class A stockholders a larger dividend than it pays its class B stockholders. However, its class A stock has no voting rights.

■ What Is Preferred Stock?

Another type of stock is preferred stock, which also represents an equity ownership in a company. *Equity* is defined as capital invested in a company by its owners; debt is capital lent to the corporation, which must be repaid. Preferred stock is a hybrid type of security in that it has features resembling both debt and equity.

Fixed Dividend

Unlike common stock, the dividend rate on preferred stock is usually fixed. It may be stated as a percentage of the par value of the preferred stock or as a fixed dollar amount. The *par* value is a stated value and, hence, a preferred stock issue with $100 par value that has a dividend of 8 percent would pay a dividend of $8 per share (8 percent of $100).

The fixed dividends of preferred stocks appeal to investors who rely on regular returns of income. In this regard, preferred stock resembles the regular returns of interest on bonds. However, the downside to a fixed dividend rate is that the price of the preferred stock is sensitive to changes in market rates of interest. For example, if an investor has bought preferred stock for $100 a share that pays a dividend of $6, and market rates of interest subsequently go up to 8 percent, there will be downside pressure on the price of preferred stock. New investors will not want to buy this preferred stock for $100 when the dividend is only $6 (a return of 6 percent, 6/100), when current investments will return 8 percent. Thus, price fluctuations of preferred stocks tend to be greater than those of long-term bonds (Mayo 233).

To counter these swings in preferred stock prices, many financial institutions and utility companies introduced *adjustable-rate preferred stock* in the early 1980s when market rates were high. Dividend payments fluctuate with changes in market rates of interest as measured by the changes in a combination of U.S. Treasury securities. Dividends would move up and down within a stipulated minimum and maximum limit. For example, Bank of America Corporation's 9.25 percent (at offering) adjustable-rate preferred stock had a 6 percent minimum dividend rate and a 12 percent maximum rate. The rate was adjusted to changes in interest rates on a quarterly basis.

The advantage of adjustable-rate preferred stock is that the price of the preferred stock does not fluctuate as much with changes in market rates of interest.

Multiple Classes

Most companies have one class of common stock, but it is quite common to see companies with more than one series of preferred stock. Table 1–3 illustrates the different preferred stock issues of the Long Island Lighting Co., listed on the New York Stock Exchange.

Each class of preferred stock may have different features, such as different dividend rates; one might be a cumulative preferred issue which gives the holder the right to receive all missed dividend payments before common shareholders are paid, and another in the series a convertible preferred issue with a call provision. Convertible preferred stock may be converted by the holders into a fixed number of shares of the common stock of the underlying company. A call provision allows the issuing company the right to repurchase the preferred stock at a specific price (normally a premium over its par value). These issues could also be differentiated in their priority status with regard to claims on assets in the event of bankruptcy.

Claim on Income and Assets

As the name implies, preferred stock has a preference over common stock with regard to claims on both income and assets. Companies must pay the dividends on preferred stock before they can pay dividends to common stockholders. In the event of bankruptcy, preferred stockholders' claims are settled before those of common shareholders. This makes preferred stock less risky than common stock but more risky in comparison to debt. This is because bondholders have priority in claims to income and assets over preferred stockholders. Interest on debt must be paid by a corporation because in the event of a default, bondholders can force the corporation into bankruptcy, whereas divi-

---

Table 1–3   Different Issues of Long Island Lighting Co.'s Preferred Stock

52 Weeks											Net
Hi	Lo	Stock	Sym	Div	%	PE	Vol	Hi	Lo	Close	Chg
29 5/8	22 5/8	LIL Co	LIL	1.78	7.7	11	1379	23 3/8	23 1/8	23 1/4	...
28 1/4	22 5/8	LIL Co	pfA	1.99	7.5	..	7	26 5/8	26 5/8	26 5/8	−1/8
110	102 1/2	LIL Co	pfC	7.66	7.2	..	1	106	106	106	...
70	53	LIL Co	pfE	4.35	7.6	..	41	57 1/2	56	57 1/2	+ 1
26 3/4	24 5/8	LIL Co	pfQ	1.76	6.8	..	3	25 7/8	25 7/8	25 7/8	+ 1/4

dends on preferred stock (and common stock) are declared at the discretion of the board of directors.

In the case of multiple classes of preferred stock, the different
issues may be prioritized in their claims to income and assets.

Cumulative Dividend

Most preferred stock issues carry a cumulative feature, which means
that if the company fails to pay the dividend it will have to make it up
before it can pay any dividends to its common shareholders. This cumulative feature protects the rights of the preferred stockholders. A
preferred issue that does not have a cumulative feature is called a
noncumulative preferred stock.

Convertible Feature

Some preferred stock issues have a convertible feature that allows the
owners to exchange their preferred stock for common shares. The conditions and terms of the conversion are set when the preferred stock is
first issued. This would include the conversion ratio, which is the
number of common shares the preferred stockholder will get for each
preferred share and the conversion price of the common stock.

For example, Company XYZ issues a new convertible preferred
stock, which is sold at $100 per share and is convertible into 5 com-
mon shares of XYZ Company. The conversion ratio is 5:1, and the conversion price is $20 per share for the common stock ($100/5 shares). If
the market price of the common stock is $15, it would not be advanta-
geous for the preferred stockholder to convert, because the value after
conversion is $75 (5 shares at $15). However, if the price of the common stock rises to $20, there is parity. The preferred stockholder
would not convert because the preferred stock pays a dividend. If the
common stock rises above $20 per share, the preferred stockholder can
share in the capital appreciation of the common stock by converting to
common stock.

The decision to exercise the conversion option depends on three
factors:

- The market price of the common stock. It would have to be
  greater than the conversion price for the holder to share in
  capital gains.
- The amount of the preferred dividend.
- The amount of the common dividend.

The conversion feature provides the investor with the possibility of sharing in the capital gains through the appreciation of the common stock as well as the relative safety of receiving the preferred dividends before conversion.

Participation Feature

Some corporations include a participation feature to make the preferred stock issue more attractive to investors. This feature allows preferred stockholders to share in earnings beyond the stated dividend. After the preferred stockholders and common stockholders have received their stated dividends, the additional amounts of the company's earnings are available for distribution to the preferred and common stockholders.

The good news is that the participation feature is very appealing to preferred stockholders. The bad news is that not many preferred issues include this feature.

Call Provision

A preferred stock issue with a call provision entitles the issuing company to repurchase the stock at its option from outstanding preferred stockholders. The call price is generally more than the preferred stock's par value.

The call provision is advantageous to the issuing company, not to the holder of the preferred stock. This is because when market rates of interest fall significantly below the dividend rate of the preferred issue, companies are likely to exercise the call provision—by retiring the issue and replacing it with a new preferred stock issue with a lower dividend rate.

The savings to the issuing company represent a loss of income to the preferred stockholders. When interest rates went down in 1989, Long Island Lighting Company retired several of its callable preferred stock issues.

Thus, not only do preferred stockholders suffer a loss of income when their high-dividend-rate preferred stock issues are called in, but the call provision also acts as a ceiling limit on the price appreciation of the preferred stock. When interest rates decline, there is an upward push on the price of high-dividend preferred stock issues. However, the price of the preferred stock will not rise above the call price. For example, if a preferred stock issue has a call price of $55, potential buyers of the preferred stock would be unlikely to pay more than this amount when interest rates decline significantly. Investors who pay more than this ceiling price would lose money if the issue is called.

The Securities and Exchange Commission (SEC) encourages companies issuing preferred stock to include a call provision. The reason for this position is to prevent companies from being stuck with high-dividend-rate preferred stock issues that they can't retire when market interest rates decline. As a result, most preferred stock issues have call provisions.

To entice investors to buy preferred stock issues during periods of high interest rates, companies include a *call protection* feature. This prevents the company from calling the issue for a period of time, generally for five years, but this may vary. After the call protection period, the issue is callable at the stated call price per share.

Investors should examine the terms of the call feature before investing because the terms vary greatly from issue to issue.

■ Summary

Investors invest in common stock and preferred stock for different reasons due to their inherently different characteristics.

Preferred stock, which is considered an equity security, has many features that resemble debt securities. With a call provision, preferred stock does not have the indeterminate life of common stock. Another characteristic resembling debt is the fixed dividend payment of preferred stock. However, with the recent increased volatility in market rate of interest, the fixed dividend is being replaced by adjustable-rate preferred stock issues.

The protective features that are included with some preferred stock are similar to the restrictive provisions of debt securities. In the event of a default on the payment of dividends, some preferred stock issues confer voting rights. This lessens the risks to the preferred stockholders.

However, when preferred stock is compared to common stock, the preferred stockholders are more like the silent partners. They do not have voting rights (if the events leading to the protective provisions are absent), and therefore they have no say in the running of the company. However, the preferred stockholders have preference over the common stockholders with regard to:

■ Dividends. The company must pay its preferred stockholders before paying common stock dividends

■ Bankruptcy. The claims of preferred stockholders must be settled before those of the common stockholders.

The common stockholders are the true owners of the company, and as such are the true claimants to the residual assets and income. The returns on common stocks have historically outperformed those of preferred stocks and debt, but the returns on preferred stocks have been inferior to those on bonds. Thus, investors invest in common stocks for three reasons:

▮ To provide income.

▮ To use common stocks as a store of value.

▮ To provide capital gains.

Both bonds and preferred stocks provide income and tend to be less risky than common stocks as to the first criterion. Interest on bonds must be paid, and dividends on preferred stocks take precedence over those on common stocks. In fact, common stocks of small-growth companies do not pay dividends.

All investors are concerned about preserving their capital, and again bonds are the least risky. (If they are held to maturity, bondholders receive the par value [$1,000 per bond] of their bonds.) Although bonds also appreciate when interest rates decline, common stocks provide greater appreciation, and hence are a better store of value over a long period of time.

Capital gains provide the wealth building for investors and over long periods of time common stocks have outperformed the other investments. The risks of investing in common stocks are discussed in Chapter 2.

▮ References

Faerber, Esmé. *All About Bonds.* Chicago: Probus Publishing Co., 1993.

Gottschalk, Earl C. Jr., and Barbara Donnelly. "Despite Market Swings, Stocks Make Sense." *The Wall Street Journal*, October, 1989.

Hall, Alvin D. *Getting Started in Stocks.* New York: John Wiley and Sons, 1992.

Hausman, W. H., R.R. West, and J.A. Largay. "Stock Splits, Price Changes and Trading Profits: A Synthesis." *Journal of Business*, 44 (January 1971), pp. 69–77.

Mayo, Herbert B. *Investments*, 2d ed. Chicago: Dryden Press, 1988.

Ibbotson, Roger G, and Rex A. Sinquefield. *Stocks, Bonds, Bills and Inflation: Historical Return (1926-1990).* Homewood, IL: Dow Jones-Irwin, 1991.

Petty, J. William, et al. *Basic Financial Management.* 6th ed. Englewood Cliffs, NJ: Prentice Hall, 1993.

Chapter 2

Should I Invest in Common Stocks?

Key Concepts
- Types of Risks
- Rate of Return
- Inflation and Taxes
- Selection of Investments

The main advantage of investing in common stock, as pointed out in Chapter 1, is that investors have historically received greater returns than those received from most other investments. These returns are in the form of dividends and capital gains as well as common stocks, acting as a store of value for the future.

The U.S. stock markets (and bond markets) have performed admirably into the early 1990s due to low market rates of interest. Many traditional certificate of deposit (CD) investors have found their low returns (around 3 percent) to be unpalatable. These traditional CD investors moved into the stock market in the latter part of 1993 and early 1994 to participate in the higher returns. The Dow Jones Industrial Average had risen about 20 percent over the year February 1993–1994. Thus, investors who had bought some of the Dow Jones Industrial Average stocks would have seen their value increase by an average of 20 percent. Of course, there are some stocks in the Dow Jones Industrial Average that have not appreciated in value.

It is this factor that makes some investors more nervous than others about investing in common stocks. You could lose some of your investment capital if the price of the stock falls below the purchase price. However, if you invest $10,000 in U.S. Treasury notes and hold them through maturity, you will receive your $10,000 back. In other words, there is no erosion of capital.

To get the most from your investments, not only do you have to understand the investments, their risks and their returns, but you also need to have an investment plan with specific objectives. The investment plan provides the direction you need to take in order to achieve the stated objectives. The first step is to review your financial position. This includes a budget review, in which you would list the following:

▮ All of your sources of income: salary, bonus, interest, dividends and so on.

▮ Your monthly living expenses, including taxes.

▮ Your expenses for insurance: life, disability, health, home, auto.

The excess of income over expenses will be used towards funding your objectives. List the objectives, their time frame and the total amount of money needed to fund them. This process is illustrated in Table 2–1.

The next step is to choose the investments that are most likely to help you achieve those objectives. The shorter-term objectives will need investments that are high in liquidity, while with the medium- and long-term objectives there is more flexibility as to the types of

---

Table 2–1   Personal Objectives

Objective	Time Needed	Total Cost	Priority	Amount Needed to Fund Objectives
Emergency fund				
Buy a car				
Save for a house				
Education fund				
Savings and investment fund				
Retirement fund				

All of your objectives should be listed along with the time frame and total costs. The latter should be realistic. The priority is the degree of urgency.

investments. Your objectives will govern your investment decisions not only from the time perspective (short-term, medium-term or long-term) but also as to whether the emphasis is on current income and/or growth. The most common investment objectives for most people fall into the following three categories:

■ Provide current income.

■ Fund expenditures.

■ Save funds for retirement.

These objectives will determine the limits of the risks you can take with the different types of investments. For example, if you are reliant on current income to meet your living expenses, you do not have much latitude in the levels of risk that your investments can be exposed to. Similarly, if you are investing money to fund a college education which begins three years hence, you do not want to find an erosion of your capital due to the nonperformance of a particular investment. However, funds set aside for long periods of time can withstand the volatility of the stock market in order to receive greater returns.

■ What Are the Types of Risks and How Much Can I Tolerate?

Understanding the risks associated with the different types of investments is an important step in investing. *Risk* is the uncertainty related to the outcome of the investment, and all investments are subject to risk of one type or another. Even passive investments such as keeping money in an FDIC-insured checking account at a large bank earning the meager interest rates currently offered will not keep up with the rate of inflation. However, with FDIC insurance, investors will not lose their capital. Merely holding cash involves the risk of loss due to inflation. By understanding the types of risks, investors can reduce their exposure to them with different types of investments.

Business Risk

Business risk is the uncertainty that pertains to the company's sales and earnings. Some companies by their nature are riskier than companies in other industries and will see greater fluctuations in their sales and earnings. If sales and earnings decline significantly, not only will there be downward pressure on the stock price but there will also be the risk that the company will not be able to cover its interest, principal and dividend payments. The company could experience losses and, at worst, go out of business, which makes their securities (stocks and bonds) worthless.

Investors' expectations of a company's earnings will affect the price of the stock. When there is an anticipated decline in earnings, shareholders may sell their shares, which puts downward pressure on the stock's price. Similarly, if there is an anticipated increase in earnings, investors will be willing to pay higher prices for the stock.

The stock prices of cyclical companies tend to fluctuate up and down along with the business cycles of the economy. Common stocks of auto, home building, construction, and durable goods companies are referred to as cyclical stocks. Their earnings and stock prices move directly up and down with the expansion and contraction of the economy.

For the more conservative investors, business risk can be reduced by investing in the common stocks of companies with stable earnings rather than those of the cyclical companies. Bear in mind that business risk affects not only the common stocks of companies but also their bonds and preferred stocks.

Financial Risk

Financial risk refers to the amount of debt a company has in relation to its equity. The greater the debt-to-equity ratio, the higher the financial risk, because the company will need to earn at least enough to pay back its fixed interest and principal payments. Failure of a company to meet these commitments can lead to bankruptcy.

Companies with very little or no debt have very little or no financial risk. Looking at a company's balance sheet reveals the amount of debt relative to its total assets and equity. At worst, financial risk, like business risk, can lead a company to bankruptcy—which may make their securities more or less worthless or may dampen the expectations of future earnings. Financial risk can be reduced by investing in companies with low debt-to-equity ratios (or debt-to-total-asset ratios).

Unsystematic Risk

Unsystematic risk or *diversifiable risk* refers to the risks associated with investing in one company—putting all your eggs into one basket. For example, had you invested all your funds in IBM company's stock a few years ago when it was trading at $150 per share, you would have lost two-thirds of your investment, as IBM is currently trading at $50 per share.

Instead of investing all your funds in the securities of one company, you could invest in several companies. You can also diversify by investing in different types of securities, such as government bonds, corporate bonds and American and foreign stocks. Diversification also lessens the business and financial risks.

Market Risk

Although investors may choose investments that have minimal business and financial risk, *market risk* is more encompassing. Market risk refers to the movement of security prices, which tend to move together as they react to external events (unrelated to the fundamentals of the company).

When the stock market goes up, most stocks go up in price, including those with less than spectacular sales, growth and earnings. Similarly, if there is a sell-off in the stock market, it will include those stocks with better than average sales, growth and earnings.

The external events that move security prices are unpredictable. It could be news of a war in a remote part of the globe, an uprising in the Middle East, a coup d'etat in a developing nation, the death of a prominent leader of a foreign nation, changes in the inflation rate, labor strikes or floods in the Midwest that trigger a sell-off in the stock market. The fact that these external events cannot be predicted means that investors in the stock markets cannot do very much to avoid these volatile, short-term fluctuations in stock prices

Investors should bear in mind that over long periods of time stock prices tend to appreciate in relation to their intrinsic value (their growth and earnings). Diversification of stocks does not help when an external event causes a landslide in the stock markets. Diversification is the process of investing in the securities of different companies in different industries. Over the short term, investors could hedge their positions using options. This concept is explored in Chapter 10.

Market risk highlights the dangers for investors who invest short-term money in the stock market. If the money is needed when the market has declined, investors will need to sell out at losses. Thus, investors should have a long time horizon so that they will not have to sell out in a down market.

Purchasing Power or Inflationary Risk

Putting money under the mattress may avoid market risk, but this action may not alleviate *purchasing power risk.* If prices in the economy keep rising (inflation), the real purchasing power of the investor's dollars is reduced. Purchasing power risk has the greatest effect on investments that have fixed returns (bonds, savings accounts, certificates of deposit) and no returns (non-interest-bearing checking accounts and the hoard under the mattress).

Assets whose values move with general price levels, such as common stocks, do better during periods of slight to moderate inflation. To protect against purchasing power risk, investors should choose investments whose anticipated returns are higher than the anticipated rate of inflation.

Interest Rate Risk

Interest rate risk refers to the changes in market rates of interest affecting all investments. Fixed-income securities (bonds and preferred stocks) are most directly affected. In periods of rising interest rates, investors who hold fixed-income securities will find that their market prices will fall to make them competitive with new issues on the market. This causes a loss of income for existing fixed-income security holders. Similarly, in periods of declining interest rates, prices of fixed-income securities will rise, resulting in capital appreciation. Bonds are not riskless investments.

Interest rates affect common stocks but less directly than fixed-income securities. High market rates of interest tend to depress stock prices and low interest rates tend to go hand in hand with bull markets. High market rates of interest prompt many investors to sell their stocks and invest in the higher coupon rates of bonds.

Investors should be aware of market rates of interest and should analyze trends so as to protect against substantial losses due to adverse changes in market rates of interest.

Political Risk

Political risk refers to changes in the political environment that affect companies' stocks and bonds. For example, government intervention in the private sector (pharmaceutical stocks battered by fears of the price controls of the Clinton health plan), currency devaluations, changes in government and taxes could all affect a company's profits. Nelson Mandela's rhetoric to nationalize the gold mines in South Africa put the brakes on the stock prices of the South African gold mining companies, while the North American and Australian gold mining company stock prices soared.

Since political events often occur overnight or with very little warning, it may be difficult for investors to anticipate which foreign companies will be adversely affected. It is easier to avoid investing in companies in troubled countries than to anticipate the possible political events that could send stock prices plunging.

Liquidity Risk

Liquidity risk refers to the uncertainty about converting an investment into cash without losing a significant amount of the funds invested. Certain investments are more liquid than others; the greater the liquidity of the investment, the easier it is to buy and sell the investment without sacrificing a price concession. When investing in a particular investment, investors should consider the following two factors:

■ The length of time to sell that investment.

■ The relative certainty of the selling price.

Funds that are to be used in a short period of time should be invested in securities high in liquidity (savings accounts, Treasury bills, money market mutual funds). A Treasury bill can be sold very quickly with a slight concession in selling price, whereas a 20-year-to-maturity junk bond may not only take time to sell, but may also sell at a significant price concession.

This is especially true for bonds that are thinly traded—where relatively few of these bonds are traded and the trades take place only with large spreads between the bid and asked prices. Thinly traded bonds are not *marketable*, which means that they cannot be sold quickly.

Common stocks listed on the stock exchanges and on the over-the-counter markets may be marketable, but not liquid in that the spreads between the bid and asked prices may be wide and the sale price may be less than the purchase price, resulting in losses.

Foreign Currency Risks

If you decide to escape it all by investing in stocks of foreign companies, these are subject to *foreign currency risks.*

A rise in the dollar against a foreign currency can decimate any returns and result in a loss of capital when the stocks are sold.

It is evident that risk cannot be avoided even with the most conservative investments (savings accounts and Treasury bills). By understanding and recognizing the different levels of risk for each type of investment, the total risk can be better managed in the construction of an investment portfolio.

There is a direct correlation between risk and return. The greater the risk in an investment, the greater the potential return to entice investors. However, in most cases, investing in securities with the greatest return and, therefore, the greatest risk can lead to financial ruin if everything does not go according to plan.

How much risk you can tolerate depends on many factors, such as the type of person you are, your investment objectives, the amount of your assets, the size of your portfolio and your time horizon for the investments.

How nervous are you as an investor? Do you check your stock prices every morning in the financial newspapers? Can you sleep well at night if your stocks have declined below their acquisition prices? If you do watch the prices of your stocks every day, call your broker every time that your stocks fall by a point and do not sleep well at night when your stocks are down, you do not tolerate risks well. In this case, your portfolio should be weighted towards conservative investments that generate income through capital preservation. The percentage of your portfolio allocated towards stocks may be low to zero, depending on your comfort zone. Figure 2–1 illustrates the continuum of risk tolerance. If you are comfortable with accepting more risks you would invest a greater percentage of your portfolio in stocks. This would be so even if you are the type of person who monitors your stocks on a daily basis. The difference would be if you can sleep well at night when your stocks go down in value.

Moving along the continuum of greater risk seeking, if you buy stocks and forget about them until you are reminded about them by someone else, your tolerance for risk is much greater, and your portfolio can include a large percentage of stocks.

The risk seeker or speculator will look for investments with the greatest rates of return even though the investments may be extremely volatile and there may be a good chance that some of the funds could be lost.

Figure 2–1   Continuum of Risk Tolerance

0%   % Allocated to Stocks   100%
|——|
Nervous   Moderate   Risk Seeker,
Investor   Risk   Speculator

Bear in mind that there are other factors you need to consider when allocating your investment funds to different types of investments. Understanding your tolerance for risk is an important step in determining how much of your portfolio can be allocated to stock.

■ Rate of Return

Investors invest in order to earn a return that may be in the form of income (interest and dividends) and/or capital appreciation (when the price of the investment rises between the time of purchase and sale). Some investments, such as savings accounts and certificates of deposit (CDs), offer only income with no capital appreciation; while others such as common stocks, which may or may not pay dividends, also offer the potential for capital appreciation. If the price of the stocks goes down, there will be capital losses. The simple definition of total return includes both income and capital gains and losses.

Why is calculating a return so important? There are two reasons. First, it is a measure of the growth or decline of your investments. Second, it is a yardstick with which to evaluate the performance of your investments against your objectives.

The total rate of return can be calculated as follows:

$$\text{Rate of Return} = \frac{(\text{Ending Value} - \text{Beginning Value}) + \text{Income}}{\text{Gross Purchase Price}}$$

Spreads and commissions should be included in the calculations. For example, if a stock was purchased at the beginning of the year for $1,000 (including the commission), was sold for $1,200 (net proceeds received after deducting the commission) at the end of the year and earned a dividend of $50, the rate of return would be 25%:

$$\text{Rate of Return} = \frac{(1,200 - 1,000) + 50}{1,000}$$
$$= 25\%$$

This rate of return is not very accurate, particularly if the investment is held for a long period of time. This is because the time value of money is not taken into account. The *time value of money* is a concept that recognizes that a dollar today is worth more in the future because of its earnings potential. A dollar invested at 3 percent for one year would be worth $1.03 at the end of one year. Similarly, a dollar to be received at the end of one year would be worth less than a dollar at the beginning of the year.

This simple average rate of return of 25 percent discussed above does not take into account the earnings capacity of the interest received. In other words, the $50 of dividends received would be reinvested, which would increase the rate of return above 25 percent.

Using the time value of money to calculate the rate of return will give a more accurate rate of return figure. However, it is more difficult for the average person to calculate. The rate of return on a stock will equate the discounted cash flows of the future dividends and the expected sale price of the stock to the current purchase price of the stock. This formula works better for bonds than for common stocks because the cash flows for bonds are much more certain than those for common stocks. The coupon rate for bonds is generally fixed; dividend rates on common stocks may fluctuate. When companies are experiencing losses, they may cut their dividends, as Westinghouse Electric Company did in 1994. On the positive side, if earnings increase, companies may increase their dividend payout ratios. There is even less certainty over the sale price of a stock into the future. Bonds are retired at their par price ($1,000 per bond) at maturity; but when selling a stock in the future, you would be guessing at the sale price.

Whichever formula you use to calculate the rate of return on stocks, you need to be aware that there could be wide fluctuations in return from year to year. This is due primarily to the fluctuations in the price of the stock, since dividend income tends to be relatively stable. Thus, at any point in the future, the price of the stock could be up or down from the acquisition price.

However, between 1926 and 1992, there have been only 20 down years in the stock market. If investors had time on their side during these down years and stayed in the stock market, they would have recouped their losses (Clements, 13).

Clearly, many investors dream of trebling their investments overnight by buying stocks. This may happen, but it is not the order of the day. The rate of return that investors ought to expect from investing in a diversified stock portfolio should be greater than the returns received on bonds and money market securities. Historically, over long periods of time the stock market has outperformed both long-term and short-term bonds, and although there are no guarantees this trend will likely prevail in the future. The superior results obtained by stocks are compelling.

According to the Ibbotson and Sinquefield study (1991) common stocks of large companies had nominal average yearly returns of 12.1 percent over the 64-year period from 1926–1990, while returns earned by common stocks of small companies averaged 17.1 percent per year during the same period. Those average returns are useful yardsticks of performance. Investors should follow the various stock market indices, such as the Dow Jones Industrial Average and Standard & Poor's 500 Index, as a measure of the performance of the stock markets.

Investors in the stock markets need to be aware that their money will always face the risks of price fluctuations despite the long-term profitability of the stock markets. Investors who have low tolerance for risks and who need investments with capital preservation should not invest in common stocks. Similarly, if investors need their money in less than five years, they should avoid stocks.

If investors have a long time horizon, they can invest in a diversified portfolio of stocks, which will more than likely generate superior returns to other investments despite all the risks.

■ Inflation and Taxes

There are two important factors affecting the rates of return on investments—inflation and taxes. If an investor earns 5 percent per year, and inflation is 3 percent for the same period, the *real rate of return* is only 2 percent. If inflation rises to 5 percent or above, investors holding fixed-income securities yielding five percent will not be jumping for joy at the prospect of zero to negative rates of return. That is why market prices of fixed-income securities (bonds) decline so rapidly when the inflation rate rises: bondholders receive fixed amounts of interest. Market prices of existing bonds on the secondary markets will go down in price in order to make their rates of return more competitive (to include the rate of inflation), which will entice additional investors.

The Ibbotson and Sinquefield studies (1991) report the highest real rates of return (adjusted for inflation) for common stocks (over Treasury bills and bonds) for the 64-year period 1926–1990. In years when inflation was low, common stocks had their highest real rates of return; but in years when inflation was high (above 6 percent), the real returns on common stocks were negative. However, to put this in perspective, in relation to other investments, the returns of stocks were less negative than those of bonds and Treasury bills.

Consequently, the stock market offers investors the most favorable real rates of return in a low-inflation economy, whereas a high-inflationary environment produces negative real rates of return on most investments (bonds and stocks). If you anticipate inflation, choose those investments that will yield rates of return that will protect against the inflationary erosion of purchasing power.

Taxes also diminish the investor's rate of return. Dividend and interest income is taxed at ordinary rates at the federal level. At the time of this writing, long-term capital gains (with a holding period of greater than one year) are taxed at a lower rate than the top marginal tax bracket rate. Currently, for 1994, the highest tax rate bracket is 39.6 percent and the long-term capital gains rate is 28 percent.

The reinstatement of the lower capital gains rate is advantageous for investors in the higher tax brackets who have investments that generate long-term capital gains. For these investors, common stocks with capital appreciation potential become attractive investments.

As taxes (federal, state and possibly local) are levied on dividends (interest) and capital gains, the after-tax rate of return on different investments should be compared. The after-tax rate of return is calculated as follows:

After–tax rate of return = (1 – tax rate) (before tax rate of return)

For example, an investor in the 39.6 percent marginal tax bracket who invests in securities yielding 10 percent has an after-tax rate of return of 6.04 percent:

After–tax rate of return = (1 –.396) (.10)

= 6.04

This rate of return can be compared to the rate of return of a municipal bond, which is tax-free at the Federal level. In many cases, taxes affect the choice of investments. Effective tax planning may reduce the level of taxes paid.

Rates of return are diminished by inflation, taxes and commissions. Investors should consider these factors to ensure that after they have been deducted, their investments yield positive returns.

∎ Selection of Investments

Understanding the risk-return trade-off is an important step in the invesment process that goes back to choosing the level of risk you feel comfortable with. Returns on common stocks may be potentially higher than those received on other investments, but the risks of holding common stocks are greater than those of bonds and Treasury bills.

There are no ideal investments, and so investors should understand the different types of investment securities, their risk characteristics and their expected returns. Keep in mind that these may change over time, and so investors may need to anticipate these changes in order to be successful.

As mentioned earlier in the chapter, there are two elements that reduce some of the risks: diversification and time. Diversification reduces unsystematic risk, which consists of business and financial risk. By investing in the different types of securities of various companies in different industries, the risks of loss in the total portfolio is reduced. For example, when the stock of one company in the portfolio declines, there may be increases in the other stocks which will offset the losses. However, diversification does not reduce market risk. If the stock market declines, the stocks of a diversified portfolio will generally also decline. In fact, the bond and stock markets often move together, so even a diversified portfolio during these times is not immune from market risk. for finance final

Time is the other element that can help combat market risk. With a long time horizon, investors can wait for stock prices to recover from a down market.

The decision about the types of securities to invest in will depend on the investor's objectives, the characteristics of the investor (marital status, age, family, education, income, net worth and the size of the portfolio), the level of risk, the expected rate of return and the economic environment. The flow chart in Figure 2–2 looks at some of the factors in the selection of the different types of investments.

For example, if an investor's objectives are to seek capital growth and this investor is a young, single professional with an excellent salary, he or she may tolerate greater risks in order to receive higher returns. With a long time horizon, a greater portion of this investor's portfolio should be invested in common stocks. If economic conditions are favorable for the stock market, the *asset allocation* in this case could be as follows:

Stocks	80%
Bonds	10%
Money Market Equivalents	10%

A more conservative asset allocation model would be as follows:

Stocks	50%
Bonds	40%
Money Market Equivalents	10%

Figure 2–2 Selection of Investments

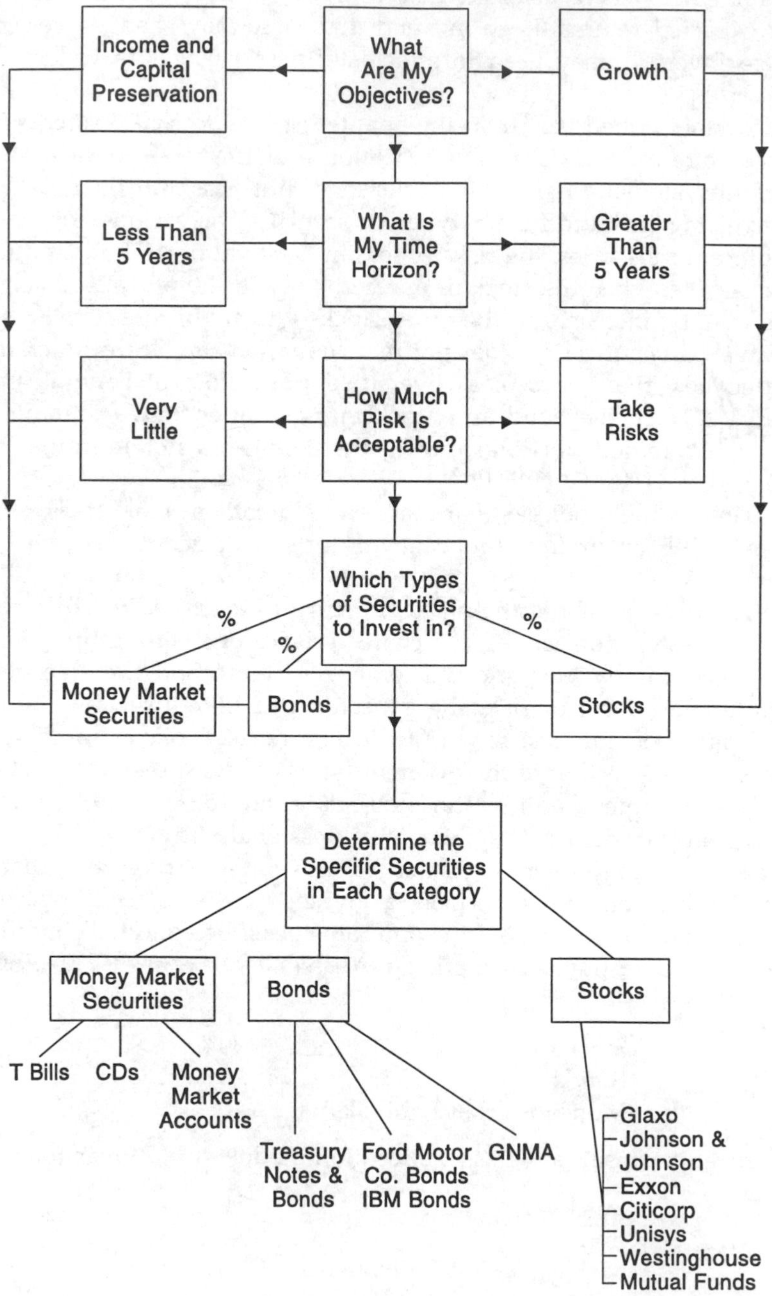

At the other extreme, an older, retired couple with limited net worth whose objectives are income and capital preservation will have an entirely different allocation of their assets. They would not be able to tolerate very much risk, and their time horizon may be shorter. In order to generate regular income, a greater portion of their investment portfolio will go into fixed-income securities with varying maturities. Generally, the longer the maturities the greater the returns, even though the risks increase with the length of the maturities. Depending on their circumstances, there could be a small percentage allocated to common stocks to provide some capital appreciation. Their suggested asset allocation model might be set up as follows:

Stocks	10%
Bonds	70%
Money Market Equivalents	20%

The percentage amount allocated between bonds and money market equivalents will vary from couple to couple depending on their circumstances.

Asset allocation depends on the investment objectives and financial characteristics of each investor. What works for one family may not be appropriate for another. For example, the financial characteristics of two couples may be identical, but the one couple may need greater amounts set aside in money market securities to meet medical bills.

The important aspect of investing is having an asset allocation plan that signifies the broad mix of investments to strive for. This allocation plan is not cast in stone and should change to accomodate changes in personal and economic circumstances. For example, when market rates of interest are declining, a greater percentage of the portfolio may be allocated to stocks. Similarly, when inflation and interest rates are rising, investors could park more of their funds in money market equivalents until economic conditions become more favorable toward stocks.

The next step is the choice of individual securities. This requires a thorough investigation. In many cases, investors invest in stocks suggested by friends and associates without even looking at the financial status of the companies. The easiest way to loose money is to make a few bad investments in stocks and bonds. There are many ways to choose individual securities. Investors can rely on "hot tips" they hear at the hairdresser's, or they can be more scientific about their choices of investments.

Most people work hard to generate savings and then spend very little time investing it. This is partly due to the fact that generally some knowledge about investments is required in order to be successful. Those who do not have the knowledge or the inclination to manage their investments hire others to do so for them; or they can choose to invest in mutual funds, which are managed by professional managers.

For those investors who decide to manage their own portfolios, the question becomes, Which individual investments should I buy?

The focus of this book is on common stocks, and so the option of buying bonds and money market securities will not be addressed. There are many books written about bonds and money market securities to help you with the choice of these securities. (My book *All about Bonds* [1993] is one such book.)

Choosing individual stocks is guided by the investor's objectives and degree of risk tolerance, among other factors. These are many different types of stocks with different levels of risks. *Blue-chip stocks* are the stocks of well-established companies that pay dividends. These stocks appeal to investors looking for income and capital appreciation. Generally, the dividend yield on these more conservative stocks tend to lessen the stock price volatility when the stock market declines. During such declines, even good-quality stocks carry moderate risks of capital losses. Growth and emerging company stocks are risky in that they may have higher business and financial risks as well as their stock prices being more volatile. In addition, these stocks may not pay dividends, and therefore would appeal to investors looking for capital appreciation.

After allocating the amount of money to put towards common stocks, the investor must decide which stocks to buy. Other than using "hot tips" to select stocks, one other method is fundamental analysis, which identifies industries in the economy with the potential for doing well. Companies within those industries are evaluated for their earnings and growth capacities. (Fundamental analysis is discussed in Chapter 5.)

Technical analysis uses past information about stock prices and volume movements to identify buying and selling opportunities for stocks. (Technical analysis is discussed in Chapter 6.)

Most of the approaches used for selecting individual stocks fall into either of these two classifications: fundamental or technical analysis. Once the individual stocks have been identified, the next step is to determine the amounts to allocate to each stock. Timing, which involves forecasting price movements and diversification, will also play a part in the selection process. Through diversification of the investments in the portfolio, the risks of the entire portfolio can be minimized.

Due to changes in an investor's objectives, the portfolio should be revised from time to time and evaluated for overall performance.

■ Summary

There is no ideal investment. Because different investments and markets perform in different ways, you need to start with a comprehensive investment plan. This includes your objectives, which will determine the types of investments and the time horizon.

Your attitude towards risk will also determine the types of investments you make. If you do not take enough risk, you may not be able to fund your long-term objectives. Similarly, if you take too much risk, you may not be able to sleep at night. You need to find a comfortable balance between the risks and returns of different investments. Your attitude will determine whether you feel comfortable investing in common stocks.

Common stocks have outperformed bonds and Treasury bills over long periods of time. Thus, it is essential for investors when investing in common stocks to have a time horizon of at least five years to be able to ride out any down years in the stock markets.

Certain risks are reduced through diversification. Different types of investments will react differently to inflation and other economic events. Further diversification within the different types of investments should be considered. For example, within common stocks, investors could buy the stocks of small, medium, and large companies as well as domestic and foreign stocks. However, diversification will not counter market risk. Currently, rising interest rates have depressed not only the U.S. stock markets but also those in Europe. Diversification of investments can help investors achieve greater levels of return for the amount of risks they are willing to bear.

How you allocate your money to the different investments will depend on your objectives, income, net worth, age, family responsibilities and your attitude toward risk. For example, the percentages of your total investment portfolio that will be invested in liquid money market equivalents, bonds and common stocks will vary according to these factors.

The next steps are the selection of individual securities within these categories and then the evaluation of the portfolio from time to time.

For investors with a long time horizon, the high returns of common stocks may outweigh the risks of losses in that investors can wait for an opportune time to sell their common stocks. As the time horizon gets closer, investors should allow enough time to sell their common stock investments. If left to the last moment they may be forced to sell their stocks when prices are down.

The risks of owning common stocks cannot be entirely eliminated, and investors should realize that individual stock prices may also go down over the long term. This requires a well-diversified portfolio of individual stocks; investors will need at least $75,000 to achieve this diversification. Investors who do not have the inclination or large amounts of money to invest in individual stocks should consider equity mutual funds (discussed in Chapter 8).

∎ References

Clements, Jonathan. "Why It's Risky Not to Invest More in Stocks," *The Wall Street Journal*, February 1, 1992, pp. C1,13

Ibbotson, Roger G, and Rex A. Sinquefield. *Stocks, Bonds. Bills and Inflation: Historical Return* (1926–1990). Homewood, IL: Dow Jones-Irwin, 1991.

Chapter 3

How to Read the Financial Pages[*]

Key Concepts

- The relationship between the economy and the financial markets
- Monetary policy and the markets
- Fiscal policy and the markets
- The dollar and the markets
- Stock markets and how to read stock quotations
- Options exchange and how to read options quotations

The aim of this chapter is to explain and simplify some of the every-day economic and financial jargon bandied about in the financial pages of the newspapers. It is not meant to be a comprehensive guide to the understanding of economics and finance (or I would still be writing!). This chapter will help investors understand some of the theories that affect the financial markets and enable them to follow the progress of their investments in the newspapers.

For many people, the financial pages of the newspapers are diffi-cult to read. There is a wealth of confusing interrelationships between the economic events and the stock markets. Terms like CPI, GNP, S&P 500 Index, M1, M2, M3 and short interest are bandied about like the codes to a secret society. In fact, economic data can be extremely eso-teric, in that the same data can be used by different economists and

---

[*] Portions of this chapter have been previously published by Esmé Faerber in *Managing Your Investments, Savings and Credit*, Probus Publishing, 1992, and in *All About Bonds*, Probus Publishing, 1993.

financial analysts to come up with different conclusions about the
state of the economy or financial markets.

To help you better understand the relationship between stock
prices and the influence of the economic environment, the first part of
this chapter includes a brief overview of some of the key terms used
to measure the economy. The latter part of the chapter will focus on
stock indices and the different stock and option price quotations in the
newspapers.

The double-digit returns from both the bond and stock markets
during the 1980s and early 1990s have made investing in bonds and
stocks very glamorous and exciting. In the coming years, it may not be
as easy to repeat those successes, and investors may have to be more
discriminating in their choice of investments to equal their earlier stel-
lar returns.

The clearest picture of the economy and financial markets is presented through hindsight, but then, after-the-fact information is too
late for investment decisions. By interpreting economic and market indicators, investors are looking for early warnings of anticipated
changes in the direction of the stock and bond markets. On the other
hand, the astute reader will say, if economists and financial analysts
can't agree on the state of the markets or the economy, how is the lay
individual able to come up with any more definitive answers?

For individual investors, it is not that important if the forecasted
numbers are not in agreement because, after all, economists and analysts all base their forecasts on the same information. What is important, however, is to be able to use either their forecasts or the key
statistical indicators to predict changes in the direction of the economy
and financial markets. Fluctuations in the economy will affect the financial markets. An understanding of the economic indicators can
help you make timely decisions in the stock and bond markets.

▮ What Is the State of the Economy?

No longer can investors make money by leaving their funds in money
market accounts and CDs when interest rates are low. With increasing
taxes, uncertainty about jobs, rising tuition for higher education and
low interest rates, investors will need to take on more risks in their
investment strategies. This means placing a greater emphasis on stocks
and longer term securities that offer higher returns. Investors must
then contend with the gyrations of the financial markets, which react
to different economic and political events.

Investors are better equipped to plan their investment strategies if they are able to understand and forecast the state of the economy. This section explains the effects of the most common economic indicators that can be used to identify trends in the economy.

Gross National Product (GNP) is a measure in dollar value of all the goods and services produced by a country in a year. Comparing the current GNP with previous periods indicates the economy's rate of growth (or lack of it). An increasing GNP indicates that the economy is expanding.

Inflation distorts the accuracy of this growth, and so there is a measure of the real growth of the nation's output, referred to as _real GNP_. Real GNP is adjusted for price level changes and measures each year's goods and services using prices that prevailed in a selected base year. A comparison of real GNP figures with those of prior years provides a more accurate measure of the real rate of growth. Gross National Product is therefore a measure of the economic health of a country.

A more narrowly focused measure of a nation's output is _industrial production_, which measures the manufacturing output.

The _unemployment rate_ is the percentage of a nation's labor force that is out of work, and it is another indicator of the economy's strength (or lack of it). Currently (1994), the United States has a tight job market, which is still seeing layoffs in various sectors of the economy.

Governments become concerned when the unemployment rate rises above a certain level (currently the unemployment rate is above 6 percent), and they will stimulate the economy through monetary and fiscal policies to reduce the unemployment rate. These actions may also stimulate inflation.

In the early 1980s the United States experienced both high rates of unemployment and inflation. The government dealt with the inflation first by pursuing restrictive economic policies. This sent the economy into a recession, and the unemployment rate increased further. In 1992, the United States experienced low inflation but high unemployment. The government's approach was to stimulate the economy by lowering interest rates through the Federal Reserve Bank.

Inflation is defined as the rate at which the prices for goods and services rise in an economy. Inflation prevails in a growing economy where the demand for goods and services outstrips the supply, which then leads to rising prices. In other words, too much money is chasing too few goods and services. At the time of this writing, it is difficult to determine whether inflation is about to increase. Some economists expect the rate to go below 2 percent, while others argue for a 5 percent rate of inflation for 1995. Several indicators are used to measure changes in prices and anticipate the level of inflation.

The Consumer Price Index. (CPI) is one measure of inflation that is calculated monthly by the Bureau of Labor Statistics. The Bureau monitors the changes in prices of items (such as food, housing, clothing, transportation, medical care and entertainment) in the CPI. It is a gauge of the level of inflation and is more meaningful when it is compared relative to the CPI of previous periods.

Some economists believe that the CPI fuels inflation similar to a cat chasing its tail. Social security payments and many cost of living increases in employment contracts are tied to the increases in the CPI. The CPI may, in fact, exacerbate the level of inflation.

When the level of inflation is high (relative to previous periods), governments will pursue restrictive economic policies to try and reduce the level of inflation.

The Producer Price Index. (PPI) is announced monthly and monitors the costs of raw materials used to produce products. The PPI is a better indicator of inflation than the CPI because when prices of raw materials increase, there is a time lag before consumers experience these price increases.

Another key indicator is the Commodity Research Bureau's *commodity price index* which measures prices of raw materials. When this index rises significantly over a six-month period it is a warning that inflation is on the horizon.

When other indicators such as the *Leading Inflation Index*—an index that anticipates cyclical turns in consumer price inflation, developed by Columbia University's Center for Business Cycle Research—moves up with commodity prices, it is a clear signal inflation is ahead.

When an economy is in recovery, the *manufacturing capacity utilization rate* becomes a key indicator to watch. This indicator measures how much of the economy's factory potential is being used. Economists worry about inflation when the nation's factory capacity rises above 82.5 percent. For example, when the recovery is robust and the economy is growing rapidly, while interest rates remain low, there will be a decline in unemployment, which will give rise to increasing wages and prices.

Inflation has a detrimental effect on the bond and stock markets as well as on the economy. When the level of inflation increases, real GNP falls (in 1980 in the United States); and, similarly, when inflation declines, real GNP increases (in 1983 in the United States). This inverse relationship may not always hold, as evidenced by the economy in

1992. Despite lower levels of inflation, real GNP showed insignificant growth, which translated into the economy taking a long time to move out of the recession.

Housing Starts, released monthly, represent the strength in the rate of housing production. An increase in housing starts relative to previous months indicates consumer confidence in the economy.

Leading Indicators: Economists have designed an index of leading indicators to forecast economic activity. This index of leading indicators includes data series ranging from stock prices, new building permits, and average work week to changes in business and consumer debt. By analyzing this monthly index, economists hope to be able to forecast economic turns, so as to give advance warning of a turn in the stock market. However, in reality, when the leading indicators forecast an economic turn, the stock market has already reacted to the change.

These are some of the pieces to the overall economic picture. By examining these indicators and statistics, investors are better able to fine-tune their opinions and forecasts of the economy. This is not to suggest that, with a brief overview of some economic terms, you are now an expert who can dispense with all the economists' forecasts. On the contrary, it is difficult to predict economic behavior; economists are notorious for differing in their forecasts of economic growth, inflation and unemployment. These differing interrelations highlight the complexities of the economy, which does not mean that the investor should throw in the towel and discount the economy. Instead, by using a consensus of economic forecasts, investors are better prepared to decide how to invest their funds.

■ The Effects of the Economy on the Stock Markets

As publicly held companies make up a large part of the economy, they will be affected by the state of the economy. Generally, there is a strong correlation between how well companies do, which is tied to their stock prices, and the strength of the economy. When the economy is strong (real GNP is growing, unemployment is falling, raw material orders are increasing, investment spending is up), most firms see sales increase followed by an increase in earnings, which allows for an increase in dividends and/or growth in the companies. This generally results in higher stock prices.

The relationships between the components of the economy are exceptionally complex and must not be oversimplified. For example, an expanding economy can also result in rising prices (inflation), higher wages, increased competition, higher interest rates and higher taxes, which could have a detrimental effect on companies' earnings. Thus, the relationship between the economy and the stock market is not a simple one. It is generally true, however, that during periods of prosperity, the stock prices of earnings-driven companies have a tendency to go up.

The opposite is true during a recession, where there is a downturn in economic activity and companies will eventually feel the effects of the poor economic activity. Sales slow down and eventually decline, which leads to reduced earnings and, therefore, lower stock prices.

This points to the overall relationship of economic activity, earnings and stock prices. An expanding economy is generally accompanied by a strong stock market and a declining economy with a weak market. However, we should be wary of blanket generalizations. Not all companies will suffer during periods of economic downturn and, similarly, not all companies will do well during periods of economic growth. Investors will still need to analyze the individual company as to its potential sales and earnings growth and its financial position to ascertain whether and when they should purchase that company's stock.

Investors are always worried about inflation. Rising prices in an economy have a detrimental effect on the bond markets, which may then affect the stock markets. With rising prices, the fixed returns received on bonds buy less and less over time. This drives bond prices down, which may then cause jitters on the stock markets. This happened in February 1994, when the Federal Reserve Bank raised the short-term federal funds rate by one-quarter point to combat inflation and keep the economy from overheating. This rate increase caused the bond markets to decline, which then brought about a sell-off in the stock markets, as well as fueling uncertainty over the short-term prospects of the stock markets.

In the 4-week period after the rate hike, the U.S. Treasury 30-year bond fell roughly 6 percent in price and the Dow Jones Industrial Average fell roughly 3.5 percent. This raises the question as to whether the stock markets will continue to fall with the bond markets or whether they will part company and go in separate directions. For the past 3 years, the stock and bond markets have moved up together during an economic period characterized by low inflation and falling interest rates and an economy struggling to move out of recession.

Some analysts argue that the stock market will rally, whereas, the bond market will fall in price. Their premise is a stronger economy with strong corporate profits and low inflation. Other analysts predict higher interest rates, which will continue to depress both the bond and the stock markets. Thus, by forecasting the direction of the economy, investors can better anticipate the direction of the stock market.

■ Monetary Policy and the Financial Markets

Monetary policy can have a substantial impact on the economy and thus on the financial markets. The Federal Reserve Bank (Fed) regulates the nation's supply of credit and money, and can thus affect the country's economic growth, inflation, unemployment and production.

How the Federal Reserve Changes the Supply of Money

The principal tools used by the Federal Reserve Bank to change the supply of money are open market operations, reserve requirements and the discount rate.

Open Market Operations. The Federal Reserve will buy and sell securities in the open market to change the money supply and the reserves of commercial banks. When the Fed buys government securities, it is expanding the nation's supply of money. The Fed will pay for the securities by check, which will increase the reserves in banks. As a result, banks will be able to increase their loans and deposits.

When the Fed wants to contract the nation's money supply, it will sell government securities from its portfolio on the open market. This has the effect of siphoning off money from the nation's money supply; commercial banks' reserves are reduced, therefore reducing banks' abilities to lend money.

Reserve Requirements. The Federal Reserve Bank requires banks to maintain reserves with the Fed. The percentage of banks' deposits held as reserves is determined by the Fed and is called the reserve requirements. The Fed can increase the money supply by reducing the reserve requirements: banks will need to keep lower reserves and can therefore increase their lending. The reverse is true when the Fed increases the reserve requirements.

Not only will the money supply increase or decrease due to changes in the reserve requirements, but there will also be a multiplier effect on the money supply. This can be illustrated by a simple example.

Suppose I deposit $100 in Bank X, and the reserve requirement is 10 percent. Bank X now has $100 on deposit, of which $10 is kept on reserve and $90 is lent to Corporation A. Corporation A deposits this $90 check in its bank, Bank A. Bank A will keep $9 on reserve and will lend the remaining $81. This process is repeated, which shows how the original $100 is increased through the banking system to expand the money supply. Figure 3–1 illustrates the multiplier process.

Thus, the Fed can stimulate the multiplier effect by lowering reserve requirements, which correspondingly increases the banks' capacities to lend.

Discount Rate. The discount rate is the Fed's third tool. The discount rate is the rate of interest that the Fed charges banks when they borrow from the Fed. When the discount rate is too high, banks are discouraged from borrowing reserves from the Fed. When the discount rate is low or lowered, banks are encouraged to borrow. Thus, by changing the discount rate, the Fed can expand or contract the money supply.

Defining the Money Supply

Before looking at the relationship of money supply and the financial markets, we need to define the different ways of measuring the money supply. This can be likened to measuring our own money supply.

How much cash do we have? The cash in our pockets, wallets, under the mattress and in our checking accounts. However, savings accounts, money market funds and some investments can easily be

Figure 3–1   The Multiplier Process

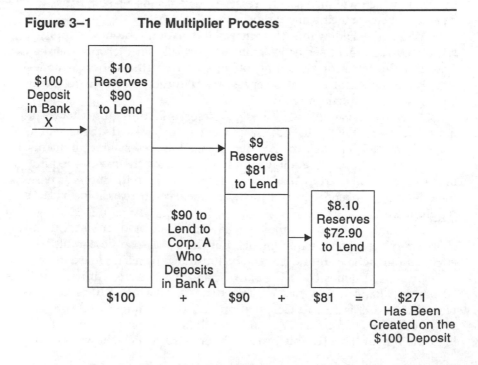

converted into cash. Similarly, the narrowest measure of the nation's money supply is referred to as M-1, a broader measure M-2 and the broadest measure as M-3.

M-1 consists of the nation's cash, coins, traveler's checks, checking accounts (NOW accounts, which are interest-bearing checking accounts, are included) and demand deposits.

M-2 includes M-1 but also adds savings and time deposit accounts (e.g., CDs, money market deposit accounts of less than $100,000).

M-3 includes M-1 and M-2 as well as time deposits and financial instruments of large financial institutions.

Which is the best measure of the economy's money supply? Economists continue to argue this point. The Federal Reserves' preferred measure is M-2, which is America's broad money supply. Some economists argue that the slow growth of M-2 in the United States (1.7 percent from January–August 1992) stunted the economic recovery and that the Fed's policy of broad monetary growth was too tight. Others complain that the nation's narrow money supply, M-1, was too lax, as evidenced by a 12.3 percent jump ("Monetary Smoke Signals," 95).

Interest rate changes explain this discrepancy. Short-term interest rates fell; which caused investors to move their savings out of low-yielding bank deposits (including M-2) into higher yielding bonds. Thus, economists argue that portfolio shifts make the definitions of the money supply unreliable as indicators of the economy. For example, you can see at once that M-1 could increase when people transfer money from their savings accounts to checking accounts without affecting M-2. There will be discrepancies between the classifications of the money supply from week to week, but the investor should be more concerned with the overall changes over a period of time so that a trend can be established. By monitoring the Fed's open market transactions, changes in the reserve requirements and the discount rate, and the rate of growth or decline in the money supply, investors are better able to make investment decisions.

Evidence suggests that changes in the money supply have an influence on nominal economic activity, but the influence on real economic growth is still hotly contested.

Impact on the Financial Markets

When the Fed pursues a restrictive monetary policy, it may sell securities on the open market to siphon money from the money supply and/or raise the reserve requirements that reduce the bank's capacity to lend money, and/or raise the discount rate to discourage banks from borrowing money.

These changes in the monetary conditions will have an effect on corporate earnings. When the money supply is decreased, interest rates will go up, making it more costly for companies and individuals to borrow money. This will cause them to delay their purchases, which will lead to reduced sales. With lowered sales and higher credit costs, companies will have decreased earnings, which translate to lower stock prices.

When interest rates are rising, investors will earn more by investing in fixed-income securities and money market instruments. Therefore, many investors will take their money out of the stock markets and invest in liquid short-term securities and longer-term debt securities, which puts more downward pressure on stock prices. Higher interest rates also translate into higher borrowing costs for margin investors. These investors will move their money to debt instruments to justify their higher interest costs.

Monetary policy has a direct effect on interest rates, and there is a strong correlation between interest rates and the stock market. Rising interest rates tend to depress stock market prices, while falling interest rates have the opposite effect. This was evidenced by the actions taken by the Federal Reserve Bank on February 4, 1994. The Fed increased the short-term Federal funds rate by one-quarter point, which sent both the stock and the bond markets reeling downwards. The stock market regained some of its losses a short time after, but interest-sensitive stocks (stocks of financial companies and utilities) still have not fully recovered.

Stock market investors will move their money into the bond markets when interest rates are high, and when interest rates fall they will move back into the stock markets.

The open market operations of the Fed have a direct impact on interest rates and the bond markets. When the Fed buys Treasury securities on the open market, it competes with other buyers, driving up prices and causing a decrease in Treasury yields. This creates a rate discrepancy between the yields on government debt and corporate debt. As a result, investors will purchase corporate debt, causing prices to go up and yields to decrease. The reverse is true when the Fed sells government securities on the open market.

This suggests that if investors anticipate changes in monetary policy, they can make the appropriate changes to their investment strategies.

■ Fiscal Policy and the Markets

The goals of both monetary and fiscal policy are the same: the pursuit of full employment, economic growth and price stability. The government can use its fiscal policy to stimulate or restrain the economy. The tools of fiscal policy are taxation, government expenditures and the government's debt management. Changes in fiscal policy can affect the financial markets.

Taxation. The federal government uses taxation to raise revenue and also to reduce the amount of money in the economy. Taxation policies can stimulate or depress the economy and the stock markets. When taxes are increased, consumers have less money to invest and spend on goods and services; corporations have reduced earnings which will lead to lower dividends.

Tax cuts, however, have the opposite effect. Individuals will have more money to spend and invest, and corporations will experience the benefits of greater consumer spending along with lower corporate taxes, which generally leads to higher sales and higher earnings.

Government Spending. A tax cut has a similar effect to an increase in government spending. A tax cut has a favorable effect on savings and investments, whereas government spending has a greater effect on the goods and services produced in the economy. Government spending can also be used, therefore, as a tool to stimulate or restrain the economy.

Debt Management. When the government's revenues are less than its expenditures, it runs a deficit. Deficit spending can have a significant effect on the financial markets in general, and the stock market in particular.

The government can finance its deficit by borrowing in the financial markets or increasing the money supply.

Borrowing in the Financial Markets. By borrowing in the financial markets, the government will drive up yields on the bond markets, which will have a depressing effect on the stock market. By selling securities on the market, prices of government securities will go down, which increases their yields. To counter the rate differential (between corporate and government securities), investors will invest in government securities rather than in corporate securities. This will reduce the prices of corporate bonds, which leads to increased yields on them. Thus, borrowing in the market by the government has the effect of depressing bond prices and increasing interest rates. The opposite is true of the government buying securities in the market: bond prices are pushed up and interest rates are lowered.

When a government is faced with financing an increasing deficit from year to year, it will have to pay high rates of interest to attract buyers to invest in all its securities. This leads to higher interest rates in the economy, which as we saw has a depressing effect on stock prices.

Increasing the Money Supply. If the government increases the money supply, inflation may raise its ugly head, and inflation has a negative effect on the economy and the bond and stock markets.

In summary, when a government is unable to reduce the growth of its deficit spending, there will be an effect on the stock and bond markets. Investors will constantly be looking for policies or budgets that can effectively change the direction of growth of the deficit and have a beneficial effect on the stock market.

Increased government spending can be inflationary and can bring an immediate response from bondholders. Due to computerized global trading, bondholders can unload millions of dollars of U.S. Treasuries within hours and can send bond prices plummeting and long-term yields soaring. This can have the effect of an earthquake on stock markets globally, sending them plummeting.

Fiscal policies affect the security markets; by anticipating changes in these policies, investors can formulate their investment strategies.

∎ The Dollar and the Financial Markets

Great attention is paid to the relative value of the dollar, the trade deficit and whether the Japanese and Europeans will continue to fund the budget deficit through Treasury auctions. The financial markets react to these financial events. In fact, by now you have come to realize that the stock and bond markets react on a daily basis to almost all economic and financial announcements. In some cases, the markets will anticipate these announcements. For example, the stock market may go up in anticipation of the announcement of favorable balance of trade figures for the quarter.

International Trade and the Dollar

There is a relationship between the markets, international trade, and the relative value of the currency. Readers of the financial press will come across an assortment of terms such as *balance of payments, trade deficit* (not the same as a budget deficit), *current account surplus and foreign portfolio investment* and wonder how these can guide (or misguide) economic policy makers. Great care should be used in interpreting balance of payments figures because of the complexities and ramifications involved.

Balance of payments is an accounting of all the transactions that take place between the residents of a country and the rest of the world. The balance of payments will show whether a country is a net importer or exporter of goods and services; whether foreigners are net investors in that country or whether that country is a net exporter of capital; and the changes in the country's reserves.

Balance of trade is the difference between a country's exports and its imports of merchandise. A balance of trade surplus indicates that the country exports more goods than it imports, and a deficit indicates the opposite.

A balance of trade deficit is not necessarily a bad financial omen and should not be judged in isolation from the rest of the country's balance of payment figures. For example, Switzerland has had balance of trade deficits, but it also has surpluses in its balance of services account. As long as a country can finance its balance of trade deficit through its other current accounts and capital accounts, it is economically acceptable.

Current account is the first major section of the balance of payments and includes all of the country's imports and exports of merchandise (balance of trade), services (balance of services) and transfers (includes foreign aid). A country with a current account surplus will be able to contribute to its capital and reserve accounts. A country with a current account deficit will either have to finance it from capital inflows from abroad or run down its reserves.

Capital account indicates whether the country is a net importer or exporter of capital. In other words, has the rest of the world invested more in this country, or has this country invested more in the rest of the world? A country with a current account deficit will need to finance this deficit with imported capital, or it will be forced to run down its reserves.

Reserve account includes liquid assets such as gold, foreign currencies, special drawing rights (SDRs) and the country's reserve position at the International Monetary Fund. All of these can be converted into foreign currencies to settle the country's international claims.

International trade, investments and the country's actual or relative reserves affect the value of its currency. When Americans buy goods from abroad, they pay in U.S. dollars, which are exchanged at the going rate into the foreign currency. Since 1973, most of the currencies of the industrialized nations have been allowed to float against each other. Thus, the value of one currency is measured against the value of other currencies through the forces of supply and demand. When there is great demand for a currency, it will appreciate in value relative to other currencies; when demand is low, the currency will lose value. Prices of currencies are determined on the foreign exchange market, which is composed of international banks and foreign exchange traders.

Inflation and interest rates are also important economic factors influencing a currency's value.

Inflation High inflation in a country will cause its currency to depreciate. For example, if inflation rises in the United States, the price of goods that originally cost $100 might increase in price to $105. American consumers may, therefore, prefer to buy imported goods for the equivalent of $100. This will increase demand for foreign currencies and put downward pressure on the dollar. The theory of purchasing power parity addresses this issue by stating the following: if the prices of goods go up in one country relative to another, in order to keep parity in prices of goods between the two countries, the currency must depreciate.

Inflation will also have a detrimental effect on foreign investments, as foreigners will not want to invest in financial assets that will lose value. Therefore, higher inflation will put upward pressure on interest rates, which is necessary to attract foreign investors.

Rising interest rates, as we saw earlier, will put downward pressure on the stock and bond markets.

Interest Rates When interest rates are higher in one country relative to another, foreigners will then invest in that country's T-bills, CDs and other higher-yielding investments. This will mean a greater demand for that country's currency and, theoretically, an appreciation in value of that currency. The opposite holds true for low interest rates and lower rates of inflation.

The relationship between interest rates, inflation and the value of the currency all add an important dimension to international investments.

This discussion points to an overall relationship between economic activity and the financial markets. Generally, an expanding economy may be accompanied by a booming stock market if companies are experiencing greater earnings.

However, economic expansion could also spook the bond markets that react to fears of inflation. Great care should be taken in not oversimplifying the relationships. A declining bond market could have the same detrimental effects on the stock markets during economic expansion due to inflationary fears and anticipation of higher interest rates. Similarly, a declining economy may be associated with a rising bond market due to lower interest rates, which would have a positive effect on the stock markets.

▮ The Stock Markets and How to Read Stock Prices

The stock markets, where you buy and sell shares of stock, and the news and listings of the different stocks seem to take up a major portion of the financial pages. Stocks may be listed on the New York Stock Exchange, American Stock Exchange and/or regional exchanges. If stocks are not listed on these exchanges, they may be traded on the over-the-counter markets.

Exchanges

The New York Stock Exchange (NYSE) is the largest and the oldest exchange in the United States, and has the most stringent listing requirements. Generally, the largest, best-known and most financially secure companies that meet the listing requirements are listed on the NYSE. When a buy or sell order is placed for a company listed on the NYSE, the broker or registered representative transmits the order electronically to the floor of the exchange. The order is then taken to the trading post for that stock, where the specialist will execute the order.

The ticker tape reports all the executed transactions; investors can watch the trades on the ticker tape, shown on CNBC T.V. during the day. The investor receives confirmation of the trade from the brokerage firm.

The *American Stock Exchange* (AMEX) has less stringent listing requirements than the NYSE and generally has the listings of the younger, smaller companies.

There are 14 *regional exchanges* (the Philadelphia and Pacific Exchanges to name two) that list the stocks of companies in their geographic areas. A company can be listed on the NYSE or AMEX and also be listed on a regional exchange.

A number of companies that issue stocks to the public may not be listed on any of the exchanges, due to a variety of reasons. Instead, they are traded over-the-counter. The *over-the-counter market* (OTC) is linked by a network of computers and telephones.

The most actively traded issues are listed on the NASDAQ (National Association of Securities Dealers Automated Quotations) national market system, and the less-heavily traded issues are listed on the NASDAQ bid and ask quotations. The least-actively traded issues are listed on the Additional Over-the-Counter Quotes. A stockbroker can, therefore, provide the bid and asked price for a particular stock by punching that company's code into the NASDAQ computer system. There are many large, reputable companies, such as Apple Computer and MCI, that have chosen to remain on the OTC market rather than move up to the AMEX or NYSE. The listing fees are lower on the over-the-counter market, which is another reason why a majority of the companies are small, capitalized companies.

In the OTC, orders are executed differently. A customer's order to buy is sent to the trading desk of the brokerage firm where the trader will contact the *market makers* or *dealers* in that stock for the lowest asked price. Market makers are the firms that buy or sell stocks out of their own inventories. A markup is added to the asked price; this amount can be ascertained from the listings of the stocks in the NASDAQ National Market Issues in the newspapers. Similarly, when selling a stock, an amount called a markdown is subtracted from the bid price. For OTC trades, a brokerage firm cannot charge a commission and act as the market maker in a trade. Thus, the brokerage firm would have to choose between charging a commission or the markup/markdown.

The financial newspapers quote the prices of the most actively traded foreign companies listed on the major European, Asian, Australian, South African and Canadian Exchanges (*foreign exchanges*).

Stock Market Indices

Stock investors are always anxious to know how the stock market is doing—whether the market is going up or down, and when to buy and sell stocks. There are a number of stock market indices that will give investors different measures of the stock markets.

The question many investors ask is, Why should we be so concerned with these aggregate measures of the stock market?

The obvious answer is that these aggregate measures will have a direct effect on individual stocks in the market. However, before becoming panic-stricken and ordering your broker to sell your stocks when you read that the Dow Jones Industrial Average has dropped 50 points in one day, or becoming jubilant and ordering champagne for the neighborhood when the Standard & Poor's 500 Index goes up, you should see how these indices relate to the overall composition of your stock portfolio before taking any action.

Individual measures of the market are convenient indicators or gauges of the stock market. These indices indicate the direction of the markets over a period of time. By using these measures, it is possible to compare how well individual stocks have performed against a comparable market indicator for the same period.

There are two measures of stock market prices: an average and an index. An *average* is calculated by adding stock prices and then dividing by a number to give the average price. The Dow Jones Averages are computed this way. An *index* is a more sophisticated weighting of stock prices that are related to a base year's stock prices. Examples are the Standard & Poors 500 Composite Index, the NYSE Composite Index and the OTC Index.

The *Dow Jones Industrial Average* (DJIA) is the oldest and most widely quoted average. The DJIA is composed of the stock prices of 30 large, blue-chip companies (see Table 3–1) that are listed on the NYSE. Stock prices are added and then divided by an adjusted divisor. This divisor is a very small number (.434 in 1994), which makes the DJIA a greater number than the average of the stock prices.

Other Dow Jones averages are the *Dow Jones Transportation Average* (DJTA), which is composed of the stocks of the 20 major transportation companies; the *Dow Jones Utility Average* (DJUA,) which includes 15 major utility stocks; and the *Dow Jones Composite Average*, which combines the three Dow Jones Indices and consists of all the stocks of the 65 companies. See Table 3–1 for a listing of the companies.

Much criticism surrounds the DJIA. First, the stocks are not equally weighted; consequently, an increase of a higher-priced stock will have a greater impact on the DJIA than an increase of a lower-priced stock. Second, with a sample of only 30 large, blue-chip stocks, the DJIA is hardly a representative measure of the market.

Yet the DJIA can be of use to investors. First, by looking at a chart of the DJIA over a period of time, investors can see the ups and downs of the market, which can help them decide when to buy and sell stocks. Second, the DJIA can be used as a yardstick for comparing how your stocks have performed in comparison to the DJIA for the same period of time. However, since the DJIA is composed of only 30 stocks (approximately 25 percent of the total market value of all the stocks traded on the New York Stock Exchange), investors can benefit from looking at more broad-based measures of the market.

Standard & Poor's Index (S&P 500) consists of 500 stocks listed on the New York Stock Exchange and on the OTC. The 500 companies in the S&P 500 Index can also be monitored on the following: the S&P Industrial Index, which consists of 400 industrial stocks; the S&P Transportation Index of 20 companies; the S&P Utilities Index of 40 companies; and the S&P Financial Index of 40 companies.

The S&P 500 Index is a market-value-weighted index, which is computed by calculating the total market value of the 500 companies

Table 3–1   Companies in the Dow Jones Averages

Dow Jones Industrial Average

Allied Signal	Eastman Kodak	J.P. Morgan & Co.
Alcoa	Exxon Corp.	Phillip Morris Co.
American Express	General Electric	Procter & Gamble
AT&T	General Motors	Sears, Roebuck
Bethlehem Steel	Goodyear Tire	Texaco, Inc.
Boeing	IBM	Union Carbide
Caterpillar Inc.	International Paper	United Technologies
Chevron	McDonald's Corp.	Walt Disney Co.
Coca-Cola	Merck & Co.	Westinghouse Electric
Du Pont	Minnesota Mining & Mfg.	Woolworth

Dow Jones Transportation Average

AMR Corp.	Consolidated Freight	Santa Fe Pacific
Airborn Freight	Conrail	Southwest Air
Alaska Air	Delta Airlines	UAL Corp.
American President Lines	Federal Express	Union Pacific Corp.
Burlington Northern	Norfolk & Southern	U.S. Air
CSX Corp.	Roadway Services*	XTRA Corp.
Carolina Freight	Ryder System	

Dow Jones Utility Average

American Electric Power	Consolidated Natural Gas	Panhandle Eastern Corp.
Centerior Energy	Detroit Edison	Peco Energy
Columbia Gas System	Houston Industries	Peoples Energy
Commonwealth Edison	Niagara Mohawk Power	Public Service Enterprises
Consolidated Edison	Pacific Gas & Electric	So. Cal. Edison Corp.

* NASDAQ National Market System.

in the index and comparing the total market value of the 500 companies to the previous day. The percentage increase or decrease in the total market value from one day to the next represents the change in the index.

Approximately 80 percent of the total market value of all the companies listed on the NYSE are represented in the S&P Index, making it a broader-based gauge of market activity than the DJIA.

The *New York Stock Exchange Composite Index* is a more broad-based measure than the S&P Index, because it includes all the stocks traded on the NYSE. It is a market-value-weighted index and, like the S&P 500, relates to a base period, December 31, 1965. On that date, the NYSE Composite Index was 50. In addition to the NYSE Composite Index, the NYSE also has indices for industrials, utilities, transportation and financial stocks.

The *NASDAQ Composite Index* is a measure of all the stocks traded on the NASDAQ (National Association of Securities Dealers Automated Quotations) system. The NASDAQ Index shows more volatility than the DJIA and the S&P 500 Index because the companies traded on the over-the-counter market are smaller and more speculative. Thus, an increase in the NASDAQ Composite Index can be interpreted as investor enthusiasm for small stocks.

Other Indices

The *American Stock Exchange Index* (AMEX) is value weighted and includes all the stocks listed on that exchange.

Wilshire 5000 is the broadest index and includes all the companies listed on the NYSE and AMEX as well as many of the larger stocks traded on the over-the-counter market. (See Table 3–1.)

The *Value Line Composite Index* differs from the other indices in that it is calculated using a geometric averaging technique of 1,700 stocks listed on the NYSE, AMEX and OTC markets.

The obvious question is, Which is the best index to use? Unfortunately, there is no obvious answer to this question. Studies have shown that all the indices are highly correlated with each other. In other words, they will all move in the same direction together, but there will be some differences. The NASDAQ and the AMEX indices are not as highly correlated with the S&P 500 and the DJIA. This can be expected, as the NASDAQ and AMEX stock indices are composed of companies that are younger, smaller and riskier than the stocks of the larger companies of the DJIA and S&P 500 Index.

The best approach is to choose the index that closely resembles the makeup of your stock portfolio.

∎ How to Read Common Stock Quotations

The format for reading stock price quotations is the same for stocks listed on the NYSE, AMEX and NASDAQ National Market System.

The market prices of listed stocks are quoted daily in the financial pages of newspapers. For example, a typical listing of a common stock from the financial pages would appear as follows:

365 Day				Yld		Sales				
High	Low	Stock	Div	%	P/E	100s	High	Low	Last	Chg
22	14 3/4	Glaxo	.84e	4.1	15	46341	20 5/8	19 7/8	20 1/4	...

Reading from left to right:

- The first two columns indicate the range of trading of the stock for the year. Glaxo traded at its high of $22 per share and a low of $14.75 per share.

- The column to the right of the name of the stock is the estimated amount of the dividend, $0.84 per share. Corporations change the dividends they pay. This is based on the last quarterly or semiannual dividend payment.

- The dividend yield for Glaxo is 4.1 percent. This can be calculated by dividing the expected dividend by the last, or closing, price of the stock (.84/20.25).

- The P/E (price/earnings) ratio indicates what price investors are willing to pay for a stock in relation to the stock's earnings. In other words, Glaxo buyers are willing to buy the stock at 15 times its earnings. High P/E ratios indicate that buyers are willing to pay more for a dollar of earnings.

- Sales in 100s indicates the number of shares traded for that day. In this case, 4,634,100 shares of Glaxo were traded. By following the average daily volume, you can tell if there is any unusually heavy trading activity in a day.

- The next three columns indicate the high, low and last price of the stock for the day. For that day, Glaxo traded at a high of $20.625 and a low of $19.875. It closed at $20.25 per share.

- The last column is the change in price from the previous day's close. In this case, there was no change.

The reporting of the stocks on the over-the-counter markets is more or less the same as for the stocks on the exchanges. The only differences are that the P/E ratios and dividend yields may be omitted.

■ Preferred Stock Quotations

Preferred stock is a hybrid of debt and common stock and is listed with the common stocks on the stock exchanges. Preferred stock is designated with a *pr* or *pf* after the name of the stock. Preferred stock pays dividends at a rate that is fixed at the time of its issue. Although the payments of preferred dividends are not legal obligations of companies, the companies cannot pay dividends to common stockholders before they have paid their preferred stockholders. Bearing in mind these differences, preferred stock is read the same way as common stock in the stock exchange quotations.

■ Options Exchanges and How to Read Options Quotes

Options

Options are traded principally on the five exchanges (American Stock Exchange, Philadelphia Stock Exchange, Chicago Board Options Exchange, New York Exchange and Pacific Exchange) and over-the-counter.

AMEX offers options on individual stocks, general stock market indices, oil and gas index, oil index, transportation index, T-bills, T-notes, computer technology index and institutional index. The *Philadelphia Exchange* offers options on individual stocks, foreign currencies, gold and silver index and general stock market indices. Equity options on individual stocks are also offered on the Chicago Board Options Exchange, New York Exchange and Pacific Exchanges.

How to Read Option Quotations

Readers who are not familiar with stock options should read Chapter 10 on stock options first before reading this section. Options are quoted daily in the financial newspapers. The following is a typical option quotation:

Option	Strike	Exp.	Call		Put	
			Vol	Last	Vol	Last
Merck						
31	25	Jul	53	5 5/8	88	1/4

∎ The first column shows the closing price for Merck stock at $31 per share on the New York Stock Exchange.

∎ The strike price for Merck options is $25 per share. For calls this is the price at which an option buyer could buy the stock. For put options, this is the price at which the stock could be sold.

∎ The expiration for these options contracts is July.

∎ The call volume indicates the number of Merck (call) contracts traded.

∎ The last indicates the price for the right to buy one share of Merck, which is $5.625. Each option includes 100 shares, and so one contract would cost $562.50.

∎ The put volume is 88 contracts.

∎ The price for the right to sell one share of Merck is $0.25. A put contract would cost $25.

∎ References

Faerber, Esmé. *Managing Your Investments, Savings and Credit.* Chicago: Probus Publishing Co., 1992.

———. *All About Bonds.* Chicago: Probus Publishing Co., 1993.

"Monetary Smoke Signals." *Economist*, October 10, 1992, p. 95.

Chapter 4

How to Buy and
Sell Stocks

Key Concepts

■ How to Select a Stockbroker

■ Types of Accounts at Brokerage Firms

■ Types of Orders

■ How Short Selling Works

■ How the Security Markets Work

■ How Orders Are Executed for Stocks on the NYSE

■ How Orders Are Executed for Stocks on the OTC

Most people work hard to earn their money, and when they invest in stocks they hope to earn significant returns. They buy and sell stocks for investment or speculative purposes. Most investors buy stocks when they anticipate that the price of the stock will go up over time. This is known as establishing a *long* position, which is another way of saying that the investor owns the stock. The phrase *selling long* means that investors are liquidating their ownership positions in the stock. This may be because the investor has made enough profit on the stock or because the money could better be invested elsewhere. The opposite of the long position is the *short sale*, where investors speculate on the price of the stock going down. With a short sale, investors place a sell order, which means that they sell the security first and buy the security back when the price is lower. In other words, they are hoping to sell high and buy low. Short selling is much more risky and complex than taking a long position; it will be discussed in more detail later in this chapter. Therefore, investors can profit by not only looking for undervalued stocks but also from overvalued stocks.

∎ How to Select a Stockbroker

Investors buy and sell stocks and bonds through stockbrokers who act as their agents. Selecting a stockbroker is a personal decision. The good news is that there are many brokers and brokerage firms to choose from. The following guidelines may be helpful.

Services Required

Stockbrokers charge commissions for executing trades. These commission costs vary considerably among brokers, which can impact on the profits or losses from the investments. The commissions charged depend on both the number of shares traded and the share price.

Full service national brokerage firms generally charge the highest fees and commissions, followed by *regional* service brokerage firms which tend to be marginally cheaper. The *discount* brokerage firms discount their commissions and either charge no fees or reduced fees for miscellaneous services. Commissions are discounted even more at the *deep discount* brokerage firms. For example, on a 100-share trade of a stock with a price of $30 per share, the typical commission charged at the different types of brokerage firms are (Welsh, 170):

	Range
National full-service brokerage firms	$83 – $91
Regional full-service brokerage firms	$78 – $82
Discount brokerage firms	$40 – $55
Deep-discount brokerage firms	$25 – $35

Paying $91 versus $25 for the same trade certainly makes a difference on the total return. In this example, paying 3 percent of the stock price (at the full-service broker) versus less than 1 percent (at the deep discounted broker) means that the stock would have to go up 6 percent to cover the transaction costs with the full-service commission broker as compared with 2 percent for the deep-discount broker. The more trades that you make the greater the significance of the commissions.

The discount brokerage firms offer reduced services compared with the full-service brokerage firms. The deep-discount firms offer virtually no ancillary services other than the execution of orders. Due to competition, some discount brokers offer some services such as providing information and research. The large, national, full-service brokerage firms offer a diversified range of financial services in addition to information, research reports and the execution of trades.

The types of brokerage services that you require depend on you. If you do not require information and research, you may not need the services of a full-service brokerage firm. On the other hand, if you are new to investing and would require information and research about the market and the types of securities to buy, a full-service brokerage firm (or a discount firm that offers these services) would be worth the extra transaction costs.

Another consideration is the number of trades you will make in a year. If you are likely to just have a few trades a year, the difference in the commissions between a full-service and a discount broker may not be significant. However, if you expect to buy and sell securities on a frequent basis, the additional commissions charged by a full-service broker will be significant. With the increased competition among brokerage firms, many full-service brokers will discount their commissions if asked.

Reputation

Selecting a broker or brokerage firm is a difficult decision that can be likened to choosing a physician. The choice can be approached in two ways: you can either choose a broker or you can choose a brokerage firm and then find a broker in that firm. There have been many complaints by investors of wrongdoing by brokers and brokerage firms; investors should ask about the reputation of the broker/brokerage firm in question.

Both a firm's size and membership in stock exchanges affect its reputation. Large, national firms are known throughout the world. However, a small, local firm may be renowned in the local community. If a stockbrokerage firm is a member of the New York Stock Exchange, its brokers have most likely passed the exam given by the New York Stock Exchange and the National Association of Securities Dealers. In addition, member firms have a stricter set of rules of conduct.

Another consideration is the level and area of expertise of the broker. If the broker's expertise is in bonds or commodities and you are interested in stocks, you ought to continue your search for a broker with specialized knowledge in that area.

Above all you ought to feel comfortable both with talking to your broker and with your broker's investment philosophy. Before making your final decision, find out whether any complaints have been lodged against your broker, by calling the National Association of Securities Dealers' toll free number, 800-289-9999 (Welsh, 171).

You should also ask about the fee structure for custodial services, account management and transaction fees before making your final choice.

Caveats

The following are caveats as to what to expect and what not to expect from your broker:

∎ Most stockbrokers make their living from commissions from trading securities. If the broker's salary is purely from commissions, as opposed to a straight salary, the broker may be biased towards encouraging you to make frequent changes to your portfolio. Brokers who encourage excessive trading, known as *churning*, in order to earn more commissions may be exposed to lawsuits and should be avoided, especially if your investment philosophy is a buy-and-hold strategy. Keep in mind that if brokers are paid a salary, they may have sales quotas to fill in order to cover some of the fixed costs of the brokerage firm.

∎ Most brokers are not financial analysts, and you should not assume they are experts in all aspects of investing. They may have an excellent feeling and working knowledge of many companies and their relative prices. However, if investors need information about stocks not followed by their broker, the broker will obtain the relevant research information from their in-house research department or from sources available to their brokerage firm.

∎ Brokers are required professionally not to offer unsuitable investments to their clients. For example, if a broker suggests a risky, speculative security when the investor's objectives are income generation and safety of principal, the broker may be held accountable for the losses. To protect yourself, state your objectives in writing and give a copy to your broker (Clareman, 167). Don't rush into investments suggested by your broker if you are not sure about them. Ask for more information and weigh the advice or recommendations carefully before making your decision.

∎ Check your monthly statements for accuracy. If you see excessive buying and selling of securities in your portfolio or any unauthorized trading, put your complaint in writing immediately. Do not acquiesce to any unauthorized trades even if profitable (it could be disadvantageous for future unauthorized trades which lose money) (Clareman, 168). In the case of excessive trading, you may be asked to sign an activity letter from the brokerage firm. Signing such a letter means that you approve of the excessive trading or unauthorized trades. If you don't approve, don't sign (Clareman, 168).

■ Types of Accounts at Brokerage Firms

Opening an account at a brokerage firm is as easy as opening a bank account. You will be asked basic information, such as your occupation and social security number, as well as more specific information about your financial circumstances. Brokers are required to get to know their customers in order to be able to use their judgement with regard to sizeable transactions and whether credit can be used by their customers to finance their trades.

You will be asked how you want your securities registered. If you decide on leaving the stock certificates in the custody of the brokerage firm, they will be registered in *street name* (in the name of the brokerage firm). Dividends on the securities are mailed to the brokerage firms, where they are then credited to the customer's accounts. The main disadvantage of registering stocks in street name is that the brokerage firms may not forward all the mailings of reports and news from the company to you. The advantage of holding securities in street name is that when you sell securities, you do not have to rush in to sign and deliver the certificates within the five days before the settlement of the transaction, (three days after June 1, 1995).

If you decide to have the securities registered in your own name, you can either have the certificates stored in the broker's vaults or have them mailed to you. In the latter case, you must store the certificates in a safe place. It is a good idea to store your stock certificates in a safe deposit box as they are negotiable securities. If they are stolen you could face losses.

Three types of accounts can be used for buying and selling securities: cash account, margin account and discretionary account.

Cash Account

With a cash account, the investor is required to pay in full for the purchase of the securities on or before the *settlement date.* The settlement date is currently five business days after the order has been executed. Thus, if a stock is bought on a Monday, the payment is due on or before the Friday of that week, assuming that there are no public holidays within those five days. The Monday is referred to as the *trade date.* Should you not pay for your stocks by the settlement date, the brokerage firm will liquidate the securities. In the event of a loss, the brokerage firm can come back to you for the additional amounts.

When stocks are sold, the certificates must be delivered within five days (if securities are not held in street name) to avoid any charges. After the settlement date, the proceeds of the sale less commissions will either be mailed to you or deposited into a cash account with the brokerage firm. This depends on the arrangements you have made with the firm. It is a good idea to ask whether there are any fees charged for the management of the cash/money market account. If fees are applied, have the checks with your proceeds mailed to you. Interest rates on money market funds are currently so low (around 2-3 percent) that a 2 percent management fee could send your returns after taxes into negative territory.

Margin Account

A margin account allows the client of the brokerage firm to buy securities without having to pay cash in full. The balance is borrowed from the brokerage firm. The maximum amount that the client can borrow depends on the margin requirement set by the Federal Reserve Board. For example, with a margin requirement of 50 percent, an investor buying stock worth $12,000 would have to put up at least $6,000 in cash and would borrow the other $6,000 from the brokerage firm. The brokerage firm would use the stock as collateral on the loan. These securities held in street name may also be loaned to other clients of the brokerage firm who are selling short. Short selling is discussed later in this chapter.

The brokerage firm charges interest on the amount borrowed by the margin investor. The risks are greater in margin trading because using borrowed funds to buy stocks could lead to greater losses if the stocks decline in price and when the interest costs are factored into the calculation. However, if the price of the stock goes up significantly, the rate of return is greater for the margin investor than for the cash investor because the margin investor has invested less money.

If the stocks decline in a margin account, the brokerage firm will send the client a *margin call.* This is a notice requesting that the investor pay additional money to maintain the minimum margin requirements. If the investor does not deposit additional funds, the firm can liquidate the securities. The investor would be liable for any losses incurred by the brokerage firm.

Certain transactions can only be performed with a margin account: selling stocks short and writing uncovered stock options. The latter is discussed in Chapter 10.

Discretionary Account

With this type of account, the investor agrees to allow the brokerage firm to decide which securities to buy and sell as well as the amount and price to be paid for buying and selling securities. For the unethical broker, a discretionary account is the answer to all prayers!

An investor should monitor the activity in a discretionary account on a monthly basis to determine if there is any excessive trading by the broker for the sole purpose of earning more commissions. There is churning if stocks are turned over frequently even though they have only moved up or down a few points. Unless you know and trust your broker implicitly, be careful with a discretionary account.

■ Types of Orders

The size of an order will determine whether it is considered a round lot or an odd lot. A *round lot* usually means that the number of shares traded is 100 or multiples of 100. For the very cheap stocks (penny stocks), a round lot may be 500 or 1,000 shares, and for very high priced shares, a round lot could be considered 10 shares. These 10-share round lots are referred to as *cabinet stocks.*

An odd lot for cabinet stocks consists of a trade of between 1 and 9 shares. On regular priced shares, an odd lot is from 1 to 99 shares, and for very cheap stocks it is less than 500 shares.

Investors trading in odd lots will pay more to trade than investors trading in round lots. The commissions to execute the odd lot trades are generally higher, in addition to the fact that the price of the shares quoted may include a hidden fee.

Orders for stocks in excess of 10,000 shares are called *block trades.* These are typically placed by institutional customers and are handled in a variety of ways. Commissions are much lower and orders are executed very quickly. By knowing the types of orders to use and how they are executed, investors may be able to lower their transaction costs and avoid any misunderstandings with their brokers.

Market Order

The most common of all orders placed is the *market order*. The market order is an instruction to buy or sell a stock at the best available price.

If you obtain a price quote from your broker on Citicorp stock, for example, and you order your broker to buy 100 shares without specifying the price, you are placing a market order. Market orders are given priority in the communications system of the brokerage firm so that the order can quickly reach the exchange floor or the over-the-counter desk. Generally, market orders are executed within a few minutes (or even a few seconds) of being placed. There are a few situations where a market order may not be executed: when there are curbs on the exchange floor or if trading on that particular stock has been halted.

The good news is that market orders are filled soon after they are placed. The downside is that the investor may not know what price the order will be executed at. Generally, the order is executed at or close to the quoted price, due to the prompt execution of the market order. However, if the stock is actively traded at the time the order is placed there may be a greater price deviation from the quoted price. For example, a market order placed to buy a newly issued stock that begins trading for the first time on the secondary market could be executed at a very much higher price than the offering price. The issuance of new stocks is discussed more fully later in the chapter.

Market orders are usually *day orders*, which means they expire at the end of the day. In other words, if the order is not executed on the day it is placed, it expires. The investor can specify a time limit when the order is placed. This can be for a week (GTW—good through the week), a month (GTM—good through the month) or an open order (GTC—good until cancelled).

Limit Order

A *limit order* is an instruction to buy or sell a stock at a specified price. The specified price may be different from the market price. For example, if you think the price of a stock is going to fall from its current price, you could place a limit order to buy that stock at a specified, lower price. If you want to buy 100 shares of Citicorp, which over the past months has fluctuated between $36 and $43 per share, you could place a limit order to buy Citicorp at $36 or lower even though the market price is currently $41 per share. The length of time that the order stands before being executed or expiring depends on the instructions given to the broker:

∎ For the week (GTW).

∎ For the month (GTM).

∎ Until cancelled (GTC).

If you do not specify a time limit, it is assumed to be a day order; and if the price of Citicorp does not go down from $41, the order will be cancelled at the end of the day.

Similarly, a limit order to sell stock is placed above the current market price. For example, when Unisys Corporation's stock is trading at $15 per share, an investor who thinks the stock will continue on an upward trend might decide to put in a limit order to sell at $17 per share or better.

The advantage of a limit order is that investors have an opportunity to buy (or sell) shares at a lower (or higher) price than the market price. The obvious disadvantage is that the limit orders may never be executed if the price never reaches the limit price.

Stop Order

A *stop order* is an instruction to buy or sell a stock when the stock trades at or past a specified price. The stop order may be used to protect existing profits or reduce losses. Although the stop order may appear similar to the limit order, there are some differences.

Stop orders cannot be used for over-the-counter stocks. However, they can be used for all stocks listed on the exchanges (NYSE, AMEX and regional exchanges).

The stop order differs from the limit order in that once the stock's price reaches the stop order price, the stop order becomes a market order. For instance, assume you bought a stock at $20 per share and it is now trading at $30 per share. If you sell now, you would receive a $10 a share profit. To protect your profits from the stock falling rapidly in price, you could place a stop order to sell at $28 per share. If the stock drops to $28, your stop order will become a market order and will be executed at the prevailing market price. If the stock is sold at $27.75 a share, you have protected your profit of $7.75 per share. On the other hand, if the stock keeps going up from $30 a share when you place the stop order, it will lie dormant (if it has no time limit GTC) until the share price falls to $28.

Similarly, an investor can protect profits on a short sale by using a stop order to buy. Short selling is explained in the next section of this chapter.

In addition to protecting profits, stop orders may be used to reduce or prevent losses. Say a stock is bought at $10 anticipating a rise in price, but soon after the purchase news of the company suggests that the price may go down rapidly. The investor could place a stop order to sell at $9, which would limit the losses should the price of the stock decline.

Limiting losses on a short sale is the other use for stop orders which will be explained in the section on selling short.

Technical analysts use stop orders to get into a stock on strength and/or out of a stock on weakness. When a stock goes above a resistance level, the technical analyst will use a stop order to buy in order to benefit from an expected rise in price. Similarly, a sell stop order for a short sale will be placed below a support level to benefit from the expected decline in price. Technical analysis is discussed in Chapter 6.

Despite the advantages of the stop order, there are some disadvantages that should be noted. In volatile markets (when the price of stocks rise or fall rapidly), when the limit is reached, the stop order becomes a market order, which then may be executed a few points away from the stop order price. Consequently, with a stop order you are never sure of the exact price you will obtain for your stock.

The second weakness is in the choice of the stop order price. If the stop order price is placed too close to the market price, a temporary surge or fall in the price of the stock to the stop order price will trigger the execution of the market order. Then if the stock price moves back in the anticipated direction, you no longer have a position in that stock. On the other hand, if the stop order price is set further away from the current market price, then less profits can be protected or greater losses will be incurred. The use of stop orders does not increase profits if the direction of the market price is not correctly anticipated. However, stop orders may limit losses.

There are other special types of orders that are not that widely used by small investors. The most popular types of orders placed by small investors are market orders, followed by limit orders. Understanding how these three frequently used orders work and what their risks are allows investors to place their orders more effectively.

∎ How Short Selling Works

Most investors invest in common stocks by buying them first and then selling them at a later date. This is defined as taking a *long position*. The opposite of this process is the *short sale*, which is based on the expectation that the price of the security is going to decline.

In a short sale, the investor borrows stocks to sell, hoping the price will decline so that the stock can be bought back later at a lower price and then returned to the lender. An example will better illustrate this process.

Ms. X thinks that the stock of Merck (the pharmaceutical company) is going to drop in price. She puts in an order with her broker to sell short 100 shares of Merck, which is transacted at $35 per share (the total proceeds are $3,500 without taking commissions into account). The brokerage firm has five business days to deliver 100 shares of Merck to the buyer. The brokerage firm has several sources from which to borrow these securities. They may borrow the 100 shares of Merck from their own inventory of stocks, if it has any, or from another brokerage firm. The most likely source is from its own inventory of securities held in street name from its margin accounts. Assume that the brokerage firm finds from its own inventory of street name securities the 100 shares of Merck that are held in a margin account belonging to Mr. Y. The brokerage firm will send these shares to the buyer who bought the shares sold short by Ms. X, and Merck will be notified of the new ownership.

All the parties in this transaction are satisfied. The buyer has acquired the shares. The short seller, Ms. X, has $3,500 less commissions in her margin account, and the brokerage firm has received the commissions on the trade. The $3,500 (less commissions) is held in the margin account (and cannot be withdrawn by Ms. X) as protection should Ms. X default on the short sale.

Mr. Y, who more than likely signed a loan consent form when he opened his margin account, is indifferent to the process. He still has all his rights to the ownership of the 100 shares of Merck. This process is illustrated in Figure 4–1.

Figure 4–1   Illustration of a Short Sale

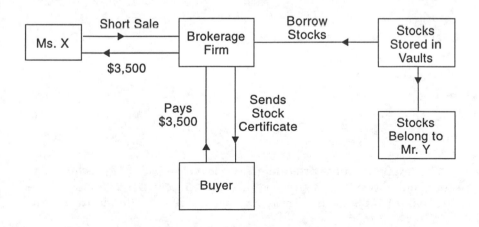

The question that comes to mind is, Who will pay the dividends? Before the short sale, the brokerage firm would have received the dividends on the 100 shares of Merck held in street name in Mr. Y's margin account, and this would then be paid into his account. However, those shares have been used in the short sale and forwarded to the new buyer who receives the dividends from Merck. Mr. Y, however, is still entitled to his dividends. The short seller, Ms. X—who borrowed his securities—is the one who will pay in the amount equal to the dividends via the brokerage firm to Mr. Y.

When Merck declines to $29 per share, Ms. X puts in a buy order to cover her short position. The securities are returned to the brokerage firm, and Ms. X has made a profit of $6 per share, not counting the commissions on the trades and the dividends.

As mentioned earlier in the chapter, short sales are transacted in margin accounts. There is always the possibility that Ms. X could skip town, and the brokerage firm would be minus its 100 shares of Merck. By using a margin account, the short seller (Ms. X) would have to leave the proceeds from the short sale in the account and would also have to pay in an additional amount of cash, known as the margin requirement. Assuming a margin requirement of 50 percent, the following example illustrates the margin account of Ms. X:

Proceeds from short sale of 100 shares of Merck at $35	$3,500
less commissions and fees	100
Net proceeds	3,400
add total margin requirement (50%)	1,700
Balance	5,100

Cost to purchase 100 shares of Merck at $29	$2,900	
add commission	100	
Total cost		3,000
Balance		2,100
less margin deposit		1,700
Profit		$ 400

Margin accounts provide greater leverage than cash accounts, as illustrated above. Ms. X put up $1,700 and received a 23.5 percent return (400/1,700). Cash transactions would require the entire investment in the stock to be put up in cash, which would reduce the rate of return. However, *leverage*, which is the use of other people's money, is a double-edged sword. In the event of losses, the percentage loss would be greater on margin trading than on cash trades.

Stop Orders

Stop orders may be used to protect profits on a short sale. If an investor sells short a stock at $40 and the stock declines to $32, the investor may be reluctant to buy to cover the short position because he or she anticipates that the stock may decline further. To protect his or her profits against an unanticipated rise in price, the investor places a stop order to preserve the profits.

Similarly, the use of a stop order can reduce the amount of losses that can be incurred on a short sale. An investor who sells short a stock at $15 may place a stop order to cover a short position at $16. This limits the losses should there be a rise in the price of the stock. Without a stop order, the investor could potentially face a large loss if the stock keeps going up in price.

Short selling is primarily used by professional traders and hedge funds who hedge their long stock positions against a decline in the prices of the stocks. Beginning investors should not be encouraged to use short selling, due to the speculative nature of the transaction—selling something you do not own. Although perfectly legal with common stocks, this concept of selling what you borrow with other types of assets could land you in jail!

With a long position in stocks, the most that an investor could lose is the entire investment (if the company goes bankrupt and the stock falls to zero with nothing left for the shareholders). However, with short selling, if the price of a stock keeps rising the losses could theoretically be unlimited.

Selling short may be risky for investors who do not have the stomach to watch the price of the stock turn in an unanticipated direction.

There are rules governing short sales on the New York and American Exchanges. Short sales may not be made when stocks are falling in price because this will exacerbate the price decline. On these exchanges, short sales may be made for a higher price than that of the previous trade, on an *uptick*, or for a price which is equal to the previous trade but more than the trade prior to that, on a *zero-plus tick*. These rules do not govern short selling on the over-the-counter markets.

What Is Short Interest?

Short interest is the number of shares of a company's stock that has been sold short and has not been bought back. In other words, the shares borrowed have not been bought back and returned to the lenders. Both the New York and American Stock Exchanges and NASDAQ publish monthly figures of the short sales of listed companies. These are published in the financial newspapers monthly. See the short interest theory discussed in Chapter 6.

▮ How the Security Markets Work

The securities markets are where financial assets are traded. These are also referred to as the *secondary markets*, which are the markets for existing securities, as opposed to the *primary market*, which is the market for new issues of securities.

Primary Markets and Initial Public Offerings (IPOs)

New issues of stocks that are sold for the first time are called *initial public offerings* (IPOs). If a company that has already issued stock on the market wants to issue more stock, this is referred to as a *new issue*. Boston Chicken and Snapple Beverage are examples of two extremely hot IPOs on the market.

With both IPOs and new issues, the companies receive the proceeds from the sale of the stocks. These issues are marketed and sold through underwriters (brokerage firms). Commissions are not charged for the sale of these new shares. Instead the brokerage firms that underwrite these issues receive their compensation from a fee included in the issue price.

In 1993, some extremely profitable IPOs made a lot of money for those who were able to buy the shares at the offering price. For example, the shares of Casino Data Systems were offered to the market on April 5, 1993, at $5 per share, and as of the first week in April 1994 the stock was trading at $33.75 per share (Zweig, Spiro and Schroeder, 84). This is more than a 600 percent return in one year.

Many investors have also been burned in the IPO market. Absolute Entertainment came to the market at $10 per share on April 29, 1993, and as of the first week in April 1994, it was trading around $4 per share (Zweig, Spiro and Schroeder, 84).

This is a 600 percent loss in one year.

There are several disadvantages to the IPO market that individual investors should be aware of before trying to jump in:

■ Institutional investors get very large allocations of shares, leaving a small percentage available for individual investors.

■ Institutional investors are privy to better information than individual investors. The latter rely on information primarily from a prospectus; institutional investors can attend road shows and meet company executives to obtain earnings projections not available in a prospectus.

■ Individual investors are penalized for selling their shares immediately after issue, while institutional investors are allowed to flip their shares. According to a study done by Christopher B. Barry and Robert H. Jennings in 1993, the greatest returns, on average, on IPOs are earned on the first day. Professor Jay Ritter has concluded that the long-term performance of IPOs is very much poorer than that of companies trading on the secondary markets (existing shares traded on the markets). In light of these studies, the Wall Street practice of imposing penalties on brokers who sell their client's shares immediately after issue is disadvantageous for small investors (Zweig, Nathans, Spiro and Schroeder, 84–90).

Currently, the IPO market favors the institutional investor. Individual investors who still like to participate in the IPO market should be aware of the disadvantages facing small investors. They might also consider mutual funds that concentrate on IPOs.

Secondary Markets

After new shares have been sold, investors can trade them on the secondary markets. The company does not receive any proceeds on these trades. Instead, the profits or losses on these trades are borne by the investors.

The secondary markets include the stocks listed on the exchanges and the over-the-counter markets. Stocks may be listed on the New York Stock Exchange (NYSE), which is the largest and has the most stringent listing requirements; the American Stock Exchange (AMEX); and/or the regional stock exchanges. The AMEX has its own listing requirements, which are not as stringent as those of the NYSE. This is why the largest and most prestigious companies are listed on the New York Stock Exchange: they meet the exchange's listing requirements.

However, there are many large, well-capitalized companies that have chosen not to move to the NYSE. Instead, these companies, along with many other small, capitalized companies, have chosen to be

listed on the *over-the-counter* (OTC) markets. Some of the large companies are Intel, Apple Computer, Microsoft and MCI. The listing fees are
lower on the OTC than on the exchanges, and orders are executed differently on the OTC.

■ How Orders Are Executed for Stocks Listed on the NYSE

An example can best illustrate the process of order execution on the
NYSE. Mr. X is interested in buying 200 shares of Exxon. He calls his
broker for a quote, which is $62 7/8 bid and $63 asked per share. (The
broker has on-line access to current quotes of listed stocks on his television monitor.) The *bid* means that the specialist is willing to buy
Exxon shares at $62.875 per share, and the *asked* means that the spe-
cialist is willing to sell Exxon shares at $63.00 per share.

Mr. X decides to buy 200 shares at the market price, which means
that it should be transacted close to the $63.00 per share if the order is
put in shortly after receiving the quote and if the market price of
Exxon has not been fluctuating widely.

The broker fills out the buy order (see Figure 4–2), which is trans-
mitted electronically to the floor of the exchange. There, the *commission
broker* will take the order to the Exxon trading post to execute the buy
order either from another commission broker who has a sell order for
200 Exxon shares or from the *specialist*.

If Mr. X had placed a limit order to buy Exxon at $62 3/4 or
better instead of a market order, the commission broker would see if
the order could be filled from the "crowd" (other commission brokers). However, if the limit order does not fall within the quotes of the
current bid and asked prices, the order will be given to the specialist.
If it is not executed by the specialist, it will be entered in the specialist's book for future execution. In this case, the specialist is acting as a
broker for the commission broker. If the price of Exxon falls later in
the day, the limit orders in the specialist's book will be executed in the
order that they were entered (on a FIFO basis—first-in, first-out). The
specialist will receive part of the customer's commission for executing
this limit order.

Besides acting as a broker, a specialist may act as a dealer by
being allowed to trade the assigned stocks in his or her own account,
and to profit from these trades. However, specialists are required to
maintain a fair and orderly market in the stocks assigned to them. For
example, they are not allowed to compete with customer's orders. If

Figure 4–2 Example of a Buy and Sell Order

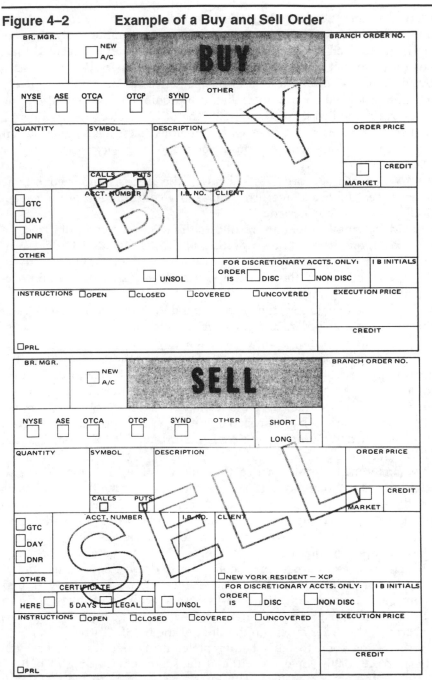

Source: Bryn Mawr Investments Group, Inc. Reprinted by permission.

there is a market order to buy, the specialist may not buy for his or her own account ahead of the unexecuted market order. Similarly, the specialist cannot sell from his or her account ahead of an unexecuted market order to sell. The purpose of allowing the specialist to act as a trader is to minimize the effects of imbalances in the supply and demand of assigned stocks. Specialists are prohibited from manipulating stock prices, which is also unlawful. The SEC monitors the trading activities of specialists, but even with numerous rules, maintaining an orderly market along with the profit motivations of specialists is a gray area.

When Mr. X's order is executed, the price is reported on the ticker tape. The brokerage firm will send a confirmation of the execution on the next business day.

Many small orders are routed to the electronic computerized order execution system known as *Super-DOT* (Designated Order Turnaround). The subscribing brokerage firms send their orders directly to the specialist, where they can be executed very quickly (within seconds).

On the opening each day the expanded Super-DOT system pairs the buy and sell orders for specialists, which allows stocks to open more quickly than they would without the system.

Although the New York Stock Exchange studies show that the auction process on the exchange floor results in a better price for customers in over one third of all trades, there have been some developments taking place that investors should be aware of. Some orders for NYSE trades are being transacted off the exchange floor through a process called *preferencing*, which is disturbing the "Big Board," the NYSE (Torres, C2).

Preferencing is a practice that allows large brokerage firms to trade their customers' orders against their own order flow from their retail customers or correspondents. According to Torres, large brokerage firms such as Shearson, Pershing and others use preferencing to turn their orders into greater profits for themselves. This all takes place on the Cincinnati Stock Exchange, which is a computer based in Chicago. Shearson uses its own computer to determine if a customer's buy or sell order for a NYSE listed stock can be profitably traded against its own account; if it can, the trade with itself takes place in "Cincinnati." If the computer determines it is not going to be a profitable trade, the order is sent to the floor of the NYSE (Torres, C2).

It is too soon to tell whether preferencing does in fact find the "best" price for the investor while at the same time finding a "better" price for the brokerage firm. This practice is similar to the way large brokerage firms trade their customers' over-the-counter stocks.

■ How Stocks Are Executed in the Over-the-Counter Markets

Transactions of stocks listed on the over-the-counter (OTC) are not executed on a central exchange floor, but involve the use of *dealers* who buy and sell securities out of their own inventories using an electronic computer system. The National Association of Securities Dealers (NASD) implemented the National Association of Securities Dealers Automated Quotation system (NASDAQ), which allows subscribing brokerage firms to obtain price quotations on the stocks in the system.

The largest and most actively traded OTC stocks (over 4,000 companies) are listed in the financial newspapers under the NASDAQ National Market System (NMS). The rest of the OTC stocks are listed in the "NASDAQ Bid and Asked Quotations" or "Additional NASDAQ Quotes" sections of the financial newspapers. Many low-priced and foreign OTC stocks are listed in the pink sheets (available in brokerage firms), and their prices are not quoted in the financial newspapers.

Customer orders on OTC stocks are executed differently. A customer places an order with the brokerage firm, who writes up a buy order, or a sell order if the customer is selling stock (Figure 4–2). The order is sent to the brokerage firm's trading department, which then "shops" among that stock's market makers for the best price. When customers buy OTC stocks, a percentage amount is added to the price of the shares. This is known as the *markup.* Similarly, when selling OTC shares, a percentage amount is deducted from the proceeds of the sale, known as the *markdown.*

The amounts of the markups and markdowns are disclosed on the 4,000 plus stocks listed on the National Market System. For the additional OTC stocks, the customer does not know what the markups and markdowns are. If the brokerage firm has acted as a principal (market maker or dealer) in the trade, the brokerage firm may charge the customer either a commission or a markup (or markdown) but not both. The SEC periodically examines these markups and markdowns to see that they are reasonable.

Many criticisms have been leveled at the execution of trades on the OTC market. The fact that brokerage firms can simultaneously act as agents for their customers and self-interested dealers may be a juxtaposition of two mutually incompatible ideas. As an agent, the broker should find the best price for the customer. This responsibility becomes blurred when the brokerage firm is also looking to profit from the deal. There is no need to look for more competitive prices if the brokerage firm can fill the order as a market maker and thereby fulfill its profit objective.

Spreads on OTC stocks tend to be wide, allowing a lot of latitude for market makers to take advantage of investors. According to Torres, certain brokerage firms take advantage of these wide spreads by using the semiprivate system, Selectnet, created by NASD. This is a special electronic dealer market for NASDAQ stocks. The spreads between the bid and asked prices are narrower, allowing dealers to trade stocks without having to change their bid and asked prices (Torres, C2).

The existing dealer system of executing trades on OTC stocks is not conducive to the efficient handling of limit orders. They are frequently missed, which, needless to say, is frustrating to investors.

The SEC's study ("Market 2000") of the securities markets has proposed some suggestions for addressing these and other shortcomings on the OTC markets:

▮ Making public customers' limit orders, which will circumvent the ease with which they are currently missed.

▮ Moving ultimately towards pricing and recording stocks in decimals, rather than the current pricing increments of one-eight of a dollar.

▮ Giving non-member firms access to the semiprivate computerized trading system Selectnet.

▮ Disclosing the payments that brokers receive for directing their order flow to market makers.

Many of these recommendations by the SEC may end up being just that, recommendations. Implementation will require action from the markets themselves.

As of this writing, the SEC has proposed two changes regarding customer limit orders and short selling. The rule on customer limit orders would ban brokers from trading ahead of their clients' limit orders. The second change aims to restrict short sales on NASDAQ stocks during a falling market. In other words, a short sale could not be placed when the bid price is at or below the previous bid. This would prevent some of the volatility in a falling market.

▮ Summary

Transaction costs include not only the brokerage commissions but also the bid-asked spreads. For example, if a stock is quoted at $24 bid and $25 asked, the stock will be purchased at $25 per share and sold at $24 per share. For 100 shares traded, a broker's commission may range from $30 to $120. This means that if the investor needed to turn around and sell the stock (after buying at $25 per share plus commissions), the price of the stock would have to go up by at least four points to break even, assuming a $100 commission for each trade plus the one-point spread. In other words, the stock would have to appreciate by 16 percent before the investor could sell it just to get back the amount of the investment.

Spreads between bid and asked prices vary. For large, actively traded stocks on the New York Stock Exchange, the spreads are very much narrower than the thinly traded stocks on the over-the-counter markets.

Sorting out the commission structure between full-service brokerage firms and discount brokers can also be a complex puzzle. This is because brokerage firms advertise prices which may be lower than other firms for one kind of trade but a lot higher for other trades. For example, a firm might quote a commission of $50 for a 100-share trade, which may be lower than other firms, but may charge very much more than the others for 500 and 1,000 share trades. Generally, deep-discount brokers may be cheaper than discount brokers, which may be cheaper than full-service brokers. However, this may not be so for all kinds of trades. In addition to the fee structure, investors should consider the level of services they require.

By understanding how the markets work and the types of orders that can be placed, investors can make more informed choices in the placement of their orders.

■ References

Clareman, Lloyd S. "Keep Your Broker Honest." *Fortune Investor's Guide 1994.* Autumn, 1993, pp. 167–168.

Torres, Craig. "How Wall Street Turns Your Trades to Gold." *The Wall Street Journal,* February 16, 1993, pp. C1–C2.

Welsh, Tricia. "How the Brokers Stack Up." *Fortune Investor's Guide 1994.* Autumn, 1993, pp. 170–171.

Zweig, Philip L., Leah Nathans Spiro and Michael Schroeder. "Beware the IPO Market." *Business Week,* April 4, 1994, pp. 84–90.

Chapter 5

Fundamental Analysis

Key Concepts

- Industry Analysis
- Company Analysis
- Ratio Analysis

This chapter discusses the fundamental approach to selecting stocks. Fundamental analysis starts with a broad analysis of the economy with regard to economic growth, inflation, unemployment and the level and direction of interest rates. By considering these indicators affecting the economy, financial analysts can forecast future levels of GNP. These forecasts are used as a basis for projecting the future sales of different industries in the economy which is then used to project the forecasted sales and earnings of companies within these industries. Common stocks within the favorable sectors of the economy are then selected by fundamentalists. This method of forecasting sales and earnings is known as the *top down approach*.

The other approach financial analysts use is the *bottom-up approach* which starts with sales projections for companies in different industries. The total forecasted sales for the companies in each industry forms the basis for industry projections. Financial analysts tend to use both of these approaches.

Because companies operate in the economic environment, they are somewhat dependent on the state of the economy. For example, during periods of prosperity there are more people employed, which means that the nation's income is growing. With increased income, there will be more spending, which translates into greater sales. Companies will spend more on property, plant and equipment to increase their capacity to produce more goods in order to share in the future increases in sales.

For individual companies, these higher sales translate into increased profits, leading to an increase in dividends and higher stock prices. Generally, even poorly run companies may see increased sales and profits.

The opposite occurs during a recession. There is a downturn in economic conditions, which leads to declining sales, earnings and stock prices.

Forecasting the direction of the economy may be a more important step than selecting individual stocks. This is not easy. Economists differ in their analyses and projections, which leaves little hope for the rest of us to defy their outcomes. However, it is not the difference between economists figures that is important to investors, but their consensus as to the direction and change in the economy.

Currently, the U.S. economy has been expanding, with increased sales and earnings resulting in a bull (increasing) market for stocks that has lasted 27 months into early 1994. The Federal Reserve Bank's hike in the Fed funds rate (the rate at which banks borrow from one another) at that time put the brakes on stock prices, which saw a pull back to the 3,600s for the Dow Jones Industrial Average, which was approaching the 4,000 level.

Rising interest rates not only dampen the stock and bond markets but make the selection of sectors in the economy more critical in terms of future stock investments.

∎ Industry Analysis

Not all companies are affected by the economy in the same way. Industries (and companies in these industries) that move in the same direction as the economy and are referred to as *cyclical industries.* The stage in the business cycle of the economy becomes important as to the timing of the investments in these cyclical companies. For example, you would not want to invest in the stocks of automobile companies at the peak of an economic expansion because their stock prices would be high (at their upper limits).

During an economic expansion, the stock prices of cyclical companies increase; during an economic recession, they decline. Cyclical companies are in industries such as automobiles, building and construction, aluminum, steel, chemicals, and lumber. Since these stocks are sensitive to changes in economic activity, investors should time their purchases of these cyclical stocks to the early phases of an expansionary period. Figure 5–1 breaks down the cyclical industries into fur-

Figure 5–1   Industry Selections

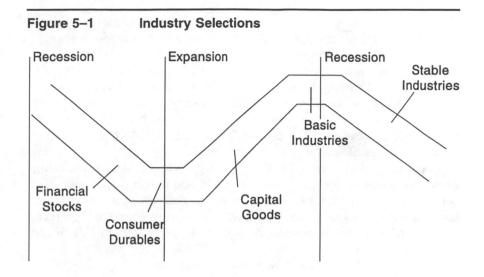

Source: Susan E. Kuhn, "Stocks Are Still Your Best Buy," *Fortune*, March 21, 1994, pp. 130–144.

ther categories: consumer durables, capital goods and basic industries (Kuhn, 140).

Financial stocks tend to do well coming out of a recession because of the lower interest rates, whereas, at the expansionary phase, consumer durables are the stocks to buy. This was evidenced in 1993 when the auto stocks—General Motors, Ford and Chrysler—took off on their bull run, in part due to pent-up demand. During the recession, consumers delayed purchases of automobiles, large appliances and houses (Kuhn, 140). Cyclical stocks fluctuate with the state of the economy and are always hit hard by rising interest rates.

Into the expansionary cycle, capital goods companies benefit from increased sales in the business sector. With increased business sales comes an increase in the demand for raw materials and commodities (Kuhn, 140).

This is the typical pattern in most business cycles. By timing purchases into these different industries, investors may be able to improve their returns.

Investors who are uncomfortable with the risks of cyclical stocks might prefer to invest in the stocks of companies in the stable industries, also referred to as *counter-cyclical* industries. These industries include the food, beverage and retail companies, and certain public utilities. Sales and earnings in these companies do not fluctuate as much as do those of the cyclical companies, especially during recessions. Many of these companies' stocks tend to hold their market values.

The difference between cyclical companies and stable industry companies is that the latter will be less risky in terms of stock price fluctuations. However, the other side of the coin is that cyclical stocks will generally outperform the stable industry stocks during an economic expansionary cycle. Over long periods of time, these fluctuations in stock prices will even out. Their overall growth will depend on the earnings of the individual companies.

Stocks that experience high rates of growth in sales and earnings are called *growth stocks*. A growth stock is one that has sustained high growth of 15–20 percent in earnings over a period of time as opposed to most other stocks, which see growth rates in the region of 5 percent. Because of their rapid growth they tend to trade at high P/E multiples.

Identifying those growth industries early on in their lifecycle is difficult. It is only when that they have established a growth record and matured somewhat that most investors become aware of their existence. Technology has been the main basis for the evolution of previous growth industries such as pollution control, video games and genetic engineering. It seems likely that future growth industries will evolve as a result of a combination of changes in technology and satisfying the ever-changing needs of consumers.

Using industry analysis, financial analysts hope to identify those industries that will experience superior growth in sales and earnings. It is not always the industries with the greatest profit potential that consistently provide the greatest investment opportunities. Often the investments that do well are those that surprise the market expectations. Therefore, investments in industries that may not look as promising could exceed market expectations and should not be discounted.

∎ Company Analysis

After identifying the attractive industries, the financial analyst will evaluate the financial conditions of the companies within those industries. Any changes in a company's earnings may have an effect on both the dividends and the stock price. If earnings are greater than the expectations on Wall Street, more investors will want to buy the company's stock, pushing prices up. Similarly, if earnings fall short of the expectations for that company, investors may sell their stocks if they perceive this to be a long-term trend, putting downward pressure on the stock price. When the company's earnings increase steadily, there is the expectation of increases in dividends, which often results in rising stock prices. The opposite is true with decreased earnings.

It is not an easy task to forecast whether companies will meet their expected sales and earnings projections, but there are a number of factors that should be considered in addition to the financial analysis.

∎ Competitive Analysis

Whether a company can achieve its sales and earnings objectives depends in part on how it competes within its industry. Industry sales and earnings may be growing, but if the company is not competitive enough it may not capture a large enough portion of the increasing sales in the industry.

How a company can compete in an industry depends on many factors:

∎ The resources the company has in relation to its competitors.

∎ The range of products versus the competition.

∎ How successful the company's existing range of products is.

∎ How innovative the company is with introducing new products.

∎ The company's ability to diversify into new markets.

∎ The strength of the company's competitors.

The above factors should be considered in determining the relative strength of the company in the industry.

Quality of Management

Access to a company's management is often difficult for financial analysts and virtually impossible for the general investing public. The most that the average investor can do to determine the quality of management is to look at the company's past and read the financial newspapers for stories about management. For example, turnover of top and middle management indicates all is not well. Generally, it is assumed that a company with effective management will be more successful in meeting its sales and earnings objectives than a poorly managed company.

Exxon, for example, has managed to increase its earnings during a period of declining oil prices. In addition, Exxon faced a negative climate due to the Exxon Valdez oil spill. Exxon's management was not deterred and stuck to their original investment objectives, which were projects with high returns. This strategy supported their profits, in contrast to the frivolous investments made by many of the other oil companies during the same period.

Financial Strength of the Company

Many investors do not have the time or inclination to study a company's financial statements to determine its financial strengths or weaknesses. Instead, many investors choose from the many sources of published information available, such as Value Line and Standard & Poor's tear sheets, in addition to the brokerage reports.

However, for many investors the starting point is the company's financial statements. These can be found in the annual reports and the 10K reports, which are filed with the Securities and Exchange Commission (SEC).

Annual financial statements are audited by independent certified public accountants (CPAs) and are distributed to shareholders and other interested parties on a timely basis. The four financial statements—the balance sheet, income statement, statement of changes in retained earnings and the statement of changes in cash—provide investors with their most important source of information.

The Balance Sheet. The balance sheet is a statement that shows the financial position of a company at one point in time. It includes the *assets* (all the resources that belong to the company), the *liabilities* (the company's obligations) and the *equity* (the amount of the stockholders' capital).

The assets (resources) minus the liabilities (obligations) equal the stockholders' equity. From this equation, the reader of the balance sheet can see how much the stockholders have contributed in relation to the total assets. See Figure 5–2 for a copy of the consolidated financial statements of Exxon Corporation.

On the asset side are current assets and long-term assets. *Current assets* include cash, marketable securities, accounts receivable, inventories and other resources that will be converted into cash within one year. The cash generated from these assets generally provides for the day-to-day expenses of operations (the working capital).

Long-term assets consist of those resources with holding periods of greater than a year. These include long-term investments, property, plant, equipment and intangible assets (goodwill, leasehold improvements). These assets are recorded at their historical cost, not their market value. The second feature is that the property, plant and equipment

Figure 5–2   Consolidated Financial Statements of Exxon Corporation

CONSOLIDATED BALANCE SHEET   F8

	Dec. 31 1993	Dec. 31 1992
	(millions of dollars)	
Assets		
Current assets		
Cash and cash equivalents	$ 983	$ 898
Other marketable securities	669	617
Notes and accounts receivable, less estimated doubtful amounts	6,860	8,079
Inventories		
Crude oil, products and merchandise	4,616	4,897
Materials and supplies	856	910
Prepaid taxes and expenses	875	1,023
Total current assets	14,859	16,424
Investments and advances	4,790	4,606
Property, plant and equipment, at cost, less accumulated depreciation and depletion	61,962	61,799
Other assets, including intangibles, net	2,534	2,201
Total assets	$84,145	$85,030
Liabilities		
Current liabilities		
Notes and loans payable	$ 4,109	$ 4,787
Accounts payable and accrued liabilities	12,122	12,645
Income taxes payable	2,359	2,231
Total current liabilities	18,590	19,663
Long-term debt	8,506	8,637
Annuity reserves and accrued liabilities	8,153	8,097
Deferred income tax liabilities	10,939	11,135
Deferred credits	770	747
Equity of minority and preferred shareholders in affiliated companies	2,395	2,975
Total liabilities	49,353	51,254
Shareholders' Equity		
Preferred stock without par value (authorized 200 million shares, 16 million issued)	668	770
Guaranteed LESOP obligation	(716)	(818)
Common stock without par value (authorized 2 billion shares, 1,813 million issued)	2,822	2,822
Earnings reinvested	49,365	47,697
Cumulative foreign exchange translation adjustment	(370)	192
Common stock held in treasury, at cost (571 million shares in 1993, 571 million shares in 1992)	(16,977)	(16,887)
Total shareholders' equity	34,792	33,776
Total liabilities and shareholders' equity	$84,145	$85,030

The information on pages F11 through F20 is an integral part of these statements.

Source: 1993 Annual Report, Exxon Corporation.

Figure 5–2   Consolidated Financial Statements of Exxon Corporation (continued)

	1993	1992	1991
		(millions of dollars)	
Revenue			
Sales and other operating revenue, including excise taxes	$109,532	$115,672	$115,068
Earnings from equity interests and other revenue, including $112 million in 1992 from gain on sale of non-U.S. investment	1,679	1,434	1,424
Total revenue	111,211	117,106	116,492
Costs and other deductions			
Crude oil and product purchases	46,124	48,552	46,847
Operating expenses	12,111	12,927	13,487
Selling, general and administrative expenses	7,009	7,432	7,881
Depreciation and depletion	4,884	5,044	4,824
Exploration expenses, including dry holes	648	808	914
Interest expense	681	784	810
Excise taxes	11,707	12,512	12,221
Other taxes and duties	19,745	21,513	20,823
Income applicable to minority and preferred interests	250	247	167
Total costs and other deductions	103,159	109,819	107,974
Income before income taxes	8,052	7,287	8,518
Income taxes	2,772	2,477	2,918
Income before cumulative effect of accounting changes	5,280	4,810	5,600
Cumulative effect of accounting changes	–	(40)	–
Net income	$ 5,280	$ 4,770	$ 5,600
Per common share – income before cumulative effect of accounting changes (dollars)	$ 4.21	$ 3.82	$ 4.45
– cumulative effect of accounting changes (dollars)	–	$ (0.03)	–
– net income (dollars)	$ 4.21	$ 3.79	$ 4.45

CONSOLIDATED STATEMENT OF SHAREHOLDERS' EQUITY

	1993		1992		1991	
	Shares	Dollars	Shares	Dollars	Shares	Dollars
			(millions)			
Preferred stock outstanding at end of year	11	$ 668	13	$ 770	14	$ 867
Guaranteed LESOP obligation		(716)		(818)		(914)
Common stock issued at end of year	1,813	2,822	1,813	2,822	1,813	2,822
Earnings reinvested						
At beginning of year		47,697		46,483		44,286
Net income for year		5,280		4,770		5,600
Dividends – common and preferred shares		(3,612)		(3,556)		(3,403)
At end of year		49,365		47,697		46,483
Cumulative foreign exchange translation adjustment						
At beginning of year		192		2,443		2,426
Change during the year		(562)		(2,251)		17
At end of year		(370)		192		2,443
Common stock held in treasury, at cost						
At beginning of year	(571)	(16,887)	(571)	(16,774)	(568)	(16,509)
Acquisitions	(5)	(323)	(6)	(358)	(8)	(466)
Dispositions	5	233	6	245	5	201
At end of year	(571)	(16,977)	(571)	(16,887)	(571)	(16,774)
Shareholders' equity at end of year		$34,792		$33,776		$34,927
Common shares outstanding at end of year	1,242		1,242		1,242	

The information on pages F11 through F20 is an integral part of these statements.

Source: 1993 Annual Report, Exxon Corporation.

**Figure 5–2   Consolidated Financial Statements of
                    Exxon Corporation (continued)**

	1993	1992	1991
	(millions of dollars)		
Cash flows from operating activities			
Net income			
Accruing to Exxon shareholders	$ 5,280	$ 4,770	$ 5,600
Accruing to minority and preferred interests	250	247	167
Adjustments for non-cash transactions			
Depreciation and depletion	4,884	5,044	4,824
Deferred income tax charges/(credits)	64	(1,285)	(43)
Annuity and accrued liability provisions	255	1,340	385
Dividends received which were less than equity in current earnings of equity companies	(9)	(33)	(151)
Changes in operational working capital, excluding cash and debt			
Reduction/(increase) – Notes and accounts receivable	965	(136)	1,003
– Inventories	156	(71)	263
– Prepaid taxes and expenses	(4)	96	62
Increase/(reduction) – Accounts and other payables	(93)	(212)	(1,463)
All other items – net	(245)	(149)	295
Net cash provided by operating activities	11,503	9,611	10,942
Cash flows from investing activities			
Additions to property, plant and equipment	(6,956)	(7,225)	(7,324)
Sales of subsidiaries and property, plant and equipment	1,095	982	1,052
Additional investments and advances	(331)	(363)	(251)
Sales of investments and collection of advances	168	134	348
Additions to other marketable securities	(1,323)	(1,079)	(279)
Sales of other marketable securities	1,246	518	234
Net cash used in investing activities	(6,101)	(7,033)	(6,220)
Net cash generation before financing activities	5,402	2,578	4,722
Cash flows from financing activities			
Additions to long-term debt	1,635	1,190	1,445
Reductions in long-term debt	(313)	(513)	(402)
Additions to short-term debt	249	271	349
Reductions in short-term debt	(1,168)	(481)	(1,005)
Changes in debt with less than 90 day maturity	(1,112)	272	(1,024)
Cash dividends to Exxon shareholders	(3,630)	(3,575)	(3,403)
Cash dividends to minority interests	(249)	(257)	(242)
Additions to minority interests and sales/(redemptions) of affiliate preferred stock	(500)	180	78
Common stock acquired	(323)	(358)	(466)
Common stock sold	131	148	113
Net cash used in financing activities	(5,280)	(3,123)	(4,557)
Effects of exchange rate changes on cash	(37)	(53)	(1)
Increase/(decrease) in cash and cash equivalents	85	(598)	164
Cash and cash equivalents at beginning of year	898	1,496	1,332
Cash and cash equivalents at end of year	$ 983	$ 898	$ 1,496

The information on pages F11 through F20 is an integral part of these statements.

Source: 1993 Annual Report, Exxon Corporation.

is depreciated (a systematic charge is recorded against income for wear and tear) over their useful lives.

Analysts will check to see if there are any significantly undervalued assets. The historical cost concept used to account for long-term assets does not recognize the increases in market value of these assets until they are sold. Thus, property on the balance sheet that may have been bought many years ago at low prices may be significantly understated (in terms of its market value).

The *liabilities* side of the balance sheet is also divided into two parts, current and long-term. *Current liabilities* are the obligations of the company that fall due within one year or less. These consist of account and trade payables, accrued (unrecorded) expenses and other short-term debts.

It is important to compare the total current assets with the total current liabilities. The cash generated from the turnover of the current assets to cash will generally be used to pay the current obligations that fall due. If current assets are equal to current liabilities, the company may have a difficult time meeting its current obligations. The warning flags should be raised. In the same vein, if current assets are less than current liabilities, cash will have to come from selling off assets or raising more debt to pay off its current liabilities. This topic is explored further in the liquidity section later in this chapter.

Long-term liabilities are the debts of the company that have maturities beyond one year.

The *equity* section represents the claims of the shareholders against the company's assets. The total assets minus the total liabilities of the company equal the shareholders' equity section. The three main parts of the equity section are the capital stock accounts, the paid-in-capital accounts and the retained earnings (or deficit).

The capital stock accounts include both the common stock and preferred issues. The value of the common stock account can be calculated by multiplying the stated or par value of the stock by the number of shares issued.

The paid-in-capital accounts represent the amounts that shareholders paid in excess of the stated (par) value in the capital accounts when the shares were originally issued by the company.

Retained earnings are the accumulated earnings that have been retained by the company; in other words, those earnings that have not been paid out in dividends. Companies accumulate earnings for various uses, such as to acquire fixed assets or pay off liabilities. Retained earnings do not represent cash; although a company may have accumulated a large amount in retained earnings, it is still restricted by its cash in terms of spending for projects.

The balance sheet provides a picture at one point in time of the company's assets and liabilities. The balance sheet shows the amount of the assets that are financed by liabilities and the amounts financed by stockholders. Leverage, the amount of assets financed through debt, is discussed in the section on ratio analysis.

The Income Statement. The income statement provides a summary of the earnings of the company over a period of time (a year for annual statements, three months and six months for quarterly and semiannual income statements).

The income statement begins with the revenues (sales) from which various expenses are deducted: the cost of goods sold, selling, general and administrative expenses. Interest expenses reflect the cost of the company's borrowing. After all the expenses and taxes are deducted, you are left with the "bottom line," which is the net income.

The income statement shows the profits (or losses, if expenses exceed revenues) over a period of time. These profits or losses can be compared with the profits or losses in previous periods.

Statement of Retained Earnings. The link between the income statement and the balance sheet is the company's net income (or loss), which is shown in the statement of changes to retained earnings. Dividends on common and preferred stocks are paid out of net income, and the balance of the earnings are added to the retained earnings in the equity section of the balance sheet. This is the third statement included in the financial statements of an annual report.

Statement of Changes in Cash. This statement analyzes the changes in the company's cash over the period. The section *cash from operations* shows how much cash was provided or used in the company's operations. The changes in the *investing* and *financing* sections summarize the uses and sources of cash from the changes in the assets, liabilities and equity sections of the balance sheet.

The financial statements provide the data for an analysis of the company's financial position as well as assessing its strengths and weaknesses. The relative financial position of the company's standings in relation to its past data and in relation to other companies in the same industry provides a more meaningful picture than merely looking at one set of financial statements in isolation. The company's strengths and weaknesses can become more apparent through ratio analysis.

∎ Ratio Analysis

You don't have to have a master's degree in business administration or be a certified public accountant to be able to perform ratio analysis on a set of financial statements. Ratio analysis uses a company's published financial information to predict whether it will meet its future projections of earnings.

Ratio analysis is simple to execute; it is the projections and extrapolations of these measures that become complex. Ratio analysis is a tool that can help the investor select stocks. There are many ratios that can be used but they are all classified into one of four groups:

- ∎ *Liquidity ratios*, which determine the ease with which a company can meet its current obligations as they come due.

- ∎ *Activity ratios*, which show how quickly the assets flow through the company.

- ∎ *Profitability ratios*, which measure the performance of the company.

- ∎ *Leverage ratios*, which indicate the level of debt.

Not all the ratios in these groups are of concern to stockholders. Stockholders are primarily concerned with the company's ability to generate sales and earnings, which then affect the price of the stock.

Liquidity

Although liquidity is of greater concern to a company's creditors, this is a starting point for a potential investor in a company's common stock. Liquidity indicates the ease (or difficulty) with which a company can pay off its current debts.

The *current ratio* shows the coverage of the company's current liabilities by its current assets, as computed below:

$$\text{Current Ratio} = \frac{\text{Current Asset}}{\text{Current Liabilities}}$$

For Exxon, the current ratio is 0.8. This indicates that Exxon has $0.80 of current assets for every $1 of current liabilities.

Generally, it is desirable for companies to have their current assets exceed their current liabilities, so that if their current assets decline, companies will still be able to pay off their liabilities. A low current ratio may indicate weakness in that the company may not be able to borrow additional funds or sell off assets to raise enough cash to meet its current liabilities.

There are exceptions to a low current ratio, as we can see in Exxon's financial statements. Exxon is one of the strongest companies in the oil industry and therefore has the capacity to borrow on a short-term basis to pay off its current obligations. In fact, in the notes to Exxon's financial statements it is stated that Exxon has an unused line of credit with its banks. Potential investors should always read the footnotes, which contain all kinds of information that may provide more insight into the figures on the financial statements.

Moreover, it is not a good idea to look at one ratio in isolation. By examining the current ratio of the company for a few years and establishing a trend, it is easier to see whether the current ratio has deteriorated, stayed the same, or improved over this period.

What may be the norm for one industry may not hold for another. Utility companies tend to have current ratios of less than one-to-one, but the quality of their accounts receivables is so good that virtually all of them will be converted into cash. (Most people pay their utility bills because if they don't, they find themselves without power). Creditors of utility companies are therefore not concerned with the low current ratios. Similarly, Exxon's liquidity is not significantly different from the rest of the oil industry. This then suggests that the oil industry also has a current ratio of around one-to-one or less of current assets to current liabilities.

Profitability

The profits of a company are important to investors because these earnings are either retained or paid out in dividends to shareholders, both of which affect the stock price. Many different measures of profitability indicate how much the company is earning relative to the base used, such as sales, assets and shareholders' equity.

Using sales as a base, the income statement is the starting point. Compare the sales for the period with the sales figures for previous years to see whether there has been a growth or a decline in sales. For example, sales may have increased from the previous year, yet the company may report a net loss for the year. This indicates that expenses have risen significantly. The investor would then examine the income statement to see whether the additional expenses were non-recurring (a one-time write-off) or increased operating costs incurred in the normal course of business. If it is the latter, the investor/analyst should question management's ability to contain these costs. Establishing a trend of these expenses over a period of time is useful in the evaluation.

There are several profitability ratios that use sales as a base: gross profit, operating profit and net profit.

Gross Profit

Gross profit reflects the company's markup on its cost of goods sold as well as management's ability to control these costs in relation to sales. The gross profit is computed as follows:

$$\text{Gross Profit} = \frac{\text{Gross Profit}}{\text{Sales}}$$

$$\text{Exxon's Gross Profit} = \frac{\$51,297}{109,532}$$

$$= 46.83\%$$

To obtain the gross profit figure of $51,297 (thousand), you need to do some calculations. The gross profit is sales minus cost of goods sold. The cost of goods sold is obtained from the consolidated income statement in Figure 5–2, which includes the crude oil purchases of $46,124 plus the operating expenses of $12,111. These added together equal the cost of goods sold: $58,235. Sales of $109,532 minus the cost of goods sold of $58,235 equals the gross profit of $51,297.

I have chosen to exclude the equity income of $1,679 from the total sales, concentrating on sales and gross profits from operations. Other revenues from nonoperations, such as equity income, would be included as other income after the operating profit margin has been calculated.

Operating Profit

Operating profit is the income from operations (or also known as the earnings before interest and taxes, EBIT) divided by sales. This includes the cost of goods sold and the selling, general and administrative expenses. The total costs shown in Exxon's income statement are $103,159. When the interest costs of $681 are subtracted from this figure, the total operating costs become $102,478. This is subtracted from sales to give the operating profit of $7,054. This ratio shows the profitability of the company in its normal course of operations and provides a measure of the operating efficiency of the company.

$$\text{Exxon's Operating Profit} = \frac{\$7,054}{109,532} = \frac{EBIT}{Sales} = \frac{Operating\ Income}{Sales}$$

$$= 6.44\%$$

✳ The operating profit or loss often provides the truest indicator of a company's earning capacity as it excludes the nonoperating income and expenses.

Net Profit

The *net profit* margin includes the nonoperating income and expenses such as taxes, interest expense and extraordinary items. Net profit is calculated as follows:

$$\text{Net Profit} = \frac{\text{Net Income}}{\text{Sales}}$$

$$\text{Exxon's Net Profit} = \frac{\$5,280}{109,532}$$

$$= 4.82\%$$

To the lay investor, it may not seem that important to calculate all these profit ratios. Instead, there may be an emphasis on the net profit margin only. This could be misleading because if tax rates or interest expenses increase or if there are some large, extraordinary items in the year, there will be a significant change in the net profit even though operating profits have not changed. *Good Point!*

Other measures of profitability, which are more specific to common shareholders in that they measure the returns on the invested funds of the shareholders, are the returns on equity and common equity.

Return on Equity

This ratio indicates how well management is performing for the stockholders and is calculated as follows:

$$\text{Return on Equity} = \frac{\text{Net Income}}{\text{Equity}}$$

For Exxon the return on equity is 15.17% (5280/34792). In other words, Exxon is earning $0.1517 for every dollar invested in equity.

Return on Common Equity

When a company has preferred stock, the common shareholders may be more concerned with the return attributable to the common equity rather than to the total equity. To determine this return, adjustments are made for the preferred dividends and preferred stock outstanding.

$$\text{Return on Common Equity} = \frac{\text{Net Income minus Preferred Dividends}}{\text{Equity minus Preferred Stock}}$$

The Effects of Earnings on Stock Prices

Corporate earnings, under the conventional stock price theory, are the most important determinant of the company's stock price. Analysts suggest buying those stocks whose earnings are expected to increase and selling those stocks with anticipated downturns in earnings. This is evidenced on Wall Street when companies turn in earnings results that are shy of the analysts' estimates. The prices of these stocks are often battered downwards.

However, there are times when stock prices appear to have no correlation to their earnings. The prices of these stocks sometimes move in opposite directions to their earnings or increase more slowly than their earnings. There are occasions when stock prices go up ahead of their earnings.

So what is the beginning investor to do when analysts correctly forecast earnings and the stock price ends up going in the opposite direction?

These anomalies in the movement of stock prices and earnings may be explained by those who subscribe to the *confidence theory*, which says that stock prices react more to trader and investor confidence than earnings. In other words, confidence or lack of confidence about a stock can drive its price up and down regardless of earnings. For example, Unisys Corporation has reshaped its balance sheet and turned losses into profits, which made it the darling of many analysts in their buy recommendations. This euphoria ended when Unisys announced quarterly earnings slightly off from analysts' forecasts. This prompted many analysts to turn pessimistic about the stock, which resulted in Unisys's stock price plummeting over 40 percent.

The difficulty of measuring and forecasting trader and investor confidence is even more nebulous than trying to forecast earnings. Where does this leave the investor? Even an accurate forecast of a company's earnings does not mean the stock's price will follow. This leads to the realization that investors cannot rely on the relationship between stock prices and earnings over a short period of time. However, over long periods of time there appears to be a relationship whereby stock prices move ahead of earnings.

The Price-Earnings (P/E) Ratio

The most commonly used guide to the relationship between stock prices and earnings is the price earnings (P/E) ratio. This is calculated as follows:

$$\text{Price/Earnings Ratio} = \frac{\text{Market Price of the Stock}}{\text{Earnings per Share}}$$

The P/E ratio shows the number of times that a stock's price is trading relative to its earnings. The P/E ratios for listed common stocks are published daily in the financial newspapers. For example, the P/E ratio for Exxon Corporation was listed in the financial newspapers on May 4, 1994, as 14 times, and the closing price of the stock was listed at $60.625 per share. This means that shareholders are willing to pay 14 times Exxon's earnings for its stock. Looked at another way, it will take 14 years of these earnings to reach the investment amount of the stock at $60.625 per share.

By rearranging the formula, the earnings per share can be determined for Exxon:

$$\text{Earnings per Share} = \frac{\text{Market Price of the Stock}}{\text{P/E Ratio}}$$

$$\frac{\$60.625}{14}$$

$$EPS \quad = \$4.33$$

Investors who obtain company information from the service organizations such as Standard & Poor's and Value Line may find there are discrepancies between the P/E ratios reported in the newspapers and those reported by information services companies. This is because the financial newspapers quote the P/E ratio based on annual earnings of the previous year, whereas the information services companies may quote the earnings based on the most current quarters available.

Theoretically, if the earnings per share increase, the stock price should rise so that the P/E ratio stays much the same. In reality, this does not often happen. P/E ratios can be volatile and can fluctuate considerably. For example, the P/E ratios of the pharmaceutical companies dropped considerably since 1992 due to nervousness concerning the price controls of the proposed Clinton health plan. Merck, the pharmaceutical company, had a P/E ratio around 24 in 1990/1991, and as of August 1994 it was trading at 13 times earnings.

As a rule of thumb, the P/E ratios of drug companies on average trade around the low 20s, while the P/E ratios of many small, emerging growth companies, such as the bio-tech companies, may be greater than the 50s. P/E ratios of companies whose stock prices have been driven down due to pessimism may be very low. Unisys Corporation, for example, is currently trading at 7 times earnings, while other computer companies are trading at higher P/E multiples.

Thus, P/E ratios by themselves are not relied on very greatly to select stocks. For example, why would an investor pay 80 times earnings for the stock of a company that may or may not succeed when there are solid companies with steady, flat earnings trading at low P/E multiples? What do P/E ratios tell potential investors?

The P/E ratio of a company will show how expensive the stock is relative to its earnings. Companies with high P/E ratios (above 20 as a rule of thumb) are characteristic of growth companies. Investors may be optimistic about a company's potential growth, and hence the stock price is driven up in anticipation. This results in a high stock price relative to the company's current earnings. Some investors may be willing to pay a high price for a company's potential earnings; other investors may consider such stocks to be overpriced.

What becomes apparent is that high P/E ratios indicate high risk. If the future anticipated growth of these high P/E ratio stocks is not achieved, their stock prices can fall very quickly. However, on the other hand, if they do live up to their promise, investors benefit substantially.

Low P/E ratio stocks (under 10) are characteristic of either mature companies with low growth potential or companies that are undervalued or in financial difficulty.

By comparing the P/E ratios of companies with the averages in the industries and the markets, investors can get a feeling for the relative value of the stock. For example, the average P/E ratios for companies on the U.S. stock markets are currently around 17 times earnings. During bull markets, these ratios go up, and during bear markets the average declines (perhaps as low as 6 times earnings, which happened in 1974).

P/E ratios fluctuate considerably, differing among companies due to many factors, such as growth rates, popularity, earnings and other financial characteristics.

Earnings Per Share (EPS)

Besides the market price of the stock, the other figure used to determine the P/E ratio is the *earnings per share* (EPS). The earnings per share indicates the amount of earnings allocated to each share of common stock outstanding. EPS figures can be used to compare the growth (or lack of growth) in earnings from year to year and to project future growth in earnings. Earnings per share is calculated as follows:

$$\text{Earnings per Share} = \frac{\text{Net Income minus Peferred Dividends}}{\text{Numbers of Common Share Outstanding}}$$

The number of shares outstanding equals the number of shares issued minus the shares that the company has bought back, called *treasury stock*. In many cases, companies will report two sets of earnings per share figures—the regular earnings per share and the fully diluted earnings per share. For the beginning investor, this can be confusing.

When companies have convertible bonds, convertible preferred stock, rights, options and/or warrants, their earnings per share figures may be diluted due to the increased number of common shares outstanding when these securities are converted into common stocks. Companies are then required to disclose their fully diluted earnings per share figures as well.

It is the trend of earnings per share figures over a period of time that is important for investors. If earnings per share are increasing steadily due to growth in sales, this should translate into increasing stock prices. However, earnings per share can also increase through companies buying back their own shares. This reduces the number of shares outstanding, and if earnings stay the same, there will be an increase in earnings per share. Conceivably, earnings per share could increase when sales and earnings decrease if a significant number of stock is bought back. The astute investor will examine the financial statements to determine whether the increase in earnings per share is due to growth in sales and earnings or whether it is due to stock buybacks. If the increase is due to the latter reason, the result could be a loss of confidence in the stock, which may lead to a decline in the stock price.

Companies with poor fundamentals may try this tactic of buying their shares back to improve their earnings per share and ultimately their stock prices, but over the long term this strategy may not work.

A large number of companies (165 out of 900 companies in the S&P 500 Stock Index) have bought their shares back over the past year

(Raghavan, May 2, 1994, C1). McDonald's Corporation's earnings per share growth slowed to 12.3 percent per year between 1987 and 1993 while the company was buying back its shares. During 1993, McDonald's bought back 10 million of its own shares. Together with this strategy, McDonald's has also slowed its dividend growth. However, since the end of 1991, McDonald's has seen a 57 percent increase in its share price (Raghavan, , C2).

Decreasing earnings per share over a period of time generally has a negative impact on stock prices. However, the reasons for the decrease are important. A decrease in EPS due to an increase in the number of shares outstanding from conversions of convertible bonds or preferred stock issues is not as negative a factor as decreasing sales. If it is due to decreasing sales, further investigation is required to determine if this is a temporary or permanent phenomenon.

Consequently, when comparing earnings per share figures with those of previous periods, you need to examine the reasons for the changes in order to get a better feeling for the potential changes in stock price.

Dividends and Dividend Yields

Investors buy stocks for their potential capital gains and/or their dividend payments. Companies either share their profits with their shareholders by paying dividends, or they retain their earnings and reinvest them in different projects in order to boost their share prices. A company's dividend policy is generally made public. For example, there are growth companies and other companies that choose not to pay dividends, and there are the blue-chip, established companies, utility companies and real estate investment trusts (REITs) that are well known for their dividend payments.

The amount of existing dividends that listed companies pay can be found in the stock listings in the newspapers. Generally, companies try to maintain these stated dividend payments even if they suffer declines in earnings. Similarly, increases in earnings do not always translate into increases in dividends. Certainly, there are many examples where companies experience earnings increases that result in increases in dividend payments, but this is not always the case. There is an imprecise relationship between dividends and earnings. There are times when increases in earnings exceed increases in dividends and other times when increases in dividends exceed increases in earnings. Thus, growth in dividends cannot be interpreted as a sign of a company's financial strength.

However, dividends are important from the standpoint that they represent tangible returns. The cash flow from dividends may be reinvested by shareholders. In contrast, investors in growth stocks that pay little or no dividends are betting on capital appreciation rather than current returns.

To determine the yield, which shows the percentage return that dividends represent relative to the market price of the common stock, the calculation is as follows:

$$\text{Dividend Yield} = \frac{\text{Annual Dividend}}{\text{Market Price of the Stock}}$$

In the current rising interest rate climate, many investors are nervous about growth stocks that either pay no or low dividends and hence have low dividend yields, and are turning to high-dividend-yield stocks. A strategy of buying high-dividend-yield stocks may offer some protection against the fall in stock market prices due to rising interest rates. Dividend yields of many utility companies, REITs, energy companies and some pharmaceutical companies may be as high as 7 percent (Gottschalk, C1). High dividend yields are characteristic of blue-chip and utility companies.

It is risky, however, to choose stocks purely because of their high dividend yields. Dividends can always be reduced, which generally puts downward pressure on the price of the stock.

When choosing high-dividend-yield stocks, you should look at the earnings to see that they are sufficient to support the dividend payments. According to Geraldine Weiss, editor of the newsletter *Investment Quality Trends*, earnings should be equal to at least 150 percent of the dividend payout (Gottschalk, C1). For example, Arco Chemical Company has a dividend yield of 5.5 percent, but its dividend payout ratio exceeds its earnings by 112 percent, suggesting an imminent dividend cut (Asinof, C1).

$$\text{Dividend Payout Ratio} = \frac{\text{Dividend per Share}}{\text{Earnings per Share}}$$

Besides earnings, you should also look at the statement of changes in cash to see the sources and uses of cash. For example, if the major sources of cash come from issuing debt and selling off assets, a company will not be able to maintain a high-dividend-yield policy.

Dividends and dividend yields are not good indicators of the intrinsic value of a stock because dividend payments fluctuate considerably over time, creating an imprecise relationship between the growth in dividends and the growth in earnings.

Book Value of the Stock

The *book value* of the stock is another statistic a potential investor can use to compare with the market value of the stock. The book value per share is the assets minus the liabilities and intangible assets divided by the outstanding common shares. In other words, if the company were to sell its tangible assets at the values stated on the balance sheet and pay off all its liabilities, the amounts left over would be for shareholders. This is a simplistic scenario because certain assets, such as buildings and real estate, are recorded at their historical costs, while their market prices may be far greater (or less). Moreover, other assets such as inventory may sell for less than their balance sheet values if the company has to liquidate in a short period of time.

Bearing this in mind, the book value is a useful additional statistic to compare to the market price of the stock. Many analysts look for companies whose stock prices are trading at less than their book values and interpret this as a buying signal. A small company quoted on the NASDAQ National Market System called Nuclear Metals Inc. posted losses for the year, which caused its stock price to fall to around $8 per share while its book value was around $18 per share. After 6 months, Nuclear Metals Inc was trading at $17 per share.

Investors looking for value stocks would place more importance on finding stocks whose book values are less than their market values. Growth stocks tend to have higher stock market prices than their book values.

Leverage Ratios

While leverage is a major concern for bondholders who use these ratios to determine the level of debt and the servicing of the contractual payments of interest and principal, it is also important for common stockholders.

By increasing the use of debt financing, a company can increase returns to shareholders. Figure 5–3 shows how returns for a hypothetical company are increased through the use of leverage (debt financing).

This example shows how both the return on equity and the earnings per share can be increased from 14 percent to 21 percent and from $1.40 to $2.10, respectively, by increasing the debt financing from 0 percent to 50 percent of its total assets.

Figure 5–3   Financial Leverage and Earnings

Company with No Leverage

Balance Sheet		Income Statement	
Assets	Liabilities	Revenues	$1,000
		Cost of Goods Sold	500
$1,000	$0	Gross Profit	500
		Expenses	300
	Equity	Earnings before Taxes	200
		Taxes 30%	60
*	$1,000	Net Income	140
$1,000	$1,000		

Return on Equity = 140/1,000   = 14%

*100 shares outstanding

Earnings per Share = 140/ 100   = $1.40

Company with 50% Leverage

Balance Sheet		Income Statement	
Assets	Liabilities	Revenues	$ 1,000
		Cost of Goods Sold	500
$1,000	$ 500	Gross Profit	500
		Expenses	300
	Equity	Earnings before Interest and Taxes	200
*	$ 500		
		Interest 10% x $500	50
$1,000	$1,000	Earnings before Taxes	150
		Taxes 30%	45
*50 shares outstanding		Net Income	105

Return on Equity   = 105/500   = 21%

Earnings per Share 105/50   = $2.10

There are two reasons for this increase. First, the company is able to earn more than the 10 percent cost of borrowing. Second, the interest cost is a tax deductible expense. The federal government bears 30 percent (the rate used in this example) of the cost of the interest payments (30 percent of $50, which is $15).

Since the use of debt increases the return to shareholders as well as the earnings per share, why should shareholders be so concerned about the level of debt a company uses to finance its assets? The answer is that the more debt a company takes on, the greater the financial risk and the cost of servicing the debt. For example, if there is a downturn in sales, the company might have difficulty covering the interest payments. This could not only lead to a default and ultimately bankruptcy, but also will significantly reduce the returns to shareholders and the earnings per share. When a company increases the amount of its debt, the costs of raising additional debt issues increase, which means that the company will have to earn more than the cost of the borrowing or it will not see the benefits of leverage. When the level of debt reaches the point where the earnings on the assets are less than the costs of the debt, the return on equity and the earnings per share will decline.

For common stock investors, a highly leveraged company means there is great risk, which will require a greater rate of return to justify the risk. This increase in the required rate of return may have a negative impact on the share price.

Thus, the use of leverage can increase the value of the stock when the level of debt used is not perceived as adding a great amount of risk to the company.

What Is the Optimal Level of Leverage?

All companies use different amounts of leverage, but some industries typically use more than others. Industries that require large investments in fixed assets, such as oil companies, airlines and utilities, will use a higher percentage of debt to finance their assets. Banks typically also use large amounts of debt because their assets are financed by deposits; this leverage results in large fluctuations in the banking industry's earnings when there are slight fluctuations in revenues.

When considering the leverage of one company, compare it to the typical leverage for that industry. Investors should look at the debt and coverage ratios of a company to see the extent of their borrowing and their ability to service their debt.

Debt Ratio

The debt ratio indicates how much of the financing of the total assets comes from debt. The ratio is calculated as follows:

$$\text{Debt Ratio} = \frac{\text{Total Current and Noncurrent Liabilities}}{\text{Total Assets}}$$

For Exxon Corporation, the debt ratio is 58.65 percent ($49,353/$84,145). This means Exxon has financed 58.65 percent of its assets with debt. The debt ratio should be compared with the average of the industry to get a better feeling for the degree and extent of the company's leverage.

A company with a large debt ratio becomes increasingly vulnerable if there is a downturn in sales and/or the economy, particularly in the latter case if it is a cyclical company.

When examining the financial statements of a company, you should always check the footnotes to see if there is any debt that has not been included on the balance sheet. If a company does not consolidate the financial subsidiaries into its financial statements, any debt that the parent company is responsible for will be reported in the footnotes to the financial statements.

Coverage Ratios

The coverage ratios measure the company's ability to cover the interest payments associated with its debt.

The *times interest earned ratio* shows the company's coverage of its interest payments. It is calculated as follows:

$$\text{Time Interest Earned Ratio} = \frac{\text{Earnings before Interest and Taxes}}{\text{Annual Interest Expense}}$$

If a company has low coverage of its interest payments, a slight downturn in sales or an increase in costs could have disastrous consequences in that the company may not be able to meet its interest payments.

■ Summary

Picking stocks using fundamental analysis starts with identifying those industries in the economy that are the strongest. Then the analyst will focus on the fundamentals of the companies in those industries in order to find the "undervalued" companies.

Fundamentalists believe that the company's stock price is determined by the industry outlook, management's abilities and the current and future earnings, outlook. By focusing on the sales, assets, earnings and management of companies, analysts hope to identify the companies whose intrinsic value will reflect an appreciation in the stock price.

Ratio analysis is used to identify the strengths and weaknesses of the company in relation to its historical pattern and in comparison with the other companies in the same industry.

Although ratio analysis may not identify the stocks that will become gold mines, it will identify the companies to avoid.

For the beginning investor, fundamental analysis may present complex relationships that may initially be difficult to sort out. However, with practice, investors will be able to sharpen their fundamental skills and focus on the relevant indicators.

Fundamental analysis is an art as well as a science in that it requires judgement as well as experience in the selection of stocks.

∎ References

Asinof, Lynn. "How to Find Good Stocks in a Dicey Market." *The Wall Street Journal*, April 29, 1994, p. C1.

Gottschalk Jr., Earl C. "Nervous about Growth Stocks? Try Some High-Dividend Ones." *The Wall Street Journal*, May 2, 1994, p. C1.

Kuhn, Susan E. "Stocks Are Still Your Best Buy," *Fortune*, March 21, 1994, pp. 138–144.

Raghavan, Anita. "As Companies Turn to Stock Buybacks, Some Market Bulls Spot 'Hidden Yield.'" *The Wall Street Journal*, May 2, 1994, p. C1.

Chapter 6

Technical Analysis

Key Concepts

■ Technical Analysis

■ Charts and their Patterns

■ Market Indicators

■ Trend Methods

■ Structural Theories

In the previous chapter, we saw that the fundamental analyst studies the outside forces to the market and then zeroes in on those companies whose stock values are expected to increase over a long period of time. For example, the fundamentalist is interested in the forecasted number of computer mainframes that Unisys Corporation will sell, the average price of the mainframes and if the market for mainframes will increase to boost the earnings of Unisys Corporation.

The *technical analyst*, on the other hand, is not all that concerned about the fundamental factors of the company and the economic environment. Instead, technical analysts focus on the company's past stock price movements and the trading volume of the stock. The technician is interested in the price appreciation of the stock generally, over a short to intermediate period of time.

Most large brokerage firms have a technical analyst on staff, but many investors and brokers use technical analysis only to assist them in the selection of their stocks. In academic circles, however, technical analysis does not have very much credibility.

Advocates of technical analysis feel that fundamental analysis is of minimal value, while those who adhere to fundamental analysis feel the same way about technical analysis. In reality, these two approaches do not work in isolation from each other. Generally, technicians are aware of the fundamentals of the stock they are interested in and fundamentalists are cognizant of the volume and trading range of the stocks they are interested in.

It is important for investors to be aware of the contradictions between these approaches, which will make it easier for them to recognize the philosophies their brokers follow. In the next chapter, the efficient market hypothesis is discussed, which refutes both fundamental analysis and technical analysis as methods of selecting stocks with above average returns.

▮ What Is Technical Analysis?

Technical analysis is not concerned with number crunching or with ratios, earnings, dividends or the types of products or services offered by companies. Instead, technical analysis focuses on past price movements of stocks, using them as a basis for predicting future stock prices. The assumption is that these price movements will be repeated in the future. Technical analysts use charts showing the patterns of stock price movements to interpret future price movements. In other words, investors determine the markets for stocks and when the same price conditions recur, investors will react to them in the same way they did in the past. This repetition of previous patterns in the stock price then becomes the basis for technicians' buy and sell recommendations.

Technicians also consider the trading volume in conjunction with price to be an important indicator of the supply and demand of the stock. For technicians, the combination of price movements and trading volume indicates the mood of the market, summarized in Table 6–1.

Table 6–1   Volume and Price Movements which Indicate Market Mood

Volume	Price	Market Mood
Increasing	Increasing	Bullish sentiment
Increasing	Decreasing	Bearish sentiment
Decreasing	Decreasing	Somewhat bullish
Decreasing	Increasing	Somewhat bearish

When both volume and stock price are increasing, investors are bullish because the increasing trading volume will continue to push prices up. However, the opposite occurs when trading volume is increasing but stock price is decreasing. This indicates bearish sentiment because there are more sellers than buyers, which is depressing the stock price.

Both decreasing price and volume indicates a mixed mood in the market. The decreasing volume shows that the market is bottoming out for this stock. When the price reaches a low enough point, more investors will start buying, which will push the price up.

Although decreasing volume and increasing price also describes a mixed market, this has a somewhat bearish tone since the increasing price will not be supported due to declining volume. The price is topping out and will start to fall.

It is easy to see why technical analysis is so much more appealing than fundamental analysis to many investors and brokers. Price and volume data is easy to get (published daily in the financial newspapers) and to use.

The approaches to technical analysis may be classified in the following categories:

■ Charts

■ Market indicators

■ Trends

■ Structural theories

There are so many technical approaches within each of these broad categories that only a few of the more popular examples in each category will be discussed.

■ Charts and Their Patterns

Technical analysts use charts to depict the stock price patterns that will tell them when to buy and sell. It is not critical to know the company or what it produces and sells. Everything is in the charts! The past price movements and patterns can be used to predict future price movements. Three types of charts used are line, bar and point and figure charts.

Line Charts

A *line chart* shows the stock price over a period of time. This type of chart is used to show, for example, hourly changes to the Dow Jones Industrial Average in a day of trading. Similarly, closing prices of stock may be plotted over a period of time to show the trading patterns. See Figure 6–1 for an example of a line chart showing the prices of a stock for 10 days in June.

Figure 6–1   Line Chart

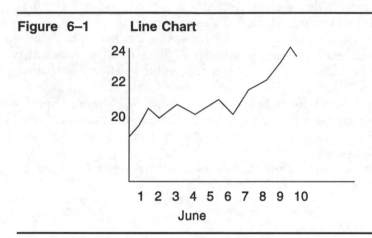

Bar Charts

A *bar chart* is similar to a line chart, but it incorporates more information. If charting stock prices on a daily basis, a bar chart would include the high, low and closing prices of the stock. On a weekly basis, the chart would show the high, low and closing price for the week. A vertical line shows the high and low price, and a horizontal line shows the closing price. Figure 6–2 shows the bar chart for these daily prices:

Price	Mon	Tues	Wed	Thurs	Fri
High	15	15 1/2	14 3/4	15 3/4	17 7/8
Low	14	14 1/2	13 7/8	14 1/4	15 1/2
Close	14 1/2	14 3/4	14 3/4	15 1/2	17 7/8
Volume	10,200	10,900	11,100	12,400	12,600

Figure 6–2   Bar Chart

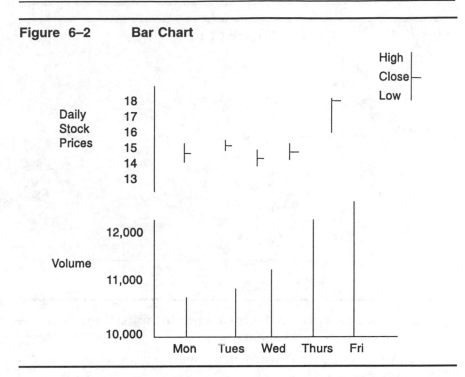

With more data plotted, a pattern would emerge which would be studied by technicians. This would form the basis for buy and sell signals.

Point and Figure Charts

Point and figure charts differ from bar charts in a number of ways. Point and figure charts record only significant changes in the stock price. "Significant—is defined by the analyst drawing up the chart. For higher priced stocks, above $50, there might be a two-point difference to activate recording the price (see Figure 6–3). For lower priced stocks, the difference might be one point. The second major difference between point and figure charts and other charts is that neither time nor trading volume is important.

The construction of a point and figure chart is relatively simple. The first step is to determine the fluctuations you consider significant. For a high-priced stock in the hundreds of dollars, three to five points might be appropriate, whereas a stock in the $10 price range might have a half- to one-point differential.

Assuming two points is decided on for a $50 range stock, the technician plots the changes in price as follows:

Figure 6–3   **Point and Figure Chart**

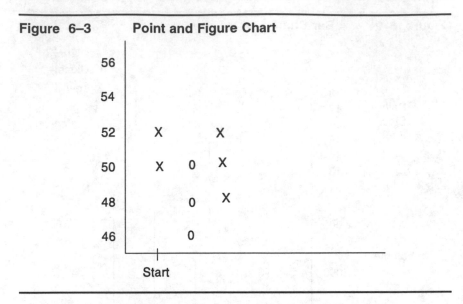

- An X is inserted on the chart when the price of the stock advances by at least two points.

- An O is inserted when the stock declines by at least two points.

For example, the following prices would result in the point and figure chart, shown in Figure 6–3.

First Week	50	51	51 1/2	52 1/4	52 3/4
Second Week	50	47 3/4	46	47 7/8	47 1/2
Third Week	48	49 7/8	50 1/4	51 1/8	53

The first X at $50 is plotted to begin the chart. The next two entries in the first week (51 and 51 1/2) are ignored because they are less than the $2 differential. The second X is placed at $52 to show the increase of the stock to $52 1/4, while the $52 3/4 is ignored.

In the second week, the stock price falls to $50, which necessitates putting an O next to $50 in the second column. The O signifies a decline in price. A second O is inserted at $48 to show the greater than two-point decline to $47 3/4, followed by a third O when the price falls to $46 per share. The third column shows the increase in price to $48, $50 and above $52. Each time the stock advances by more than $2, an X is inserted; and when it falls by more than $2, an O is inserted. Thus, at a glance, a point and figure chart will show price changes.

By plotting prices over a long period of time, many technicians believe they can predict how long a stock will advance or decline as well as identify the support and resistance levels, which are explained in the next section.

Chart Patterns

Once you have decided which type of chart to construct, you can analyze the charts by looking for emerging formations. See Figure 6–4 for some common formations.

There are some difficulties for beginning chartists. First, in practice, the common patterns such as those shown in Figure 6–4 may not emerge; second, the buy and sell signals may not be obvious to the reader of the chart.

Technicians also look for trends in their charts. A *trend* is the direction of the movement of the stock's price or the market movement of prices. It could be in an upward, downward or sideways direction. Generally, prices move in a jagged pattern. A succession of high and low points higher than the previous data signifies an upward trend.

Figure 6–4   Chart Patterns

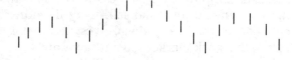

Head and Shoulders

Double Bottom

Inverted Dome

The opposite is true of a downward trend. These trends (upward and downward) are illustrated in Figure 6–5.

During an upward or sideways trend, a pricing point to which the stock rises then repeatedly falls below without breaking through is called a *resistance* level. An explanation for this level of resistance is that when the stock reaches its high side of this trading range, investors sell seeing a chance to make profits. This prevents the stock from moving higher and breaking out of the resistance level.

Similarly, during a downtrend (or sideways trend) there may be a lower level of trading called a *support level*. This is the price level at which the stock will bottom out before increasing in price due to investors buying the stock.

For technical analysts, a *breakout* below a support level or above a resistance level (Figure 6–6) is significant. Technical analysts believe that when stocks break out of their support or resistance levels, the stock prices will continue to move lower or higher, respectively, which will establish new support or resistance levels.

Charting is a lot easier than fundamental analysis and stock price information is easy to get at virtually no additional cost. However, the value of charting as a method for predicting future stock prices and profits has been questioned.

Many chartists attribute their successes to their charts, but the crux of the matter—when to buy and sell—may lie more in the chartist's judgement than in the charts themselves. If it were that simple, we would all have the stock market sewn up by now!

Figure 6–5   Trendlines

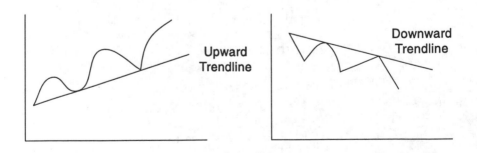

Figure 6–6   Line Chart Showing Support and Resistance Levels

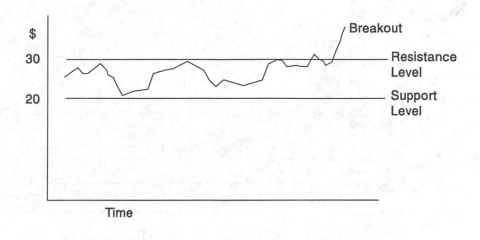

▌ Market Indicators

This group of technical indicators is used to determine the direction of the market.

Dow Theory

The oldest technical method of predicting the direction of the market prices is the Dow theory, developed by Charles Dow, the founder of the Dow Jones Company and the first editor of *The Wall Street Journal.*

The Dow theory is based on the premise that stock prices move together in patterns over a four-to-five year period. According to the theory, there are three major movements in stock prices: primary; secondary and daily or tertiary movements.

Primary price movements are the long-term movements related to the stock's intrinsic values. These may be characterized as bullish or bearish. Secondary price movements are the short-term fluctuations (weeks or months) which are based on current events, which, depending on the fluctuations, may indicate changes in the primary price trend (see Figure 6–7). The tertiary or daily price movements are inconsequential.

The Dow theory assumes that the primary trend will continue for an extended period of time. The directional change can therefore be

Figure 6–7   Dow Theory

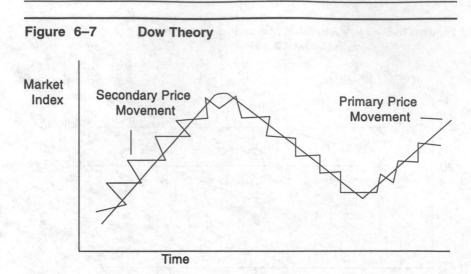

ascertained from observing the movement of the Dow Jones Industrial Average and the Dow Jones Transportation Average. According to the theory, a bull market is confirmed when the industrial average and the transportation average are moving upwards together. Similarly, a decline in both the industrial and transportation averages indicates a bear market. When the averages move in opposite directions it is an indication of uncertainty in the market, which may indicate a change in the primary trend.

Two questions can be raised about the Dow theory. First, why should the movement of the two averages be indicative of the market as a whole? This leads to the second question: How accurate is the Dow theory in predicting changes to market directions?

To answer the second question, the Dow theory is not very accurate and has missed more buy and sell signals than it has correctly predicted (Wright, 312–317). Thus, the Dow theory is not given much credence.

Volume, Breadth and New Highs and Lows

Many technicians gauge the short- and intermediate-term directions of the market by looking at the following indicators:

- Daily volume
- Breadth
- New highs and lows

Volume. As mentioned at the beginning of this chapter, technicians consider volume to be the matching shoe to price. When the daily volume on the New York Stock Exchange increases and the indices (prices as measured by the indices, Dow Jones Industrial Average, S&P 500 Index, *etc.*) are up, this is considered bullish. There are more buyers than sellers.

In a bear market, volume increases, while prices decrease due to increased selling. In a weak market, prices increase but volume declines. When both prices and volume decline, this is a somewhat optimistic sign that stock owners are reluctant to sell.

Many technicians monitor volume figures as an indicator of short-term trends. Statisticians may differ considerably in their interpretations of the combinations of price and volume. Even the more straightforward high volume can be interpreted differently by technicians. Some view this as a positive force, while others view it as a negative force (Dorfman, C18).

In practical terms, daily price and volume changes may be difficult to correlate to determine a trend in the market.

Breadth. Many technical analysts look at the breadth of the market, which is the number of issues traded. By looking at the number of stocks that have advanced, declined and remained the same on a particular day of trading, analysts feel they can determine the strength or weakness of the market.

For instance, of the roughly 2,800 issues on the NYSE, if 1,200 advance, 1,200 decline and 400 remain unchanged, a neutral picture of the market is presented for that day. A stronger picture of the market would be presented by a greater number of advancing stocks over declining stocks—a favorable sign, indicating a rising market. The opposite is true when breadth is negative: greater declining stocks over advancing stocks, indicating a falling market.

The financial newspapers list these daily statistics for the markets, and many technicians use this data to calculate the *advance/decline indicator*. This is calculated by subtracting the number of declining issues from the advancing issues and then dividing this difference by the total number of issues traded for the day. This indicator is plotted on a daily basis to show the *advance/decline line*, used to indicate the trend of the market. Two more complex indices are based on the advance/decline indicator. These are the ARMS Index and the Trading Index.

New Highs and Lows. Many technicians monitor the daily new highs and new lows on the NYSE. When a sizeable number of stocks reach their 52-week highs and they outnumber the stocks that reach their

52-week lows, and this pattern is maintained over a period of time, technicians are bullish on the market.

Many technicians place importance on the signals given by volume, market breadth and the new highs and lows. However, they are not foolproof, and possibly too much importance is placed on them as a prediction of future market activity.

Short Interest Theory

Technical analysts use the information on *short interest* as a sign of weakness or strength in the market. For instance, investors and speculators sell stocks short when they anticipate that their prices will go lower so they can buy them back at these lower prices. Analysts monitor short interest figures, and they contend that when short interest positions are large this is a bullish indicator. This is because with large short positions open, these investors will eventually have to buy back these stocks, which will drive the prices up. Small amounts of short interest are considered of no consequence to future market activity.

The short interest theory may not be all that reliable an indicator of future market sentiment because the amount of stocks sold short is a very small percentage of the shares outstanding on the NYSE. Secondly, short selling may also take place for tax purposes rather than in anticipation of a lower price. This is referred to as *short selling against the box*. An investor can defer the tax consequences of selling appreciated stock into the next year by using the short selling strategy.

For instance, an investor who owns 100 shares which was purchased at $20 a share that is currently trading at $35 wants to sell but does not want to pay the taxes that year. To defer the taxes, the investor sells short 100 shares of the stock at $35 per share and now has two positions in this stock: a long position (purchased at $20 per share) and a short position (short sale at $35 per share).

If the stock goes up in price, the gain on the long position is offset by the loss on the short position. Similarly, if the stock declines in price, the gain on the short position offsets the losses on the long position. The investor has locked in the capital appreciation of $15 per share ($1,500), and because the investor has open positions in both the long and short position, the taxes on the gain are deferred for this year. The next year, the investor can use the 100 shares from the long position to replace the stock borrowed for the short sale, and of course pay the taxes on the gains.

There are other reasons for short interest which also do not represent further purchases of the securities to cover short positions.

Therefore, the volume of short selling may not be a reliable indicator of the movement of stock market prices, despite the fact that many technical analysts religiously follow the short interest figures.

Many technicians are interested in the relationship of short sales to the total number of shares traded, known as the *short interest ratio*. The short interest ratio for the NYSE is calculated by dividing the short interest of the NYSE by the average daily volume on the NYSE for the same period. This ratio can also be calculated for other markets and for individual stocks.

$$\text{Short Interest Ratio} = \frac{\text{Short Interest}}{\text{Average Daily Trading Volume}}$$

Short interest figures are released in the middle of every month by each of the exchanges. For instance, if the short interest is 22 million for one month on the NYSE and the average daily trading volume in that same month for the NYSE is 20 million shares, the short interest ratio for that month is 1.1 (22 million divided by 20 million).

When the average daily volume is less than the short interest the ratio is greater than 1. A short interest ratio of between 1 and 1.6 is considered neutral. Technicians regard a ratio greater than 1.6 as a bullish sign, in that short sellers will have to cover their positions and buy back the stocks. A ratio of less than 1 is considered bearish.

Although this a popular indicator among technicians it too is not infallible in predicting market directions.

Barron's Confidence Index

The Barron's Confidence Index compares the yield of higher grade bonds to lower grade bonds. This relationship is used to predict future movements in the stock market. The assumption for this theory is that bond traders are more sophisticated than stock traders and their actions are much more insightful of market activity.

The Barron's Confidence Index is calculated by dividing the yield of 10 top grade corporate bonds by the yield of 10 intermediate grade bonds.

$$\text{Barron's Confidence Index} = \frac{\text{Yield on 10 Top Grade Bonds} \times 100}{\text{Yield on 10 Intermediate Grade Bonds}}$$

Yields on top grade bonds are always lower than yields on lesser grade bonds, so this index will always be less than 100 percent. Generally, the trading range is between 80 and 95 percent (Hirt and Block, 275).

For instance, if the average yield of the 10 high grade bonds is 9.5 percent and the average of the intermediate grade bonds is 10 percent, the Barron's Confidence Index is 95 percent (9.5/10 × 100). This would indicate optimism because investors are willing to bear more risk in their bond holdings. By selling lower-yielding high-grade bonds and buying more speculative bonds, the prices of the latter are pushed down, resulting in higher yields. This narrows the yield differential between high grade and lesser grade bonds, resulting in a high Barron's Confidence Index, which, according to the theory, means that the outlook for the stock market is positive.

When the Barron's Confidence Index falls to around 80 percent, the outlook for the stock market is bearish. When confidence in the economy is low, investors buy good-quality debt, which increases their prices and lowers their yields. The selling of lower grade bonds decreases their prices and increases their yields. This results in an increase in the rate differential between high quality and lower quality bonds and a lower Barron's Confidence Index.

Like all the other technical indicators, the Barron's Confidence Index has not been all that accurate in that there may be time lags between the indicator and the results; and when companies in the Confidence Index issue a large supply of bonds there is a distortion in the yields, which then distorts the indicator.

The Barron's Confidence Index is published weekly in Barron's newspaper.

Insider Transactions

Corporate directors, officers and large shareholders—referred to as insiders—have access to privileged information about their companies and therefore are required by the Securities and Exchange Commission (SEC) to report their purchases and sales of stocks. Insiders know first-hand how the company is doing; if they are purchasing their company's stocks, this is a bullish signal for that stock. Conversely, if insiders sell their stocks, this is a bearish signal.

Insider transactions are reported in the financial newspapers on a weekly basis. Many technicians follow insider activity as a method for selecting stocks. Academic studies tend to lend more support to insider transactions as a means of correlating changes in stock prices than other technical approaches (Jaffe, 410–428 and Zweig, 5).

Odd-Lot Theory

The odd-lot theory is concerned with the purchase and sale of securities by small investors. An odd-lot trade consists of fewer than 100 shares which are generally placed by small investors. *The Wall Street Journal* reports odd-lot trading on a daily basis and *Barron's* reports it on a weekly basis. Technicians calculate the ratio of odd-lot purchases to odd-lot sales, which has a range from 0.6 to 1.4 (Reilly, 334).

$$\text{Odd-Lot Ratio} = \frac{\text{Odd-Lot Purchases}}{\text{Odd-Lot Sales}}$$

Technicians view small investors as unsophisticated and frequently wrong in their investment decisions. According to the theory, small investors buy stocks at the peak of the bull market—which is the time to start selling. Similarly, after a stock market decline—the time to start buying—small investors sell their stocks.

When the ratio approaches its upper limits (1.4), this means that small investors are buying more than they are selling. This indicates that the stock market is about to turn and become a bear market. In other words, small investors become enthusiastic about the stock market when the market has reached its highs and become disillusioned after a crash in the market, which gives a low reading on the ratio.

There appears to be no validity to the odd-lot theory. In fact, there were times in the mid-1970s and late 1980s when small investors out-guessed many of the money managers (Hirt and Block, 272).

Investment Advisory Opinions

Technicians who follow the predictions of investment advisors take a contrarian view and do the opposite. When most of the advisors are bullish, technicians become bearish. Similarly, if the majority of advisors become bearish, for technicians this is a buy signal.

It seems strange to think that investment advisors who spend most of their working hours studying the market should be lumped in with the odd-lotters in their assessments of the market. However, when analysts and advisors do make their recommendations, the investing public may never be sure of their underlying reasons.

Mutual Fund Cash Position

The cash position of mutual funds is another indicator. By monitoring the cash position of mutual funds, technical analysts can then assess their potential purchasing power. Equity mutual funds hold between 5 and 25 percent of their assets in cash. When mutual funds are fully invested or hold very little of their assets in cash, they have very little purchasing power in the market. However, when they hold larger percentages of their assets in cash (15 percent or higher), their potential purchasing power in the market is significant, which could trigger an upturn in the market (Hirt and Block, 278).

∎ Trend Methods

Some analysts subscribe to the belief that it is more important to identify a trend because trends are more likely to persevere. In other words, once a trend has been identified, you should move with it: in an up market you should be buying, and in a down market you should be selling.

Moving Average

The moving average is one of the more popular methods for determining a trend. An average is the sum of the figures divided by the number of figures used in the numerator; a moving average is an average over time. For example, using a stock with closing prices for a 10-day period, the average is calculated as follows:

Day	Closing Price
1	$ 15 3/4
2	16 1/4
3	17 1/2
4	15
5	16 1/8
6	15 7/8
7	16 1/4
8	17
9	17 1/4
10	18
Total	165

$$\text{Average Price} = \frac{165}{10}$$
$$= 16.5$$

A 10-day moving average would add the stock price for the 11th day and drop the stock price for the first day. For instance, if the closing price on the eleventh day is $18 per share, the 10-day moving average will be:

$$10\text{–day Moving Average} = \frac{10\text{–day average} + 11\text{th day price} - 1\text{st day's price}}{10}$$

$$= \frac{165 + 18 - 15\,\tfrac{3}{4}}{10}$$

$$= \$16.725$$

By continuing this method of adding the next day's price and dropping the oldest day's price, the moving average is calculated over time. This moving average may be plotted to show the graphical trend over time and how the moving average compares with the daily prices of the stocks. When the moving average line crosses the line of actual prices, this indicates a change in trend. The moving average line tends to smooth out any volatility in the actual daily stock prices.

You can choose any length of time for a moving average—10, 15, 30 and 200 days. The 200-day moving average is frequently used but can be tedious for the investor to calculate, particularly if a number of stocks are followed. There would be the daily closing prices for 200 days to record and calculate as well as having to compute a moving average for each stock that is being followed.

The length of time chosen for the moving average will have an effect on the trend line. A short duration moving average results in greater sensitivity to price changes than a longer duration moving average. With the former, an investor who religiously follows the signals given with the frequent crossing of the trend line and the price line will be encouraged to trade stocks after small changes in price. In other words, when the trend line goes up, the investor should buy, and when it turns down the investor should sell. Thus, with a short moving average, a volatile stock price would encourage the investor to enter and exit the stock frequently, which means that the transaction costs could eliminate any profits. With a longer moving average, the trend line will exhibit a greater lag behind the actual price line of these stocks.

A study done by James C. Van Horne and G. G. C. Parker (1967) suggests that the use of the moving average as a tool for buying and selling stocks does not produce superior results. The fact that investors need to decide on the duration to use for the moving average and whether they should buy and sell when the lines cross suggests a somewhat arbitrary and simplistic approach to the complexities of buying and selling stocks. If there is a major uptrend in a stock, the investor will profit from it by buying early, and of course the opposite is also true. If a major downtrend is recognized early and the investor sells before the downturn, the investor is ahead of the game. However, for the stocks that exhibit volatility, this method may give equivocal signs and would encourage frequent trading, which would not take the transaction costs into account.

The moving average for the Dow Jones Industrials is used by technicians to determine the trend for the market. Emphasis is placed on the crossover of the daily price to the moving average line as an indicator of a change in trend direction.

∎ Structural Theories

The structural theories of technical analysis are based on a repetition of previous price patterns. Price patterns are believed to be regular over long periods of time. There are many structural theories, some of which are quite esoteric and literally base their stock market predictions on lunar phases. Although these exotic theories may be colorful and interesting to the reader, the author will stick with the more down-to-earth theories.

Seasonal Patterns

Those who advocate seasonality in the stock market may find patterns, but the use of such knowledge may be limited. For example, in monitoring the Dow Jones Industrial Average on a monthly basis, the statistics show a slight seasonal pattern in December, January, July and August. Some attribute the seasonal pattern in December and January to tax planning. By December, many investors sell stocks that are depressed in value to produce capital losses that can then be offset against other capital gains. This selling further depresses the prices of these stocks, which presents opportunities for investors to buy them back in January, which results in a surge in their stock prices. This is known as the *January effect*. Historically, the prices of small stocks have risen slightly in January. Gottschalk reported that since 1982 small stocks have increased by 4.2 percent as compared with 3.8 percent for larger stocks in January (C1, C16).

The January effect should not be taken too seriously because there are some nagging questions. Which stocks will increase in January? Will these include the stocks in your portfolio? Maybe, maybe not! What about a bear market? During the bear markets of 1978 and

1982, the prices of small stocks lost ground in January. Will the small percentage increases cover the transaction costs of buying and selling?

Investors should not jump for joy over the January effect because the price increases may not cover the costs of trading and may not even include the stocks that you choose for your portfolio.

The same questions can be asked about summer rallies in the markets. Research done by Hugh Johnson, chief investment officer for First Albany, has shown net gains from May 31 to August 31 in the Dow Jones Industrial Average for 21 of the past 33 years (Kansas, C1).

Birinyi Associates have found support for this premise with a longer study going back to 1915. There were only four time periods where the Dow Jones Industrial Average reported losses in all three summer months—June, July and August—since 1915. The gains on the industrial average was reported to be 0.41 percent, 1.31 percent and 1.06 percent on average per year for June, July and August, respectively over the time period from 1915. Surprisingly, even in 1929 there was a summer rally where the Dow Jones Industrial Average surged 11.5 percent in June, 4.8 percent in July and 9.4 percent in August (Kansas, C2).

There is also the weekend effect: stocks peak on Fridays and fall back in price on Mondays. Research over decades has shown some validity for this phenomenon (Hirt and Block, 475). According to this theory, investors should sell their stocks at the end of the week rather than at the beginning.

Elliott Wave Theory

This chapter would not be complete if it did not include the Elliott Wave Theory. The premise of this theory is that stock prices move in a five-wave sequence when following the major trend and in a three-wave sequence when moving against the major trend. Long waves can last longer than 100 years, while there are subwaves with rather short durations.

The Elliott Wave Theory gained a following after it was used by technicians to correctly forecast the bull market of the 1980s. However, it lost much of its following when it turned bearish in the late 1980s and early 1990s, missing out on the continuing bull market.

The problem with this structural theory and with many of the others is that what is considered a wave by some analysts would be considered a subwave by others. The Elliott Wave Theory may be too broadly defined to be conclusive; its followers often include their successes while discounting their failures.

∎ Summary

Technical analysis uses past information on price and volume to predict future price movements. Charts are used to show this data graphically. From these charts, various patterns may be identified; from these, technical analysts will identify the buy and sell signals.

This approach is much more appealing to the lay investor than fundamental analysis, which relies on number crunching. By constructing some charts and/or following the insider transactions or odd-lot purchases to sales ratios, technical analysis implies that you have an easy read on the market.

If this were the case, there would be many more self-made millionaires, and you would never see an advertisement for an advisory service that uses technical analysis to beat the market. They would be guarding their secrets while making millions of dollars instead of resorting to selling their services to investors.

There is little empirical evidence to support technical analysis in the selection of superior stocks that outperform the markets consistently. There are so many technical indicators used to predict future prices and identify buy and sell signals that, when considered together, they often give confusing and contradictory advice.

There is little academic support for technical analysis as a method of producing superior results. In fact, investors may do as well or better by randomly picking stocks and holding them than by frequently trading stocks, as suggested by following the ever-changing buy and sell signals of the technical indicators. The commissions and spreads eat into profits, reducing overall returns.

Technical analysis is in direct opposition to the efficient market theory, which states that all information is readily disseminated to investors which impacts on stock prices. In other words, the past prices of stocks have no bearing on future prices. This gives rise to the random walk theory, which is that stock prices are independent and randomly determined. These theories are discussed in Chapter 7.

∎ References

Dorfman, John R. "Technical Analysts Get a Chill as Winter Approaches," *The Wall Street Journal,* (Dec 14, 1993; C1, C18.

Hirt, Geoffrey A. and Stanley B. Block. *Fundamentals of Investment Management,* 3rd ed. Homewood, IL: Irwin. 1990.

Gottschalk, Earl C. "It's the 'January Effect' but Will It Occur in January?," *The Wall Street Journal,* (Dec. 14, 1988); C1, C16.

Jaffe, Jeffrey F. "Special Information and Insider Trading," *Journal of Business* (July 1974), pp. 410-428.

Kansas, Dave. "Analysts Expect Summer Rally, but Nothing Special," *The Wall Street Journal.* (June 6, 1994), C1, C2.

Reilly, Frank K. *Investments.* Hinsdale, IL: Dryden Press 1982.

Van Horne, James C. and G.G.C. Parker. "The Random Walk Theory: An Empirical Test," *Financial Analysts Journal.* (November–December 1967).

Wright, Leonard T. *Principles of Investments,* 2d ed. Columbus, OH: Grid, Inc., 1977.

Zweig, Martin E. "Canny Insiders," *Barron's* (June 21, 1976), 5.

Chapter 7

Buying Strategies

Key Concepts
- Theories of Stock Prices
- Implications of the Efficient Market Hypothesis
- Capital Asset Pricing Model
- Buy and Hold Strategy
- Active Investment Strategy
- Formula Plans
- Implications for Investors
- Caveats

Many investors believe they can time the markets by buying stocks when the markets are moving up and then selling their stocks before the markets start to decline from their peaks. Many investment advisory newsletters are aimed at these investors, who are known as market timers. These newsletters advise their readers when to buy and when to sell their stocks.

Correctly anticipating a correction or crash can certainly improve the rate of return for an investor. For instance, some newsletters correctly advised their readers to sell their stocks before the stock market crash in 1987 and to buy stocks after the Dow Jones Industrial Average had fallen to the lows of the year. Such a strategy would have increased investors' returns over those who stayed invested during and after the market crash. However, the trouble with market timing is if you exit the market at the wrong time, you can not only miss out on stock market gains, but you can also greatly diminish your rate of return.

Over the long term, investors who stay fully invested in the stock market reduce the risks of mis-timing the market. This strategy becomes evident in the next section, an examination of the different theories of stock prices.

∎ Theories of Stock Prices

In Chapter 5 the *fundamental theory* was discussed, which relates the movement of stock prices to earnings. Anticipating changes in earnings will precipitate a change in stock prices. According to the theory, the astute investor analyzes the fundamentals of the company as to their effects on future earnings. When future earnings are anticipated to increase, the stock price will move up in advance of the actual changes in earnings. The belief is that by buying and selling stocks in advance of the actual changes in earnings, investors will increase their profits. In other words, it would be too late to buy stocks after the actual earnings increases are announced or to sell them after decreases in earnings are announced, because the stock price has already reacted to this news.

The fundamental analyst is concerned with determining certain financial characteristics of different stocks in order to find those stocks whose prices are undervalued. When the market price of the stock is less than its intrinsic value (a reflection of estimated earnings multiplied by a price/earnings ratio), the stock is said to be undervalued. If the market price is above the intrinsic value, the stock is overvalued. This theory then implies that the markets are inefficient, which allows large profits to be made from undervalued securities. The fundamental theory is refuted by the efficient market hypothesis, which is discussed later in this section.

Since there are no assurances that stock prices move in the same direction as earnings, investors may not be able to count on correctly forecasting stock price movements. Moreover, there are a multiplicity of conditions and factors over and above the fundamentals that affect stock prices.

In Chapter 6 the *technical factors* were discussed, which, unlike the fundamental factors, affect stock prices due to conditions within the market. Technical analysis ignores the basic factors in the economy, such as earnings, dividends and interest rates as the cause of stock price changes. Instead, there is a focus on past stock prices, their patterns and the trading volumes. By charting these past price movements and volume, technicians forecast future price movements.

Their belief is that the past price patterns will be repeated into the future, which is the basis for their recommendations of when to buy and sell stocks. Besides defying logic, technical analysis has little support from the academic investment literature. Not only has the academic world not been kind to technical analysis, but there has also been disdain from supporters of the efficient market hypothesis.

The implication from both the fundamental analysis and technical analysis theories is that the markets are inefficient. By investing in stocks with low P/E ratios or high earnings yields or by purchasing stocks at the low end of their trading ranges, investors expect to receive higher returns. This may occur; but according to the efficient market hypothesis, investors will not consistently be able to outperform the markets by earning abnormally large returns.

The basic premise of the *efficient market hypothesis* is that the stock markets are efficient. Information about stocks is disseminated throughout the investment community. Thus, if investors and analysts use the same public information on stocks, it will be hard to generate superior returns because the rest of the investment community has the same information. Stock price reflects all the available information, which implies there will be very few mispriced stocks. If a stock is undervalued, investors will quickly buy it, which will drive up the price and hence reduce the returns for subsequent investors. Similarly, overvalued stocks will be sold, which will reduce the price and increase returns for subsequent investors.

In other words, stocks will not be mispriced for long. Stocks will settle at their intrinsic values, which reflect the investment community's consensus about their earnings returns and risks.

The implication of efficient markets is that investors cannot expect to consistently outperform the markets or consistently underperform the markets. On average, investors will do no better or worse than the market averages over an extended period of time with a diversified portfolio of stocks. This is not to say that investors cannot find securities that earn abnormally high returns. For example, investors who bought MCI Corporation's stock at $7 per share in 1984 and sold it at $45 per share in 1990 would have outperformed the markets. The theory of efficient markets implies that investors will not be able to consistently buy stocks such as these to earn these kinds of returns.

The question most asked concerning the efficient market hypothesis is, What is the degree of efficiency in the markets? Obviously, if investors believe the markets are inefficient, they will continue using different techniques and analyses to select those stocks that will produce superior returns. However, if markets are efficient, the value of these techniques and analyses are diminished.

There is considerable debate about the degree of efficiency in the markets and this is centered on three forms of the efficient market hypothesis: the *weak form, the semistong form and the strong form*. The degree of market efficiency has important ramifications for investors and the strategies that they develop for the selection of their stocks.

The *weak form* of the efficient market hypothesis suggests that the use of technical analysis in the selection of stocks will not produce superior returns. According to the weak form of market efficiency, stock prices reflect all historical market data. This includes the price history of the stocks, the trading volume, and all other information that forms the basis for technical analysis.

The weak form maintains that past stock prices are independent of future stock prices. In other words, there is no relationship between past and future stock prices. This would make it futile to chart past prices.

Studies testing the weak form of the efficient market hypothesis show that stock prices appear to move independently or in a random fashion (Fama, 34–105). This is also known as the *random walk hypothesis*.

Burton G. Malkiel, in his book *A Random Walk Down Wall Street*, supports the weak form of the efficient market theory by arguing that investors would do no better or worse than the market averages if they chose their investments by throwing darts at stock tables. Periodically, *The Wall Street Journal* publishes results that compare stocks picked by dart throwers and those by financial analysts. There are times when the stock picks of the dart throwers outperform those of the analysts.

Technical analysts and many on Wall Street dispute the findings of the studies that support the weak form of the efficient market hypothesis. After all, if there is no validity to the weak form, technical analysts would be able to consistently earn superior returns by charting and analyzing past stock price information to predict future stock prices. The weak form, however, suggests that the use of fundamental analysis in selecting stocks may produce superior returns.

According to the *semi-strong form* of the efficient market hypothesis, stock prices reflect all public information. This includes information in all published reports, analysts' reports, press and radio and television reports, as well as historical information. When a company announces information, it will be reflected quickly into the stock price. Therefore, analysis of this information may not produce superior returns. However, the door is not completely closed regarding superior returns. The semi-strong theory asserts that superior returns could be achieved through the analysis of this information, but over a period of time this will not consistently produce superior returns.

This conclusion may be quite rational when you consider that analysts and investors are exposed to the same public information. In their competition with each other over changes in information, analysts and investors make the pricing of stocks much more efficient. If there is a perceived change in a stock's value, investors will buy it, moving the price up to its equilibrium value.

Many studies support the validity of the semi-strong form of the efficient market hypothesis, which asserts that stock prices change very rapidly to reflect new public information and in many cases anticipate the announcements of the information to the public (Fama, *et al.*, 2–21). This implies that investors could earn superior returns by anticipating any new information before it becomes public and is reflected in the stock price. This may be the clairvoyant's dream!

However, there are some anomalies in the research done on the semi-strong form that suggest some inefficiencies in the market could produce superior returns. These will be discussed after the strong form of market efficiency.

The *strong form* of the efficient market hypothesis reflects not only all public information but all information that includes insider information. It assumes that the market is highly efficient and that stock prices react very quickly to insider information. If this is so, even corporate insiders will not have information that will benefit them because stock prices will have already reacted to this information. According to this form, no investors or groups of investors who are privy to monopolistic information (insider information) will benefit by earning superior returns because the markets are virtually perfect.

The strong form of the efficient market hypothesis has been studied and tested with regard to returns earned by specialists and the use of insider information. As discussed in Chapter 4, specialists have a book of orders waiting to be executed at different prices. The specialist buys and sells stocks from his or her own inventory, which means that the specialist has some very valuable information. For example, if there are many unfilled limit orders to buy a stock at $9 per share and the stock is trading at $12, the specialist knows the price will not fall below $9 per share. A study sponsored by the Securities and Exchange Commission reported that specialists earned on average a return of over 100 percent on their capital (SEC 1971).

Corporate insiders are another group who are privy to special information that brings about superior returns. Studies show that insiders achieve greater returns than those expected of a perfect market

(Lorie and Niederhoffer, 35–53). Insiders are defined as officers and directors of a company and those shareholders who own 10 percent of a company's stock.

Insiders are privy to information that has not been made available to the public; there is a fine line distinguishing legal and illegal use of this information.

Corporate insiders have access to privileged information but are not allowed to use this information to make profits or to engage in short-term trading (six months or less). They are allowed to trade and make profits on the stock on a long-term basis, and their trades must be reported to the SEC.

Ivan Boesky used insider information to rake up excessive profits, but he paid a high price for the illegal use of this information. He was convicted, sent to prison and paid heavy finds.

Despite the fact that specialists and insiders are able to earn superior returns, which rejects the strong form of the efficient market hypothesis, there is support for the strong form based on the performance of mutual fund managers. Mutual fund managers receive information faster than the investing public, yet they have not been able to consistently outperform the market averages (Hirt and Block, 285).

The difference can be explained as follows: the use of privileged (monopolistic) information may help generate superior returns; the use of publicly available information may not be able to assist in earning superior returns on a consistent basis.

What Are the Implications of the Efficient Market Hypothesis for Investors?

On first impressions, the logical implications to the efficient market hypothesis might be to buy some powerful telescope to watch for some astrological signals such as when the planets Jupiter and Venus are aligned as to when to buy and sell stocks. The second is to give a sigh of relief for all those hours saved in not having to crunch numbers on the earnings, sales and growth figures required by fundamental analysis. The third is not to even waste the gas in the car to go out to buy graph paper to plot the charts required by technical analysis.

According to the weak and semi-strong forms of the efficient market hypothesis, the use of technical and fundamental analysis will not produce superior returns on a consistent basis. This may be disconcerting to investors. But what about the technical and fundamental analysts, whose occupations are deemed worthless or null and void? It is no wonder that Wall Street has not embraced the efficient market hypothesis.

The fourth implication to be drawn is not to break into the headquarters of various corporations to gain access to their privileged information!

The final window of opportunity belongs to the specialist. However, those of us who do not become specialists have a bleak future with regard to choosing stocks for our portfolios. The theory suggests that all information is incorporated into the price of the stock and that stocks with good fundamentals will be bid up in price to reflect this. Similarly, stocks that are in trouble will be sold. In other words, there will be no undervalued stocks.

If there is an even chance of stocks rising or falling, it doesn't matter which stocks you choose or for that matter which stocks anyone else chooses. The random walk theory implies pure luck in picking stocks.

The efficient market hypothesis is hotly debated and the jury of academicians is still undecided on the degree of efficiency of the market. Even though the efficient market hypothesis has not aroused the enthusiasm of most investors, the implications are important because they shatter any thoughts of creating overnight wealth in the stock market.

The efficient market hypothesis suggests that few investors will consistently beat the market averages over a long period of time. For example, if the market increases by 10 percent over a one-year period, most investors will earn close to the 10 percent average. However, this does not mean there won't be those who do very much worse than 10 percent or those who earn abnormally high returns.

The following are some anomalies to the efficient market hypothesis where investors have been able to generate superior returns to beat the market:

- Small Stocks. A study done by Arbel and Strebel (1982) suggests that undervalued stocks of small companies that have been neglected by the investment community may provide greater returns than the market averages. This suggests that the security markets may not be equally efficient.

- Low P/E Ratio Stocks. Studies done by Basu (1975, 1977) show that portfolios of stocks with low P/E ratios have outperformed portfolios of stocks with high P/E ratios on a risk-adjusted and nonrisk-adjusted basis. This refutes the semi-strong form of the efficient market hypothesis because P/E ratios of stocks can be obtained from publicly available information.

Benjamin Graham, who did the pioneering work that forms the basis of fundamental analysis, realized that markets were becoming more efficient, thus making it more difficult to find undervalued stocks. Figure 7–1 lists Graham's guidelines for selecting stocks. One of his guidelines is to select low P/E ratio stocks. The greater the number of yes answers, the more ideal the stock choice, according to Graham's model.

∎ There are other possible market anomalies that suggest inefficiencies in the market that result in superior returns. The *January effect* finds that stocks that have done poorly in December may produce superior returns in January.

These anomalies should not lead investors to think that the markets are inefficient. Rather, they should be viewed as exceptions. Academic studies lend support for the weak and semi-strong forms of the efficient market hypothesis, which lends support to the conclusion that very few investors outperform the markets over long periods of time. For investors who feel the efficient market hypothesis is not equally efficient with regard to the pricing of the smaller, lesser-known stocks, there is a role for fundamental analysis.

∎ Capital Asset Pricing Model (CAPM)

The 1990 Nobel prize laureates for economics, Harry Markovitz and William Sharpe, have done work on the financial markets that has had a profound effect for investors.

Harry Markovitz's work pioneered what is now known as the *modern portfolio theory*. Concerned with the composition of investments that investors would select for their portfolios, Markovitz determined that the major properties of an investment of concern to investors are risk and return. By choosing a range of different investments for a portfolio, investors are able to determine and control the total risk in that portfolio through variance analysis of each investment.

William Sharpe further developed Markovitz's approach into the capital asset pricing model (CAPM). In this model, the risk of portfolio theory is broken down into two parts: the systematic risk and the unsystematic risk.

Figure 7–1   **Benjamin Graham's Guidelines of Stocks to**
                   Buy Rewards

1.   Is the P/E ratio less than half the reciprocal of the AAA corporate
      bond yield? For example, the current AAA yield is 7.34 percent,
      and the reciprocal is 13.62 percent (1/.0734). The P/E ratio of the
      stock would have to be less than 6.81 percent (one-half times the
      reciprocal or 1/2 × .1362) to be bought.

2.   Is the P/E ratio less than 40 percent of the average P/E of the
      stock over the past five years?

3.   Is the dividend yield equal to or more than two-thirds the AAA
      corporate bond yield? Two-thirds of the current AAA corporate
      bond yield of 7.34 percent is 4.88 percent. In order to rate the
      stock a buy, the dividend yield should equal or be greater than
      4.88 percent.

4.   Is the stock price less than two-thirds of the book value of the
      stock?

5.   Is the price less than two-thirds of the net current asset value per
      share?

Risks

1.   Is the debt-to-equity ratio less than one? The total debt of the
      company should be less than the total equity.

2.   Is the current ratio equal to two or more? The total current assets
      divided by the total current liabilities should equal two or more.

3.   Is the total debt less than twice the net current assets?

4.   Is the 10-year average EPS growth rate greater than 7 percent?

5.   Were there no more than 2 years out of the past 10 with earnings
      declines of greater than 5 percent?

Source: *Fundamentals of Investments*, Prentice Hall (1993) in Paul Sturm "What if Benjamin Graham had a P.C.?" *Smart Money* (March 1994): 32.

Systematic risk is similar to market risk in that the movement of
the security's price is proportional to the movement of prices in the
market. Systematic risk is measured by the Greek letter *beta*. A stock
with a beta coefficient of one indicates that if the market rises by 20
percent, the stock will go up in price by 20 percent. Similarly, if the
market falls by 20 percent, the stock will also see a 20 percent decline

in price. A stock with a beta coefficient greater than one should produce above-average returns in a bull market and below-average returns in a bear market. A stock with a beta coefficient of less than one
will be less responsive to market changes. Most stocks have beta coefficients ranging from 0.6 to 1.6 (Martin, 102). Investors who seek
higher returns will, therefore, be willing to assume more risk.

Increased diversification into many different stocks in a portfolio
will not eliminate the systematic risk. In other words, these stocks will
not be immune to a downturn in the market. However, diversification
into many different stocks can eliminate the *unsystematic risk,* which
are the risks that pertain to the company itself. These are financial risk,
business risk and purchasing power risk, which affect the stock price
of the company.

Sharpe's model has evoked controversy that is still being debated. One implication from the CAPM is that the selection of high
beta stocks in a portfolio is likely to produce above-average returns in
a bull market and below-average returns in a bear market. The assumption of the theory is that investors cannot outperform the market,
but through managing the risks of the stocks in the portfolio, they can
forecast returns that are correlated to the market.

As can be expected, security analysts have not embraced the
CAPM nor the efficient market hypothesis. Their view is that academicians are so immersed in their own research that they would not be
able to recognize an undervalued stock even if it was brought to their
attention. The ongoing battle between the analysts and the academicians is of little importance; however, what is important to individual
investors is an awareness of these theories from several practical
points of view.

The degree of efficiency of the market will determine the investor's strategy with regard to the selection of stocks and the length of
time to hold these stocks. If the investor believes that the market is
efficient and that all information is reflected in the price of the stock,
the strategy might be to select quality stocks with good future earnings and to hold these stocks for long periods of time (a buy-and-hold
strategy). On the other side of the spectrum, if the investor believes
the markets are inefficient, he or she can use technical analysis to determine which stocks to buy and sell over shorter periods of time and
fundamental analysis to select undervalued stocks to buy and hold for
longer periods of time. The degree of efficiency is debatable; the ultimate decision is the investor's.

The Capital Asset Pricing Model suggests that investors diversify
their investments to eliminate the unsystematic risk. The returns
earned by most investments will be consistent with those earned by

the market and the related amount of risk. Bearing this in mind, the investment strategy that is chosen should be in keeping with the investor's objectives.

■ Buy-and-Hold Investment Strategy

Buy-and-hold investment strategy is a passive strategy based on the premise that over long periods of time the returns on common stocks will exceed the returns earned from other investments, such as bonds and money market securities; and on the fact that historically stock markets have always increased in value.

The object of a buy-and-hold strategy is to do as well as the market. There is no attempt to beat the market. By holding a broadly diversified portfolio, which reduces the unsystematic risks—the risks pertaining to the companies or the industries—this type of investment strategy should approximate the returns of the market. The success of this type of strategy depends on the state of the market.

During an uptrend in the market, such as during the decade of the 1980s, a buy-and-hold strategy would have benefited most investors. Of course, in a market correction or crash, prices of most stocks will decline. However, after most stock market declines, the markets historically have recovered and moved on to greater heights.

It is always wonderful to hear the feats of investors who are able to time the markets—selling their portfolios days before the stock market crash and then moving back into the market at a lower level. However, few investors like to tell the story of how they exited the market in anticipation of the crash that never materialized. This meant sitting on the sidelines during a bull market or reentering the market at a higher level.

The buy-and-hold strategy avoids the need to time the markets or read the financial stock tables in the newspapers on a daily basis. With a long time horizon, there is no need to time the markets because the investor remains fully invested in stocks.

The second advantage of a buy-and-hold strategy is that transaction costs are minimized. Similarly, the cost of acquiring information is avoided. This does not mean stocks that are bought are forgotten about. With a buy-and-hold strategy, investors should still review the performance of their stocks with regard to growth in sales and earnings from time to time and get rid of those stocks that do not present future potential growth and earnings.

Indexing is a concept that embodies the buy-and-hold strategy, thereby minimizing the transaction costs due to the passive investment strategy. By choosing a market index such as the S&P 500 or the Dow Jones Industrial Average and choosing the same stocks in that index for the portfolio, an investor replicates the performance of the market index. It may be difficult for individual investors to replicate these indices due to the large numbers of stocks in the indices (500 for the S&P Index) and hence the enormous dollar cost. There are index mutual funds, discussed in Chapter 8, which make it easier to invest in stocks of the specific indices.

Although the buy-and-hold strategy minimizes the timing decisions of when to buy and sell, investors still need to decide which stocks to select. By approximating an index, the types of stocks to choose becomes an easy matter. Which index to follow would depend on the investor's overall objectives. A conservative investor who is looking for income and capital preservation would consider blue-chip stocks, utility stocks and some of the more established growth stocks. A more aggressive investor would include growth stocks and the small capitalized company stocks.

Investors who believe the market to be efficient would choose stocks from various industries to form a diversified portfolio and hope to replicate the performance of the market. According to the efficient market hypothesis, these stocks could be randomly selected because if the markets are efficient these stocks would be correctly valued (at their intrinsic value). Efficient markets support passive investment strategies; inefficient markets suggest actively managed investment strategies.

With a buy-and-hold strategy, investors can take advantage of the *dividend reinvestment plans* (DRIPs) that many companies offer. Companies with DRIPs allow their existing shareholders to choose whether they want to automatically reinvest their cash dividends in additional shares of the company's stock. Brokerage fees may be avoided, but some companies assess a handling fee (which is generally less than the brokerage fees). In order to encourage shareholders to sign up for these dividend reinvestment plans, many companies are willing to issue fractional shares as well as to sell their stock at small discounts to the current market price. It is important to examine the fees charged by companies. Some companies charge excessive fees, and their dividend reinvestment plans should be avoided.

The advantage of DRIPs to shareholders is that they act as a forced savings plan in that dividends are automatically reinvested to accumulate more shares. This is particularly good for investors who are not disciplined savers.

The disadvantage of a dividend reinvestment plan is that shareholders need to keep their records of the additional shares purchased for tax purposes. These dividends are taxable income to investors whether they are received in cash or automatically reinvested in additional shares. However, when the additional shares are sold, the cost (purchase price) will be used to determine whether there is a capital gain or loss for tax purposes.

■ Active Investment Strategy

Timing the market accurately will always produce superior returns. This strategy involves buying stocks before they go up in price. In other words, you would be fully invested in stocks in an increasing market and out of stocks in a decreasing market. There are many newsletters that advocate timing the market.

The greatest disadvantage to timing is that you need to be accurate in your calls of the market. If you are correct 50 percent of the time, you will earn less than if your pursued a buy-and-hold strategy, according to a study done by T. Rowe Price and Associates in 1987 as reported in Cheyney and Moses (19). During the period 1926–1983, investors who were 100 percent accurate in their timing decisions would have earned an average of 18.2 percent per year versus an 11.8 percent average yearly return for a buy-and-hold strategy. With a 50 percent accuracy rate in calling the market, the return was 8.1 percent. Thus, to earn returns in excess of the market, investors would have had to be more accurate than 70 percent of the time in calling the market during this period (T. Rowe Price Associates, Inc., 1987 in Cheyney and Moses, 19).

Technical analysis charts the past price movements of stocks to time when to buy and sell stocks. This is advocated for timing the overall market and timing stocks.

Fundamental analysis also advocates timing but with a longer time horizon and a more critical eye concerning which stocks to buy and sell.

Inefficient or weakly efficient markets suggest that investors may be able to earn returns in excess of the markets by pursuing active investment strategies. The downside to timing the markets is that you could be on the sidelines during an increasing market if a wrong call is made.

∎ Formula Plans

Many investors use formula plans to avoid having to time the markets. These plans eliminate the timing, but investors still need to select their stocks to buy and sell using these plans. By buying shares of stocks over a period of time at different prices, investors will lessen the impact of price fluctuations.

Three plans are discussed below.

Dollar Cost Averaging

Dollar cost averaging is a method of investing the same amount of money at regular intervals over a long period of time. This strategy can be used for stocks, bonds and mutual funds. By consistently investing the same amount in a security at regular periods of time, the average cost of the security will be lower than the high price of the security for the period, and higher than the low price for the security. Table 7–1 shows the dollar cost averaging method when $1,000 is invested every month to purchase stocks of Company X. The example assumes that fractional shares may be purchased, and commissions are ignored.

In January, $1,000 is invested at $7 per share, resulting in 142.86 shares being purchased. The price of the stock goes up in February to $8 per share, which means that the same amount ($1,000) will buy fewer shares (125.00) than in January. Conversely, when the price of the stock goes down to $6.75 in May, more shares are purchased (148.15) with the same investment dollars ($1,000).

Over the 12-month period, $12,000 was invested to purchase a total of 1,467.36 shares. The average cost per share is $8.18. In this example, an investor would lose money if the price falls below $8.18 and would make money when the stock price is above the average cost per share when selling. This average cost per share is $0.09 less than the average price per share during the 12-month period. Part of the reason for this is that during the months when the price per share is low, more shares are purchased for the same dollar amount. Thus, with fluctuating stock prices, the average cost per share will always be lower than the average price per share.

This does not mean that investors will always make a profit by using dollar cost averaging. If the price of the stock keeps going down, the average cost per share will be lower than the average price

Table 7–1   Dollar Cost Averaging

	Investment	Price per Share	Number of Shares Purchased
January	$1,000	$ 7	142.86
February	1,000	8	125.00
March	1,000	9	111.11
April	1,000	7.50	133.33
May	1,000	6.75	148.15
June	1,000	7.75	129.03
July	1,000	8	125.00
August	1,000	9	11.11
September	1,000	9.50	105.26
October	1,000	9	111.11
November	1,000	8.75	114.29
December	1,000	9	111.11

Total Invested	Average Price	Total # shares bought
$12,00	8.27	1467.36

$$\text{Average Cost per Share} = \frac{\text{Total Invested}}{\text{Total \# Shares Bought}}$$

$$= \frac{\$12,000}{1467.36}$$

$$= 8.18$$

per share, but the investor will still lose money if the shares are sold at a declining price.

Advantages of Dollar Cost Averaging

■ Investors avoid having to time the market.

■ Investors can use this method to systematically add to positions in a stock over a long period of time, which will average the fluctuations in the stock's price.

■ Participating in a dividend reinvestment plan in conjunction with dollar cost investing enhances the benefits over a long period of time.

Disadvantages of Dollar Cost Averaging

▮ Transaction costs are higher using dollar cost averaging to purchase shares on a systematic basis.

▮ The use of the dollar cost averaging method to buy stocks requires large amounts of money for the regular payments in order to receive the lower commissions of buying shares in round lots over 100 shares. By investing small amounts, investors will buy shares in odd lots (less than 100 shares), which means that the transaction costs will be higher. The total transaction costs will also be larger than if the shares were purchased in one or two transactions rather than twelve. Dollar cost averaging works well with no-load mutual funds where there are no transaction fees.

▮ With a rising stock price, the use of dollar cost averaging will result in a higher average cost per share than if the total amount was invested at the beginning of the period.

▮ When shares are sold, the calculation for the tax basis of the shares is complicated for most investors. This requires keeping records of all transactions and may require the use of a tax professional to compute the gains or losses for tax purposes. The success of dollar cost averaging requires sticking to the plan and investing, particularly when the stock price falls. However, from time to time, investors should evaluate the stock with regard to its overall performance. A stock that is going downhill with no bright prospects should be viewed as a sunk cost and an investor should abandon it rather than sink more money into a bad investment. Thus, dollar cost averaging does not alleviate the decision of which stocks to buy and sell.

Constant Dollar Plan

The constant dollar investment plan requires an investment of a fixed dollar amount in a portfolio of stocks, bonds, or mutual funds. The constant dollar plan works well when the total investment dollars available are split into two parts: an amount going to the more speculative portion of the portfolio and the rest invested in more conservative investments. This fixed dollar amount is maintained by either buying or selling stocks.

For example, assume you have a total portfolio of $100,000 of which you want to keep $50,000 invested in stocks and the rest in bonds and money market securities. When the value of the stock portfolio increases to an upper limit set by you, stocks would be sold off so that the stock portfolio is reduced to a total market value of

$50,000. Assume that the upper limit is $60,000. When the value of the stock portfolio reaches $60,000, $10,000 in stocks would be sold to reduce the portfolio to $50,000. The $10,000 would be invested in bonds and money market securities. If the stock portfolio declines to the lower limit set, stocks will be added to the value of the portfolio to increase the value of the portfolio to $50,000. This plan forces investors to take profits when the upper target amount is reached and to buy more shares when the lower target amount is reached.

This method of investing works well for investors who do not tolerate risks well. By maintaining a fixed dollar amount in stocks and transferring the excess profits from stocks into more conservative investments, conservative investors can still pursue the growth objective for their portfolios.

However, if the stocks keep increasing in price, this plan will not do as well as a buy-and-hold strategy. The return will be lower for a constant dollar plan. Similarly, if the stocks chosen for a constant dollar plan do not fluctuate very much in price, they will not enhance the value of the total portfolio. This plan will do well with stocks that fluctuate in price along with those that have good long-term appreciation potential.

Thus, not only does the investor have to take care in selecting securities for this plan, he or she must also make decisions about how much to set for the target dollar amount, as well as the upper and lower limits. A conservative investor might allocate too small an amount to stocks, which may result in that investor not being able to fulfill the growth objective set for the total investment portfolio. On the other hand, if a greater dollar amount is allocated to stocks, such an investor may have sleepless nights. A more aggressive, growth-oriented investor will allocate a greater dollar amount to the stock portfolio.

Setting the upper and lower limits mitigates the timing decisions of when to buy and sell the stocks, but should these upper and lower limits be 5, 10, 15, 20 or 30 percent of the dollar plan? If the percentages set are too small, investors may be churning their stocks without getting the benefits of large run-ups in the stocks or being able to average down when the stocks fall in price. Moreover, if the percentage limits are too high, the portfolio will not turn over to generated excessive profits to the more conservative investments. After a period of time, the upper and lower dollar limits should be reassessed.

There is also the reinvestment risk to consider. The money from the excess profits from the stock portfolio may be reinvested in bonds or money market securities, which may provide a lower return than if the money had been left in stocks.

Advantages of a Constant Dollar Plan

∎ The plan is beneficial to conservative, risk-averse types of investors who can limit the amount of their total portfolio that is invested in stocks.

∎ The plan increases the value of the total portfolio when the price of the stocks rise in value.

∎ Once the upper and lower limits are set, the timing decision of when to buy and sell the stocks is alleviated.

Disadvantages of a Constant Dollar Plan

∎ In a bull (increasing) market, the constant dollar plan will not do as well as a buy-and-hold strategy.

∎ Investors are faced with the risk of having to reinvest the proceeds from the sale of stocks into other investments that may produce lower returns.

The Constant Ratio Plan

The constant ratio plan is an asset allocation plan that establishes fixed percentages to the different types of securities. An example of a constant ratio plan is an allocation of 50 percent to stocks, 40 percent to bonds and 10 percent to cash (money market securities).

The percentages allocated to the different types of investments are determined by the investor's objectives and risk tolerance. A conservative, risk-averse investor who is approaching retirement and who needs income might use the following allocation:

> 25 percent to stocks.
> 70 percent to bonds.
> 5 percent to money market securities.

A younger investor, seeking growth in a portfolio would allocate a greater percentage to stocks (for example 80 percent to stocks, 15 percent to bonds and 5 percent to money market securities).

Once the investor has decided on the percentages to apportion to the different types of investments, the next step is to determine the trigger points, or percentages, of when to rebalance the portfolio. For example, in a portfolio of $100,000 with 50 percent allocated to stocks and 50 percent to bonds, the amounts in the different portfolios will change over time and the investor will need to decide when to rebalance the portfolio. If the stocks increase to $60,000 and the bonds decrease to $45,000, the constant ratio is no longer 50:50. The rebalancing decision can be on a timely basis, every quarter, every six months or yearly, with percentage limits (10 percent, 20 percent, *etc.*). If the 20 percent limit is chosen for the stock portfolio, rebalancing will occur when the stock portfolio increases to $60,000 (120 percent of $50,000) or drops to $40,000 (80 percent of $50,000).

If the total value of the portfolio has increased to $105,000 with the stock portion accounting for $60,000, which is 57 percent of the total portfolio (60,000/105,000), the stock portion will need to be decreased. To rebalance the portfolio, the investor would sell $7,500 of stocks to reduce the total stock value to $52,500, which is 50 percent of the total portfolio. The $7,500 would be added to the bond portfolio to increase that percentage back up to 50.

As with the constant dollar plan, the long-run expectation is that the stock portfolio will increase in value. When this occurs, stocks will be sold to rebalance the portfolio and increase the amounts invested in the conservative types of investment sectors.

If the stocks in the portfolio decline while the bond portfolio appreciates, bonds will be sold off to provide funds to purchase more stock.

Advantages of the Constant Ratio Plan

■ Investors can change their asset allocation plans to meet changes in personal objectives as well as changes in the state of the markets.

■ Over the long term, when stocks and/or bonds increase, the value of the total portfolio will increase.

■ Profits can be taken when the stocks and bonds appreciate to the limits or on a timely basis.

Disadvantages of the Constant Ratio Plan

■ A constant ratio plan may not produce the greatest returns. Losses may be realized in declining stock and bond markets.

■ Investors need to select the stocks and bonds for these portfolios that will meet the investor's objectives. However, this plan does eliminate the timing decision of when to buy and sell.

■ Investors face reinvestment risks when securities are sold and reinvested in other securities to rebalance the portfolio.

∎ Implications for Investors

There are formula plans and investment strategies for buying and selling stocks, but there are no "magic" plans for beating the market. Some investment strategies have produced superior returns to those earned by the stock market as a whole over various time periods. However, over long periods of time, it becomes difficult to consistently beat the market.

Investors still need to decide which stocks to invest in, in addition to deciding when to buy and sell. Fundamental analysis provides an insight into the makeup of the company and the industry, which may be helpful in the selection of stocks for the long term. Technical analysis uses past price and volume information as well as charting to determine when to buy and sell stocks.

The efficient market hypothesis (EMH) renders technical analysis a waste of time because, according to the EMH, the past stock prices reflect all available information. Therefore, the movement of past stock prices have no relationship to future prices. This reflects the weak form of the efficient market hypothesis.

The semi-strong form suggests that there are no undervalued or overvalued stocks because all public information is reflected in the stock price. This is a kick in the teeth of the fundamental analysts.

The strong form implies that the markets are perfect. They have digested all information pertaining to the stock's value.

There is little evidence to support the strong form. But there are some contradictions of the semi-strong form that suggest there are inefficiencies in the market, particularly with regard to small stocks that have been ignored by the fundamental analysts. After all, it is the fundamental analysts being in competition with each other that makes the market more efficient, which lends support for the semi-strong form.

The capital asset pricing model differentiates the risk in the portfolio into two parts: systematic and unsystematic risk. A diversified portfolio of stocks will eliminate only the unsystematic risk, which leaves the portfolio exposed to the systematic risk. Thus, in order to earn higher returns in the market, investors would need to invest in stocks with higher beta factors (a coefficient measuring the systematic or market risk) than the market.

These theories are important for two reasons:

∎ Investors will not consistently earn superior returns over those of the stock market for long periods of time.

■ The way to increase returns is to invest in riskier securities. However, if the market heads south, the riskier securities will decline by more than the averages of the market.

This then emphasizes the importance of the construction of a portfolio of investments that are compatible with the investor's overall level of risk. This can be accomplished through diversification, which can eliminate some of the risks. Furthermore, returns can be improved through the reduction of taxes, investment fees and commissions.

Tax planning can reduce taxes and increase returns to some extent. At present, long-term capital gains (securities held for longer than one year that are sold at more than their original purchase price) are taxed at lower rates than the higher marginal tax rates. Capital gains become much more important than ordinary income for high tax bracket investors.

Capital losses result when stocks are sold for less than their original purchase prices. For tax purposes, gains and losses are netted out. Net short-term capital gains are taxed at the same rates as ordinary income, and net capital losses of up to $3,000 can be offset against ordinary income. Net capital losses of greater than $3,000 can be carried forward to offset against future income.

The tax code has a regulation that prevents the abuse of the deduction of capital losses; investors should be aware of it. It is known as the *wash sale*. Capital losses cannot be claimed for tax purposes if the security is sold at a loss and then repurchased within 30 days. Thus, in order to take capital losses on a sale of a stock, the investor would have to wait longer than 30 days to repurchase that same stock.

A way to get around this regulation is to use a tax swap strategy. Assume that an investor has 200 shares of Glaxo, which was beaten down in price along with the other pharmaceutical stocks by the impending Clinton health care proposals, and the investor would like to realize these losses to offset other capital gains. The investor can sell the 200 shares of Glaxo, realize the losses, and replace the stocks with another pharmaceutical company, such as Mylan Labs, which is currently trading at a similar price to Glaxo.

Reducing or eliminating fees and sales commissions can increase returns significantly, as pointed out in Chapter 4. Since many brokers make their money buying and selling securities, they have an incentive to advise their clients to trade more than they should. This is called *churning*, the buying and selling of stocks at a rate that is not justified by their returns.

One way to reduce the costs of churning through the active buying and selling of stocks is to invest in stock mutual funds, discussed in the next chapter.

∎ Caveats for Investors

There is a direct relationship between rates of return and risk. Before investing, you should consider the following questions:

- Is the expected rate of return for the investment abnormally high as compared with similar investments?

- Is this based on past performance?

- Is the investment based on sound business sense? If not, forget the whole thing.

- Is there pressure to invest immediately or put some money up? Be cautious of schemes that require you to act immediately.

- Who are the principals? If you do not know them, have them checked out, especially with regard to their previous operations. Check if they have ever been involved in bankruptcy.

- Are there financial statements? If so, are they audited? Check the auditor's report for qualified or adverse opinions.

- Can you afford to lose the money you invest in this operation? If not, don't invest.

- Is there a guarantee? Can it be verified? Guaranteed by whom? "Guaranteed" does not mean much if the company goes bankrupt and has no assets.

- Has this investment been offered to you over the phone by someone you don't know or don't know very well? Never invest because of a telephone call.

- Always check every detail before you invest. If there is not enough time, look for something else to invest in.

- If you do invest, do not put additional money in to "help out" or for any other irrational reason. Keep your investment small.

- Be wary of investment tips from investment talk shows on the radio. There have been a number of scams where investors have lost money instead of "getting rich quickly."

■ Carefully investigate stocks that have been suggested by bulle-
tin board messages on the on-line computer services. If you
know nothing about the stocks, don't buy them.

■ Summary

Bear in mind that with the efficient market theory very few investors
consistently beat the market averages over a long period of time, and
the greater the return the greater the risk involved.

The trader's lament aptly sums up the investor's dilemma:

> Buy and you'll be sorry.
> Sell and you'll regret.
> Hold and you'll worry.
> Do nothing and you'll fret.

■ References

Arbel, Avner and Paul Strebel. "The Neglected and Small Firm Effects," *Financial
Review* (November 1982): 201–218.

Basu, S. "The Information Content of Price-Earnings Ratios," *Financial Management.* (Summer 1975): 53–64.

————. "Investment Performance of Common Stocks in Relation to their Price-
Earnings Ratios: A Test of the Efficient Market Hypothesis," *Journal of Finance* (June 1977): 663–682.

Cheney, John M. and Edward A. Moses. *Fundamentals of Investments.* St. Paul,
MN: West Publishing Co., 1992, p. 19.

Fama, Eugene F., "The Behavior of Stock Prices," *Journal of Business,* (January
1965): 34–105.

Fama, Eugene F., Lawrence Fisher, Michael G. Jensen and Richard Roll, "The
Adjustment of Stock Prices to New Information," *International Economic
Review* (Feb. 1969): 2–21.

Hirt, Geoffrey A. and Stanley B. Block. *Fundamentals of Investment Management,*
3rd ed. Irwin, Homewood, IL, 1990: 285.

Lorie, James H. and Victor Niederhoffer, "Predictive Statistical Properties of Insider Trading," *Journal of Law and Economics* (April 1966): 35–53.

Martin, John D., J. William Petty, *et al., Basic Financial Management,* 5th ed. Englewood Cliffs, NJ: Prentice Hall, 1991.

Securities and Exchange Commission. *Institutional Investor Study Report*. Washington D.C.: Governement Printing Office, 1971.

Sturm, Paul. "What If Ben Graham Had a PC?," *Smart Money* (March 1994): 32.

Chapter 8

Mutual Funds*

Key Concepts

- How Mutual Funds Work
- The Different Types of Funds
- How Performance Affects the Choice of Mutual Fund
- The Significance of the Prospectus
- The Tax Consequences of Buying and Selling Shares
- The Risks of Mutual Funds
- How to Buy and Sell Mutual Funds
- The Advantages of Mutual Funds
- The Disadvantages of Mutual Funds
- Caveats
- Whether to Invest in Individual Securities or Mutual Funds

In some respects, mutual funds have come close to being the ideal investment for millions of investors. Many of these investors are able to move their money in and out of different types of mutual funds just as portfolio managers would when overseeing a large portfolio. Mutual funds have allowed investors who do not have the time, knowl-

---

* Portions of this chapter have been previously published by Esmé Faerber in *All About Bonds*, published by Probus Publishing Co., Chicago, IL, 1993.

edge or expertise of different financial instruments on the market to invest their money in stocks, bonds and money market funds.

Since the early 1980s, the number of mutual funds has grown rapidly to the point where quotations of mutual fund prices now occupy four full pages in *The Wall Street Journal*. The fact that there are more mutual funds than companies listed on the New York Stock Exchange means that investors should be as careful in selecting mutual funds as they are in investing in individual stocks and bonds.

Moreover, the management companies of these mutual funds compete very aggressively for investors' dollars. This is evidenced by all the advertising in newspapers and magazines as well as the use of the mass medium of television.

This increase in the clutter of "infomercials" coming from their sponsors compounds the complexity of the investor's decision as to which mutual fund to choose. The decision becomes more difficult for investors who take the advertising messages literally without reading the fine print and stepping back to analyze the investment objectives of the fund.

According to the advertisements, there are no loser funds, only funds that are "number one" in something or funds that have had remarkable yields. If you read the fine print, you discover that many of the funds may have achieved that yield for a one-week or one-month period or achieved number one status in a limited setting. In fact, being number one at one point in time does not mean that the fund is assured of a rosy future. For example, the number one position may have been achieved by an exceptional manager who has long since left the fund. Results as reported by Lipper Analytical Services Inc. show that poor performing funds can at some stage or another rank as number one performers for a short period of time. According to the editor of Morningstar *Mutual Funds*, a Chicago newsletter, virtually any fund can achieve number one status in something at a point in time (Clements, "The 25 Facts").

Reacting to concerns about misleading advertising claims by mutual funds, the S.E.C. has approved new guidelines on the mutual funds' use of rankings in their advertisements. The new rules require prominent disclosure of a fund's ranking, as well as the name of the category of the ranking, the number of funds in that category and the period encompassing the ranking. The Pilgrim Group is currently fighting fines and penalties imposed by placing ads with misleading statements about their rankings.

A high yield that is quoted may only present half the picture. A fund could earn a high yield, but the total return may be negative due to a decline in the fund's share price.

The advertisements do not include the fees charged by the funds, so if investors pick a fund that was number one in something once upon a time, they will assume they have invested wisely. Well, the fund they choose could, in reality, be a poor performer. Fees charged by that fund could be higher than those charged by other mutual funds in the same category of investments. Needless to say, that fund may have chosen riskier investment assets which may make that its share price more volatile. In fact, investors should be suspicious of funds that post yields much greater than those posted by funds in the same category. This may mean that the fund is investing in derivative securities, which can enhance returns but can also pose greater risks of loss. The use of derivative investments is discussed later in the chapter.

Many investors are so confused that they turn to one of the many newsletters on the market. The hype from some of the advertisements of these advisory newsletters may overwhelm investors so as to make the choice of which newsletter even more complex than the choice of a mutual fund. Some newsletters go so far as to predict the returns for certain funds into the future (Savage).

Of course, the aim is to get investors to subscribe to the newsletter, so the messages promoted by many of them use a combination of hyperbole and fear to move investors in that direction. Implying that investors will choose the wrong fund makes investors even more unsure about choosing a fund. For example, mutual fund advisory letters touted gold and strategic metal funds, which outperformed all other funds in the first quarter of 1993. Needless to say, gold funds had the worst returns for the two years prior to that quarter when most of the newsletters were touting other types of funds.

For investors who are so confused that they are in a state of paralysis as to how to invest their money, there are *wrap accounts*, which are advertised to answer the concerns of investors who don't know how to manage their money.

These are offered by all the major brokerage firms. For an all-inclusive flat fee, they will manage your investments by diversifying into stocks, bonds and money market accounts. Sounds ideal!

Many investors have been jolted to reality by the fees charged for some of these wrap accounts. Some wrap accounts have high annual fees that are not all-inclusive. This means that they do not include the management of their cash accounts. An additional fee is charged to manage money market and cash accounts, which in today's economic environment of low interest rates means that investors are losing money on their cash funds. Not all investors like to be fully invested in stocks and bonds. This means that their money in cash accounts may be earning only 2.9 percent per annum. With a 3 percent annual management fee levied, investors will earn negative rates of return after paying taxes and adjusting for inflation.

Performance is another widely touted reason for investing in a brokerage firm's wrap accounts. However, many of the brokerage firms do not include their fees when factoring in their performance. This can make quite a difference to the actual performance of the account when investors find that they will be earning ± 2–3 percent less than the advertised rate. The high cost and the equivocal performance of many wrap accounts should also make investors think twice before jumping into them without a careful analysis. Besides cost and performance, investors should also look at potential conflicts of interest in the management of the wrap accounts. For example, does the broker favor securities underwritten by the same brokerage firm when choosing investment securities (Schultz)?

Currently, the SEC has voted to require the sponsors of wrap accounts to give investors more information about their costs, services and performance (Harlan).

The author agrees that it is confusing for investors to choose a mutual fund, especially when there are over 4,000 of them available on the market. Moreover, investors may be equally confused by all of the conflicting advice and predictions offered by many of the newsletters. Consequently, the author's advice is to go back to the basics of investments:

∎ Understand how mutual funds work.

∎ Understand the basics of the types of investments that the fund invests in.

∎ Evaluate the performance of the fund from the prospectus.

By following these steps, investors will be able to narrow their choices of the different types of funds, and then they will be in a better position to make a decision as to the overall choice of fund.

■ How Do Mutual Funds Work?

All mutual funds work in similar ways. A mutual fund makes investments on behalf of the investors in that fund. The money from investors is pooled, which allows the fund to diversify their acquisition of different securities such as stocks for stock funds and bonds for bond funds. The type of investments chosen is determined by the objectives of the mutual fund. For example, if a bond fund's objectives are to provide tax-free income, the fund should invest in municipal bonds. The fund will buy different municipal bond issues to achieve a diversified portfolio, which will also reduce the risks of loss due to default.

When these securities pay out their interest, fund holders get a proportionate share. Thus, an investor who invests $1,000 will get the same rate of return as another investor who invested $100,000 in the fund.

The prices of the securities fluctuating up or down will affect the total value of the fund. These fluctuations in price are due to many different factors such as the intrinsic risk of the types of securities in the portfolio, and economic, market, and political factors. The objectives of the fund are important because they will indicate the type and quality of the investments the fund will choose. From these objectives, investors are better able to assess the risks the fund is willing to take to improve income (return) and/or capital gains. See Table 8–1 for a classification of mutual funds by investment objectives.

Investors invest their money in mutual funds by buying shares at the net asset value (NAV). The fund's net asset value price of the shares is the total assets minus the liabilities of the fund divided by the number of outstanding shares.

It is quite easy for a fund to determine the market value of their assets at the end of each trading day. For instance, if the fund is a balanced fund, which means that it is invested in both common stocks and bonds, the investment company would find out the closing prices of the stocks and bonds for the day and multiply them by the number of shares of stock and the number of bonds that the fund owns. These are added up, and any liabilities (for example accrued fees) that the fund has are subtracted. The resulting total is then divided by the number of shares outstanding to give the net asset value price per share. A numerical example illustrates the process as follows:

Table 8–1   Types of Mutual Funds

Funds	*Objectives*
Money Market Funds	Invest in money market securities with relatively short maturities.

Equity

Aggressive Growth Funds	Seek maximum capital gains. Invest in stocks of companies in new industries and out of favor companies.
Growth Funds	Seek increase in value through capital gains. Invest in stocks of growth companies and industries (which are more mainstream than those chosen by the aggressive growth funds).
Growth and Income Funds	Seek increase in value through capital gains and dividend income. Invest in stocks of companies with a more consistent track record than the companies selected for growth and aggressive growth funds.
Income Equity Funds	Invest in stocks of companies that pay dividends.
International Equity Funds	Invest in stocks of companies outside the U.S.
Global Equity Funds	Invest in stocks of companies in the U.S. and outside of the U.S.
Emerging Market Funds	Invest in stocks of companies in developing countries.
Sector Funds	Invest in stocks of the sector of the economy stated in the objectives of the fund. Examples are stocks in the energy sector, health care sector, technology stocks, precious metals.
Balanced Funds	Seek to provide value through income and principal conservation. Invest in common stocks, preferred stocks and bonds.
Asset Allocation Funds	Invest in different types of securities (stocks, bonds and money market funds) according to either a fixed or variable formula.

Table 8–1   Types of Mutual Funds (continued)

Hedge Funds	Invest in securities (stocks and bonds) and derivative securities to hedge against downturns in the market, changes in interest rates and currency values.

Bonds

Corporate Bond Funds	Seek high levels of income. Invest in corporate bonds, Treasury bonds and agency bonds.
High-Yield Bond Funds	Seek higher yields by investing in less than investment grade bonds (junk bonds).
Municipal Bond Funds Long Term	Seek income that is exempt from Federal income taxes. Invest in bonds issued by state and local governments with long maturities.
Municipal Bond Funds Intermediate Term	Seek income that is exempt from Federal income taxes. Invest in bonds issued by state and local governments with intermediate term maturities.
Municipal Bond Funds Short-Term Maturities	Invest in municipal securities with relatively short maturities. These are also known as tax exempt money market funds.
U.S. Government Income Funds	Invest in different types of government securities such as Treasury securities, agency securities and federally backed mortgage backed securities.
GNMA Funds	Invest in Government National Mortgage Association securities and other mortgage backed securities.
Global Income Funds	Invest in the bonds of companies and countries worldwide, including those in the U.S.

Market Value of Stocks and Bonds	$5,000,000
minus	
Total Liabilities	– 150,000
Net Worth	$4,850,000
Number of Shares Outstanding	750,000
Net Asset Value	$ 6.466 (4,850,000/750,000)

The net asset value may change every day because the market value of the stocks and bonds fluctuate in price. The net asset value is important for two reasons:

∎ This is the price used to determine the value of the investor's holding in the mutual fund (number of shares held multiplied by the net asset value price per share).

∎ This is the price that new shares are purchased at or redeemed at when selling shares in the fund.

The net asset values of the different funds are quoted in the daily newspapers. Table 8–2 shows how mutual funds are listed in the newspapers. Some of the funds in two families of funds (Vanguard and Fidelity Investments) are shown for illustrative purposes.

Table 8–2   Mutual Fund Quotations

	Inv. Obj.	NAV	Offer Price	NAV Change
Vanguard Group:				
STAR	S & B	13.08	NL	+ 0.02
Intl Gr	ITL	13.87	NL	+ 0.02
Wnds II	G & I	16.83	NL	+ 0.05
Fidelity Investments Group:				
Gro Inc	G & I	22.04	22.72	+ 0.02
Latin Amer r	Itl	13.74	14.16	0.07

Source: *The Wall Street Journal*

In the Vanguard Group, the International Growth fund, which invests in international stocks (as opposed to the STAR fund, which invests in stocks and bonds) has a net asset value of $13.87 per share. The investment objectives column indicates the types of investments a fund will invest in. A NL in the offer price column signifies that the fund is a *no load* fund, which means that investors can buy and sell shares at the net asset value of $13.87. The net asset value change column signifies the change in price from the previous day's closing price. The Vanguard International Growth fund closed $0.02 up from the previous day's closing price.

The two fund examples in the Fidelity Investments Group are *load* funds since they charge a commission to buy and sell their shares. This is evidenced by the offer price, which is different from the net asset value price. To buy shares in Fidelity's Growth and Income Fund, investors would buy at the offer price of $22.72 per share and would sell their shares at the net asset value price ($22.04). The difference ($0.68 per share) between the offer price ($22.72) and the net asset value price ($22.04) represents the load or commission that investors will pay to buy or sell shares in this fund. The r after the Latin America fund indicates that there is a redemption charge over and above the load when investors sell their shares.

Investors earn money from their mutual funds in three ways:

■ When interest and/or dividends earned on the fund's investments are passed through to shareholders.

■ When the fund's management sells investment securities at a profit, the capital gains are passed through to shareholders. If these securities are sold at a loss, the capital loss is offset against the gains of the fund, and the net gain or loss is passed through to the shareholders.

■ When the net asset value per share increases, the value of the shareholder's investment increases.

Investors in funds have the option of having their interest and capital gain payments paid out to them in check form or having them reinvested in the fund. The reinvested funds will be used to purchase additional shares in the fund.

Mutual funds can be *open-end* or *closed-end*. With open-end funds, the investment company of the fund can issue an unlimited number of shares. Investors may buy more shares from the mutual fund company, or they may sell their shares back to the mutual fund company, which means that the number of shares will increase or decrease, respectively. Closed-end funds issue a fixed number of shares; after they are all sold, they do not issue any more. In other words, they have a fixed capital structure. Closed-end funds are discussed in Chapter 9.

Mutual funds pay no taxes on income derived from their investments. Under the Internal Revenue Code, mutual funds serve as conduits through which the income from the investments is passed to shareholders in the form of interest or dividends and capital gains or losses. Individual investors pay tax on their income.

Shareholders receive monthly and annual statements showing the interest, dividends, capital gains and losses, and other relevant data that should be retained for tax purposes. In fact, not only is the interest and dividend income important for tax purposes, but when investing in different mutual funds, investors should also keep track of the net asset value prices of the shares purchased and sold. This information will help in the computation of gains and losses when shares are redeemed.

∎ The Different Types of Funds

There are many different types of funds, and their differences may be significant. The overriding differences between the types of funds are that they invest in different types of investments in the markets. There are stock funds, bond funds, money market funds, hybrid funds and commodity funds.

Money market funds are the only funds that maintain constant share prices. These are mostly one dollar a share and the management company will keep the net asset value at one dollar per share. Any expenses or short-term losses from the sale of securities will be deducted from the revenues generated from the investments to keep the share price constant. This is more easily accomplished for funds that invest in money market securities, which are short-term, where there is not that much volatility in the prices of the investment assets.

However, within the past year, a few money market mutual funds have incurred some losses due to investments in derivative securities, which were aimed at increasing the yields of the funds. When interest rates unexpectedly changed direction many of these funds incurred large losses. Instead of allowing the net asset values to fall below one dollar per share, the fund's families quietly propped up the losses of these money market funds.

Stock funds vary with regard to the types of stocks that the funds choose for their portfolios; the choice is guided by the fund's investment objectives. The Securities and Exchange Commission (SEC) requires the funds disclose their objectives. For example, the objective could be to seek growth through maximum capital gains. This type of fund would appeal to a more aggressive investor who can withstand the risks of loss, because of the speculative nature of the stocks of the unseasoned, small companies that the fund would invest in.

A more conservative investor would choose a fund whose objectives are capital preservation while providing current income. Such funds would invest in high-yielding, good quality stocks, which would also provide for capital appreciation even though this may not be a primary objective.

Growth and income funds seek a balance between long-term capital gains and providing current income. See Table 8–1 for a list of some of the types of stock funds.

Many stock funds in their pursuit of higher returns have deviated from their objectives and turned to riskier types of investments. According to Clements ("Funds", C1) some blue-chip and U.S. stock funds are investing in small stocks and foreign stocks, respectively. During bull markets this strategy has boosted the returns of these funds significantly, but during a downturn in the market, these share prices will become much more volatile.

Conservative investors looking at income equity funds should look at the makeup of the fund's investments to see if the stocks are of well-established companies and that there is a broad diversification within different industries. This applies to all investors, not only to conservative investors.

Investing in equity funds does not immunize investors from the volatility of the markets. The more speculative stocks in the funds's portfolios will decline more than the more established blue-chip stocks. This means that the share prices of the aggressive funds will be more volatile than the share prices of the more conservative stock funds.

The same can be said of bond funds. Many investors think that by investing in bond funds their principal investments are safe because bonds are more conservative investments than stocks. This is not true. Investors can lose money in bond funds in the same way that they can with stock funds. When market interest rates go up, existing bond prices become depressed in order to make their yields competitive with the new issues. There are many types of bond mutual funds. Municipal bond funds are very different to zero-coupon bond funds. Similarly, short-term government funds differ from both municipal bond funds and zero-coupon bond funds. The types of securities that funds invest in will determine the risks of the fund, namely the reaction to changes in market rates of interest, credit quality and the risk of default, length of time to maturity and the yield of the fund.

Share prices of bond funds fluctuate up and down, depending on the value of the assets (investments) of the funds. Certain types of securities fluctuate more in price than other securities. For instance, Ginnie Mae securities will be much more volatile to changes in interest rates than similar maturity Treasury notes and bonds. In order to gauge the extent of the volatility in the mutual fund's price, investors should understand how the different bond securities will react to changes in interest rates.

A conservative investor should be aware that investing in a bond fund composed of junk bonds (high-yield bond fund) can fluctuate as much as 50 percent in net asset value price. During the junk bond sell-off, some funds' prices declined by as much as 50 percent. Similarly, in the past there have been occasional sell-offs in GNMA bond funds (1981 and 1982) and briefly in the municipal bond market in 1987. Currently, investors in adjustable-rate mortgage funds have seen losses and declines in net asset value prices even though market rates of interest have been declining. This is because homeowners have been refinancing their mortgages. These mortgages are paid back to their holders at 100 percent of their face value, but many funds may have bought these securities paying premiums for them. These losses translate into lower net asset value prices.

Thus, understanding how individual types of bonds react to changes in interest rates will replay more or less into how the fund prices will react to these changes. Generally, the higher the risk of the securities the greater the potential return and the greater the potential loss on the downside, for all types of funds.

To lessen the potential price volatility, investors can invest in shorter maturity bond funds, which tend to fluctuate less than longer term maturity funds. Money market funds which have constant share prices have an average maturity of 90 days. This is why money market funds are considered safe investments. Short-term funds have maturities of three years or less, which means there is less volatility in net asset value prices due to changes in interest rates than longer maturity funds. Remember, less risk does not mean no risk. During several months in 1992, two top-rated short-term bond funds chalked up declines in their net asset values. Long-term maturity funds have average maturities in the range of 20 years, which will see the greatest fluctuations in price as interest rates change. Fund managers are quick to take advantage of changing rates of interest by either increasing or decreasing the maturities of their investments. For instance, when market rates of interest are on their way down, fund managers will purchase bond issues with longer maturities, which of course will increase the yield and the fund's total return.

The credit quality of the investments will have an influence on the price volatility as well as the yield. The lower the ratings of the individual bond issues in the fund, the higher the fluctuations in price and the greater the yields. Due to the many issues held in a bond fund, credit risk does not affect bond funds in the same way as when buying individual bond issues. For instance, most individual bond issues account for less than 2 percent of the total value of the typical large bond fund, which means that a default by the issuer would not have a significant impact on the net asset value price. The exception is the high-risk bond fund. This type of fund invests in below investment grade bond issues, namely junk bonds, where credit risk and the risk of default may be of greater concern. Investors in these funds are compensated with higher yields for bearing these risks, which translate into greater net asset value price volatility.

With historically low market rates of interest, many bond and stock fund managers have been looking for exotic types of investments to boost their funds' yields. They have turned to derivative securities. Derivatives are securities that can be issued based on the performance of some other underlying security such as stocks, bonds, mortgages, currencies, interest rates or a combination of these. Generally, bond funds hold the largest amount of derivative securities. Derivatives are less prevalent in stock funds. Some derivatives to watch for in bond funds are collateralized mortgage obligations, inverse floaters, interest-only strips and principal-only strips. Collateralized mortgage obligations (CMOs) have been scooped up by not only the mortgage funds but also by funds investing in government and corporate bonds (Jereski). Some bond funds hold as much as 15% of their assets in CMOs. CMOs have the potential of boosting returns for funds but due to the complexities of the type of investment become very difficult to price on a daily basis.

Inverse floaters have mainly been acquired by municipal bond funds to boost their yields. Due to their volatility, these are also very difficult to price. In fact, Merrill Lynch, which prices most of the mortgage-backed securities in the market, will not price the volatile instruments (Jereski). How does this affect the shareholder?

At best, most shareholders are unaware of the fund's pricing problems and the fact that many funds use the approximate market values to compute their net asset value prices. This means that investors could be buying and selling shares in their bond and stock funds at inexact prices. Fidelity Investments, one of the largest mutual fund families, admitted that it reported the previous day's closing figures for its funds instead of the true prices.

Pricing errors may occur much more frequently in the future due to the following factors:

■ More complex derivative securities are being held by bond mutual funds.

▌ Many bond issues are difficult to price. These are thinly traded issues and junk bonds which are not priced on a daily basis.

Even an error of a few cents in the pricing of the fund's share price can be costly. A few cents multiplied by several million shares outstanding can add up to a significant sum. In November 1992, T. Rowe Price made a mistake in the pricing of their International Bond fund and the investment company asked some shareholders to pay them back due to the three-cent a share error (Eaton).

There is not much that the investor in bond mutual funds can do about this other than to be aware of the potential glitches that could occur in the pricing of certain of their funds' bond investments.

By understanding the characteristics of the types of investments in the fund, shareholders will be better able to gauge the extent of the fluctuations in the net asset value of the fund. Moreover, if investors don't know what the fund is investing in, it becomes harder to anticipate the changes to net asset value prices. The main reason investors don't know what the funds are invested in is that it is not clearly spelled out in the prospectus of the fund. The securities that the funds invest in are listed in the prospectus information, but the type and characteristics of the bonds are not fully disclosed. Hence, an investor might see the number of the bond in a mortgage pool with the coupon rate, but that does not tell the investor anything about the bond, such as whether it is a floating rate bond or a fixed-rate bond; its weighted average life; which tranche it is in if it is a CMO; and so on.

One suggestion is to call the fund company and ask them if they use derivatives in their portfolios. If they do, how much of the portfolio is in derivative securities, and what are the reasons for using these derivatives? Answers to these questions will give the investor a feeling for the potential risks for that fund.

Another suggestion is to compare the total returns of the funds that you are considering. If the total return of the fund that you are considering is vastly superior to its competitors in the same category, the chances are that the fund is using derivatives to boost its return.

▌ How Does Performance Affect the Choice of Mutual Fund?

The overall performance of a fund pertains to the following:

▌ Yield

▌ Total return

■ Expenses

As mentioned in the beginning of the chapter, most funds can boast attaining the number one position in some area of performance at some point in time throughout their existence. Similarly, good past performance may not be indicative of good future performance. Some funds that have performed well in the past have had poor performance thereafter. In fact, there are some funds that did well in the past that no longer exist today.

It is little wonder that with several thousand mutual funds on the market vying for investors' savings, many of the messages in their advertisements would lead you to believe that they have attained 2 + 2 = 5 performance. Even if funds do well during good times, investors should also examine how these funds have performed during the down markets. Several business magazines track the overall performance records (during up and down markets) of many of the mutual funds. This would be a better yardstick than the advertising messages of the individual mutual funds. *Forbes* magazine publishes annual performance ratings of mutual funds. From this (or from other publications) investors can see how well funds have performed in upmarkets as well as how the funds protected their capital during periods of declining prices.

New funds do not have track records; therefore, investors may not have a yardstick on performance during a period of declining prices. This is especially so for funds created during bull markets.

Some organizations such as Morningstar rate a mutual fund's performance relative to other funds with the same investment objectives, but this too can be misleading for investors trying to choose a fund. First, the funds may not be comparable even though they have similar objectives, in that one fund may have riskier assets than another fund, and hence a comparison would not be appropriate. Second, past performance may not be a reliable indicator of future performance.

In choosing a fund, investors are best off looking at what the fund invests in (as best as can be determined), and then trying to determine the volatility in terms of up and down markets.

Yield is one aspect of performance. Yield is defined as the interest/dividends that are paid to shareholders as a percentage of the net asset value price. Money market funds quote yields over a 7-day period. This is an average dividend yield over 7 days, which can be annualized. Long-term bond funds also quote an annualized average yield, but it is generally over 30 days.

Since 1988, the SEC has ruled that funds with average maturities longer than those of money market mutual must funds quote the SEC standardized yield. The SEC standardized yield includes the interest or dividends accrued by the fund over 30 days as well as an adjustment to the prices of the bonds for the amount of the amortization of any discount or premium that was paid for the bond assets. The SEC standardized yield makes the comparison of different mutual funds more meaningful. Prior to this standardized rule, comparing the yields of funds that were calculated differently was an exercise in futility if one of them used a formula that inflated its yield (Thau).

The SEC standardized yield should be used for comparison purposes and not as a means to predict future yields. This yield is a measure of the fund's dividend distribution over a 30-day period and is only one aspect of the fund's *total return*. Mutual funds pass on any gains or losses to shareholders which can increase or decrease the fund's total return.

Another factor that affects total return is the fluctuations in net asset value. When the share price increases by 6 percent, it will effectively increase the total return by an additional 6 percent. Similarly, when the net asset value price of the fund declines, the total return will decrease. This explains why funds can have a negative return. This happened when the European currencies went into turmoil towards the latter part of 1992 and affected short-term global bond mutual funds. These funds had high yields, but they were diminished by the steep declines in their net asset value prices.

The interest on reinvested dividends is another factor that may also be in the total return. When the interest or dividends paid out by the fund is reinvested to buy more shares, the yield earned on these reinvested shares will boost the overall return on the invested capital.

Therefore, when comparing the total returns quoted by the different funds, you need to make sure you are comparing the same type of total return.

As you can see total return can include the following three components:

▮ Dividends and capital gains or losses.

▮ Changes in net asset value.

▮ Dividends (interest) on reinvested dividends.

When total returns are quoted by funds, you should ask whether all of these are included in the computation. In other words, it would be a cumulative total return for the period. However, there are examples of funds who choose not to advertise a total cumulative return. Some high-yield junk bond funds have at times chosen not to emphasize total returns, as they were negative due to the deep declines in junk bond prices. Instead they touted their high yields. Thus, basing your choice of fund on yield alone can be misleading, as yields may be easier to manipulate. Investors should, therefore, look at the yield and the total return of the fund to get a more balanced picture.

Expenses are a key factor in differentiating the performance of the different bond funds. By painstakingly looking for funds with the highest yields, investors are only looking at half the picture. A fund with a high yield may also be the one that charges higher expenses, which would put that fund behind some of the lower-cost funds with smaller yields. This is because fees will reduce the total return earned by the funds.

The mutual fund industry has been criticized for the proliferation of fees and charges. Granted, these are all disclosed by the mutual funds but besides the conspicuous charges, investors need to know where to look to find the less obvious fees.

Some mutual funds are *no-load* funds in that the investor pays no commission or fee to buy or sell the shares of the fund. An investor investing $10,000 in a no-load fund will have every cent of the $10,000 going to buy shares in the fund. These no-load funds are easily identified in the newspapers by NL under the offer price column in the mutual fund quotes.

A *load* fund charges a sales commission for buying shares in the fund. These fees can be quite substantial, ranging to as much as 8 1/2 percent of the purchase price of the shares. The amount of the sales (load) charge per share can be determined by deducting the net asset value price from the offer price. Some funds give quantity discounts on their loads to investors who buy shares in large blocks. For example, the sales load might be 5 percent for amounts under $100,000, 4 1/4 percent for investing between $100,000 to $200,000, and 3 1/2 percent for amounts in excess of $200,000. When buying load funds, you have to check whether they charge a load on reinvested dividends as well.

Some funds also charge a *back-load* or exit fee when you sell the shares in the fund. This could be a straight percentage, or the percentage charged could decline the longer the shares are held in the fund.

The ultimate effect of load charges is to reduce the total return. The impact of the load charge is felt more greatly if the fund is held for a short period of time. For instance, if a fund has a yield of 6 percent and there is a 4 percent load to buy into the fund, the total return to the investor for the year is sharply reduced. If there is a back end load to exit the fund, this could be even more expensive to the investor, in that if the share price has increased it will be the load percentage of a larger amount.

Don't be fooled by some funds that tout themselves as no-load funds but assess fees by another name that come right out of the investor's investment dollars like a load. These fees are not called loads, but they work exactly like loads. Their uses are to defray some of the costs of opening accounts or buying stocks for the fund's portfolio. They vary from 1–3 percent among the different fund groups.

From the investor's point of view, it should not matter how lofty the purpose is for these fees. They reduce your investment. If you invest $10,000 and there is a 3 percent fee, only $9,700 of your investment will go towards buying shares.

You also need to watch out for redemption fees: sell $10,000 with a 3 percent redemption fee and you only receive $9,700.

Why then would so many investors invest in load funds when these commissions "eat away" so much of their returns? The author can only speculate on answers:

∎ Investors may not want to make decisions by themselves as to which funds to invest in, so they leave the decisions to their brokers and financial planners.

∎ Brokers and financial planners earn their living from selling investments from which they are paid commissions. These include load funds.

∎ No load funds do not pay commissions to brokers and financial planners.

Do Load Funds Outperform No-Load Funds?

There is no evidence to support the opinions expressed by many brokers and financial planners that load funds outperform no-load funds. According to CDA/Weisenberger, there was no difference between the performance of the average no-load funds and load funds over a five-year period (Clements, "The 25 Facts"). In fact, when adjusting for sales commissions, investors would have been better off with no-load funds.

Loads obviously make a difference to the chief executives in the mutual fund industry. According to Stephen Taub (10) 14 top executives of load funds made more money than the top compensated no-load chief executive.

12 (b)-1 fees are less obvious than loads. These are charged by many funds to recover expenses for marketing and distribution. These fees are assessed annually and can be quite steep when added together with load fees. Many no-load funds tout the absence of sales commissions but tack on 12 (b)-1 fees, which is like a hidden load. A 1 percent 12 (b)-1 fee may not sound as if it is very much, but this is $100 less per annum in your pocket on a $10,000 mutual fund investment.

In addition to the above mentioned charges, funds have *management fees* that are paid to managers who administer the fund's portfolio of investments. These can range from .5 percent to 2 percent of assets. High management fees will also take its toll on the investor's total return.

Thus, all fees bear watching as they reduce yields and total returns. Critics of the mutual fund industry have brought a sense of awareness of the proliferation of all these charges. However, investors should not be deceived by funds claiming to be what they are not. Lowering front-end loads or eliminating them altogether doesn't mean that a fund can't assess the fee somewhere else.

Funds have to disclose their fees, which means that investors can find them in the fund's prospectus. Management fees, 12 (b)-1 fees, redemption or back-end loads and any other fees charged will be disclosed somewhere in the fund's prospectus. The financial newspapers also list the types of charges of the different funds in their periodic mutual fund performance reviews.

You may want to follow these guidelines to choose a fund:

- Examine the performance records of the funds that you are interested in.

- Compare their total expenses and fees.

- Choose the fund that you feel will be the best choice in terms of performance. If there is no difference in performance, go with the fund that has the lowest expenses.

▌ What Is the Significance of the Prospectus?

Besides information about the different funds that can be obtained from business magazines, newspapers and advisory services, essential information is provided by the mutual fund's prospectus. Currently, funds are required to send a prospectus to a potential investor before accepting investment funds. However, this may change as the SEC is testing a new proposal. This will allow mutual funds to eliminate the sending of a prospectus as long as the key points of the prospectus are included in their advertisements. The information in the advertisements would be legally binding in that if any facts are not true, investors can sue. However, there is a vast grey area of puffery that has the potential for causing tremendous confusion among investors. Imagine the clever letters advertisers of mutual funds could dream up to send as direct mail to potential investors:

Dear Potential Investor:

The markets are going to tumble in addition to ......
No need for you to bear these hardships. Invest in XYZ
Fund and reap the rewards.

Sincerely,

E. Z. Prey
Chairman,
XYZ Fund

Although a prospectus is written in a manner that may vie with other literature as one of the best cures for insomnia, it still provides investors with information about the fund that they may not be able to get anywhere else.

You should look for the following in the prospectus.

Objectives

The objectives and policies of the fund will be somewhere near the front of the prospectus. The objectives describe the type of securities the fund invests in as well as the risk factors associated with the securities. For instance, if the prospectus states that the fund will buy securities which are less than investment grade, the investor should not be surprised to find that most of the bonds are junk bonds.

The investment policies will outline the latitude of the fund manager to invest in other types of securities. These may be the trading of futures contracts and the writing of options to hedge their bets, on the direction of interest rates, or the market, and/or to invest in derivative securities to boost the yield of the fund. Many so-called conservative funds, which supposedly hold government securities, "only" have used derivative securities to boost their returns (Thau). The greater the latitude in investing in these other types of securities, the greater the risks if events backfire.

Selected per Share Data and Ratios

The selected per-share data and ratios table in the prospectus summarizes the fund's performance over the time period shown. Table 8–3 gives an example of such a table. Although these may vary from fund to fund, the format will be similar.

The investment activities section shows the amount of investment income earned on the securities held by the fund; this income is passed on to the mutual fund shareholders. For instance, in 1993 all of the net investment income of $0.37 was distributed to the shareholders (line 4) but in 1992 only $0.30 of the $0.31 of net income was paid out to shareholders. In this year, the $0.01, which was not distributed to shareholders, increased the net asset value (line 7) in the capital changes section. (The capital loss and distribution of gains was reduced by this $0.01, which was not distributed.)

Capital gains and losses will also affect the net asset value. Funds distribute their realized capital gains (line 6), but the unrealized capital gains (losses) will also increase (decrease) the net asset value.

The changes in the net asset value from year to year will give you some idea of the volatility in share price. For instance, for the year 1992 the net asset value decreased by $1.01, which is a 9.17 percent decrease. How comfortable would you feel in the short term if you invested $10,000 to have it decline to $9,082.65 (this is a 9.17 percent decline)?

Investors can calculate an average total return by taking into account these three sources of return (dividends distributed, capital gains distributed and the changes in share price) by using the following formula:

$$\text{Average Total Return} = \frac{\frac{\text{Dividend} + \text{Capital}}{\text{Gain Distributions}} + \frac{\text{Ending NAV} - \text{Beginning NAV}}{\text{Year}}}{\frac{\text{Ending NAV} + \text{Beginning NAV}}{2}}$$

$$\text{Average Total Return} = \frac{.37 + .70 + \frac{[10.30 - 10.00]}{1}}{\frac{10.30 + 10.00}{2}}$$

$$= 13.50\%$$

This simple yield of 13.5 percent which indicates that an investor in this fund would have received double-digit returns due mainly to realized gains and increases in the NAV share price. The more volatile the net asset value of the fund, the greater the likelihood of unstable

Table 8–3   Selected Per Share Data and Ratios

		1993	1992	1991
Net Asset Value (NAV) Beginning of the year		$10.00	$11.01	$10.73
Investment Activities				
line 1	Income	.40	.35	.55
line 2	Expenses	(.03)	(.04)	(.05)
line 3	Net investment income	.37	.31	.50
line 4	Distribution of dividends	(.37)	(.30)	(.47)
Capital Changes				
line 5	Net realized and unrealized gains (losses) on investments	$1.00	(.75)	1.50
line 6	Distributions of realized gains	(.70)	(.25)	1.25
line 7	Net increase (decrease) to NAV	.30	(.99)	.28
	NAV beginning of the year	10.00	11.01	10.73
	NAV at end of year	10.30	10.00	11.01
	Ratio of operating expenses to average net assets	.53%	.56%	.58%
	Ratio of net investment income to average net assets	.45%	.46%	.84%
	Portfolio turnover rate	121%	135%	150%
	Shares outstanding (000)	10,600	8,451	6,339

returns. Thus, when considering whether to invest in a particular fund, don't go by the advertised yield alone—look at the total return.

The ratio of operating expenses to average net assets is fairly low in this hypothetical fund (close to 1/2 of 1 percent).

The portfolio turnover rate indicates how actively the assets in the fund are turned over. Bond funds tend to have higher turnover rates than stock funds, and 150 percent is not uncommon for a bond fund. A turnover rate of 100 percent indicates that all the investments in a portfolio would change once a year (Thau).

Annual Expenses

Although annual expenses are shown in the selected per share data and ratios section, mutual funds will have a separate table with a breakdown of their expenses in the prospectus. This would typically show the different load charges, redemption fees, shareholder accounting costs, 12 (b)-1 fees, distribution costs and other expenses.

By examining the prospectus of the funds you are interested in, you will be able to make a more informed choice than merely going by the advertised messages of the funds.

■ The Tax Consequences of Buying and Selling Shares in Mutual Funds

Tax reporting on mutual funds can be complicated. Even if you buy and hold shares in a mutual fund, there are tax consequences. Dividends paid to investors may be automatically reinvested in that fund to buy more shares. At the end of the year, the mutual fund will send a Form 1099 to each mutual fund holder showing the amount of dividends and capital gains received for the year. Individual shareholders will pay taxes on these dividends and capital gains. Therefore, these dividends and capital gains need to be added into the cost basis when the investor sells the shares in the fund.

For example, suppose that an investor who had invested $10,000 in a fund two years ago and has received a total of $2,000 in dividends and capital gains in the fund to date, wishes to sell all the shares in the fund for which $14,000 is received. Thus, the investor's cost basis is $12,000 (not $10,000), and the gain on the sale of the shares is $2,000 ($14,000 − $12,000).

When investors sell only a part of their total fund the procedure is different and may be tricky. This is further complicated when investors actively buy and sell shares as if the fund were a checking account. In fact, many mutual funds encourage investors to operate their funds like a checking account by providing check writing services. However, every time an investor writes a check against a bond fund, there is a capital gain or loss tax consequence. This does not include money market funds, which have a stable share price of one dollar. This action either causes a nightmare for the investor around tax time or will produce extra revenue for the investor's accountant in terms of the additional time spent.

The most important thing in an actively traded mutual fund (or any mutual fund for that matter) is to keep good records. For each fund keep a separate folder and store all the monthly statements showing purchases and sales of shares, dividends and capital gain distributions.

By keeping records of all transactions, investors will be able to determine the cost basis of shares sold. This can be done using either an average cost or on a FIFO basis. FIFO is first in, first out, which means that the cost of the first shares purchased in the fund will be used first as the shares sold. Table 8–4 illustrates the FIFO method of calculating capital gains or losses on the partial sale of shares in a mutual fund. The example shows that the earliest shares purchased are the first to be used in the sale of shares. After all the shares of the invested funds are sold, the basis of the dividends and capital gains shares will be used to determine any gains or losses.

Several funds provide the gains and losses on an average cost basis when investors sell shares in these funds. The average cost basis can get quite complex with additional sales and purchases of shares. Hence, some funds don't allow their shareholders to write checks against their accounts.

To minimize any tax hassles, investors are better off not writing checks from their stock and bond funds for their short-term cash needs. This only creates gains or losses. The investor would be better off investing the money needed for short term purposes in a money market fund, which alleviates these tax problems.

Whether you trade actively or not, the solution to tax computations is to keep good records. If you can't determine the cost basis of your shares, an accountant will be able to do so, provided you keep records. If you don't have all the records of your purchases and sales, you may not be able to prove your cost basis to the IRS if disputed.

▮ The Risks of Mutual Funds

The major risk with mutual funds is the *risk of loss of funds invested* through a decline in net asset value. There is *interest rate risk*. When interest rates go up in the economy, it tends to depress both the stock and the bond markets. This causes the net asset values of bond and stock funds to go down in price. Similarly, when market rates of interest go down, bond and stock prices (and the net asset values of bond and stock funds) appreciate.

The quality of the securities will determine the volatility of the fund's price swings. Stock funds that invest in small company stocks and emerging growth stocks will see greater upward swings in price during bull markets and greater downward swings during bear mar-

Table 8–4   Calculation of Gains/Losses on the Sale of Shares

Summary of Growth and Income Fund

Date	Transaction	Dollar Amount	Share Price	# of shares	Total #
06/14	Invest	$10,000	10.00	1,000	1,000
11/26	Invest	4,500	9.00	500	1,500
11/30	Redeem (sell)	12,000	10.00	1,200	300
12/31	Dividends	1,000	10.00	100	400

To Calculate Gain/Loss on a FIFO Basis

Sold 1,200 shares at $10.00 per share   Sale Price   12,000

Cost Basis

06/14	1,000 shares at $10.00	$10,000
11/30	200 shares at $9.00	1,800
Total Cost		11,800
Gain		200

Growth and Income Fund after Sale

Date	Transaction	Dollar Amount	Share Price	# of shares	Total #
11/26	Invested	$2,700	9.00	300	300
12/31	Dividends	1,000	10.00	100	400

kets than conservative income equity funds, which invest in the stocks of larger, more established companies. Some small company funds have knowingly invested in small stocks of dubious value, which has caused some losses to their funds.

As a result of some bank failures and the shaky financial status of some of the country's savings and loan associations, some investors are naturally concerned about the *risk of insolvency* of mutual funds. There is always the risk that a mutual fund could go under, but the chances of this happening is small. The key distinction between banks and mutual funds is the way that mutual funds are set up, which reduces the risks of failure and loss due to fraud. Typically, mutual funds are corporations owned by shareholders. A separate management company is contracted by the shareholders to run the fund's daily operations. The management company oversees the investments of the fund, but they do not have possession of these assets (investments). The assets (investments) are held by a custodian such as a bank. Thus, if the management company gets into financial trouble they cannot get access to the assets of the fund. However, even with these checks and balances, there is always the possibility of fraud. Two mutual funds that were cleared by the Securities and Exchange Commission and whose prices were quoted in the financial newspapers along with all the other mutual funds were in essence bogus funds.

Another safeguard is that the shareholder's accounts are maintained by a transfer agent. The transfer agent keeps track of the purchases and redemptions of the shareholders. In addition, management companies carry fidelity bonds, a form of insurance to protect the investments of the fund against malfeasance or fraud perpetrated by the employees.

Besides these safeguards, there are two other factors that differentiate mutual funds from corporations such as banks and savings and loan associations:

∎ Mutual funds must be able to redeem shares on demand, which means that a portion of the investment assets must be liquid.

∎ Mutual funds must be able to price their investments at the end of each day which is known as marking to market.

Hence, mutual funds cannot hide their financial difficulties as easily as banks and savings and loans.

Mutual funds are regulated by the SEC, but as noted earlier, fraudulent operators will always find a way into any industry. The risk of fraud is always present, but it is no greater in the mutual fund industry than in any other industry. However, investors should be aware that they can lose money through purchasing a fund whose investments perform poorly on the markets.

∎ How to Buy and Sell Mutual Funds

Buying and selling shares in mutual funds can be accomplished in several ways, depending on whether the fund is a load or no-load fund.

Investors can buy into no-load mutual funds dealing directly with the mutual fund. Most if not all funds have 800 telephone numbers. Mutual funds will send a prospectus along with an application form to open an account for first-time investors. Once investors have opened accounts with the fund, they can purchase additional shares by sending a check along with a preprinted account stub detached from the account statement. As mentioned earlier, there are no sales commissions with no-load funds, so these are not sold by brokers. Shares in no-load funds are bought and sold at their net asset values.

Load funds are sold through brokers and salespeople who charge commissions every time new shares are bought. Some funds also charge a redemption fee, which is a back-end fee or reverse load for selling shares. If the percentage loads are the same (for front- or back-end), it may be preferable to go for a reverse load rather than a front load because all the money is invested immediately with the back-end load (Faerber, *Managing Your Investments*).

Financial planners, brokers and salespeople may try to convince you to buy load funds with claims of better performance than no-load funds. There is no evidence to support this premise for both stock and bond mutual funds. In fact, according to a study by Morningstar, a Chicago firm that tracks mutual funds, no-load bond funds consistently outperformed load funds over 3-, 5- and 10-year periods through March 31, 1993 (McGough, "Who's Got the Best Funds?"). However, there may be some truth to the claim that no-load bond and stock funds are much more volatile than load funds during expanding and contracting markets.

Banks and discount brokerage firms have also entered the mutual fund arena, and they too sell mutual funds. This, of course, complicates the choice of mutual funds, but investors who feel confident enough to choose their own funds are better off with no-load funds. The difference saved may be minimal over a short period of time, but this difference can grow substantially over a 10-year period due to the compounding of interest (time value of money). A study done by Morningstar on performance and expenses among diversified U.S. stock funds found that over a 10-year period ending in 1993, the 25 percent of funds with the lowest expenses increased on average by 13.4 percent as opposed to the highest cost funds that averaged only 11.5 percent after expenses (McGough, "Use Yardsticks").

A good source of information on mutual funds is a reference book by Wiesenberger called *Investment Companies*, available in most libraries. In it, you can review the long-run performance of the funds you are interested in.

∎ Advantages of Mutual Funds

∎ Mutual funds offer small investors the opportunity to own a fraction of a diversified portfolio. For instance, investing $2,500 in a stock fund gives the investor a share of an excellent cross section of stocks. Investors would need to invest at least $50,000 in individual stocks to have a diversified portfolio of about 12 different stocks.

∎ Mutual funds provide administrative and custodial duties; recordkeeping of all transactions, monthly statements and information for tax purposes, as well as the safekeeping of all securities.

∎ Mutual funds are professionally managed. Many investors do not have the time or the expertise to manage their stock portfolios.

∎ Mutual fund companies redeem shares on demand. In the case of no-load funds, they are redeemed at net asset values.

∎ Investors have the option of reinvesting dividends and capital gains automatically for more shares in the fund or having them paid out to them.

∎ Investors in a family of funds can switch from one fund to another as market conditions change. For example, when interest rates are going up, investors can switch money from their stock funds to money market funds.

∎ Levels of risk, return and stability of income and principal vary with the type of fund chosen. Most families of mutual funds offer a range of different types of stock and bond funds with various characteristics.

∎ Disadvantages of Mutual Funds

∎ Professional management does not guarantee superior performance. Many funds underperform the market over long periods of time.

∎ When load charges and fees are included, total returns may be significantly less than if investors bought individual stocks and bonds and held for long periods of time during bull markets.

▐ Investors have no choice over the investment securities that portfolio managers make.

▐ Investors have no control over the distribution of hidden capital gains which can upset very careful tax planning. Since investment companies do not pay taxes, income and capital gains are passed through to the shareholders.

▌ Caveats

▐ Choose a mutual fund family with a wide range of different funds, allowing you greater flexibility to transfer from one fund type to another.

▐ Avoid funds with high sales charges, redemption fees and high management and expense ratios.

▐ Keep all the records of income and capital gains distributions, as well as the dates, amounts and share prices of all purchases and redemptions of shares. This can alleviate a potential nightmare at tax time.

▌ Should You Invest in Mutual Funds or in Individual Securities?

Stock and bond mutual funds have been very popular among investors, and record amounts have been invested in them over the years. The advantages of mutual funds, as stated earlier, are professional management, diversification, being able to invest small amounts of money and ease of buying and selling. For many investors, these advantages outweigh the disadvantages of mutual funds. Mutual funds may be the most practical way for investors to buy many types of securities. These would be bonds that sell in high denominations such as certain mortgage-backed bonds, certain agency bonds and some municipal issues. Another factor pointing in favor of mutual funds is the complexity of certain types of bonds. The complexities of mortgage-backed bonds, zero-coupon bonds, convertible issues and derivative securities may exclude most investors from buying them as individual bonds. Mutual funds, therefore, allow investors to own many different, complex types of bonds. Similarly, the decision of which individual stocks to select may be mind-boggling for many investors.

The diversification achieved by mutual funds minimizes the impact from any unexpected losses from individual stocks in the portfolio as well as the fact that professional managers of these funds have quicker access to information about the different issues. This means that they react sooner in buying or selling the securities in question.

However, there is a strong argument for buying individual securities over mutual funds in certain cases. Rates of return on individual stocks and bonds may often be greater than those earned from mutual funds. This is true even for no-load funds because besides sales commissions there are other fees (12 (b)-1, operating fees) that eat into the returns of mutual funds. By investing in individual securities, investors avoid these fees.

There is a powerful argument for investing in individual bonds in that if they are bought and held until maturity, interest rate risk is avoided. Changes in market rates of interest affect the price of both individual bonds and bond mutual funds. However, if investors have a set time during which they will not need their money they can invest in individual bonds with corresponding maturities (to their needs) and not worry what happens to market rates of interest. This does not apply to bond mutual funds. If market rates of interest go up, there will be a decline in the net asset value of share prices of bond funds.

Some bonds, such as Treasury securities, are easy to buy and by owning them investors can eliminate many of the fees mutual funds charge, thereby increasing their returns. Moreover, when they are bought directly from the Federal Reserve banks or branches, investors do not pay any commissions. Buying and holding Treasury securities makes more sense than investing in Treasury bond funds. However, if investors do not plan on holding the bonds through maturity, funds may be a better alternative.

If investors have small amounts of money to invest, mutual funds are a better alternative. A $2,000 investment into a stock fund will buy a fraction of a diversified portfolio of stocks, whereas individually this may allow for buying only the shares of one company.

Investing in mutual funds is good for investors who do not have enough money to diversify their investments and who also do not have the time, expertise or inclination to select and manage individual securities. In addition, there is a wide range of funds offering investors the opportunity to invest in the types of securities that would be difficult to buy on an individual basis.

■ References

Clements, Jonathan. "The 25 Facts Every Fund Investor Should Know," *The Wall Street Journal* (March 5, 1993): C1.

———. "Funds That Look Dull, Can Be Real Daredevils," *The Wall Street Journal* (March 4, 1994): C1.

Eaton, Leslie. "Price Fixing. Costly Mistakes in Valuing Shares," *Barron's* (April 19, 1993): 35.

Faerber, Esmé. *Managing Your Investments, Savings and Credit*. Chicago, IL: Probus Publishing Co., 1992).

———. *All About Bonds*. Chicago: Probus Publishing Co., 1993.

Harlan, Christi. "SEC to Require More Wrap Account Data," *The Wall Street Journal*, (April 20, 1994): C1.

Jereski, Laura. "What Price CMOs? Funds Have No Idea," *The Wall Street Journal* (April 12, 1993): C1.

McGough, Robert. "Banks vs. Brokers: Who's Got the Best Funds?," *The Wall Street Journal* (May 7, 1993): C1.

———. "Use Yardsticks to Weed through Fees," *The Wall Street Journal* (July 7, 1994): R8.

Savage, Stephen. "Refrigerator Rules. ABCs for Today's Complex Fund Climate," *Barron's* (February 15, 1993): 43.

Schultz, Ellen. "How to Unwrap a Wrap Account," *The Wall Street Journal* (February 5, 1993): C1.

Taub, Stephen. "Market Watch," *Financial World* (June 7, 1994): 10.

Thau, Annette. *The Bond Book*. Chicago: Probus Publishing Co., 1992

Chapter 9

*Closed-End Funds**

Key Concepts:

- Unit Investment Trusts
- The Risks of Closed-End Funds and Unit Investment Trusts
- Real Estate Investment Trusts (REITs)
- Guidelines for the Selection of REITs
- How to Buy and Sell Closed-End Funds
- Their Advantages
- Their Disadvantages
- Caveats
- Whether They Are Suitable Investment Vehicles

Closed-end funds bear certain similarities to open-end mutual funds, but there are some significant differences. As pointed out in the previous chapter, open-end mutual funds issue an unlimited number of shares. When investors buy more shares in an open-end fund, more money is available to the fund manager to buy more investment assets.

With closed-end funds, there is a fixed number of shares outstanding; after these are sold, the fund does not issue any new shares. Shares of closed-end funds are traded on the stock exchanges or on the over-the-counter market. Most closed-end funds are traded on the New York Stock Exchange, with some on the American Stock Exchange and a few on the over-the-counter market.

---

* Portions of this chapter have been previously published by Esmé Faerber in *All About Bonds*, published by Probus Publishing Co., 1993.

Since there is a fixed number of shares in a closed-end fund, investors who want to invest in an existing fund (as opposed to a new fund) would have to buy shares from shareholders who are willing to sell their shares on the market. Thus, the price of the shares of the closed-end fund will fluctuate, depending on not only the supply and demand for the shares, but also on other factors such as the return of the fund, the average price of the stocks in the fund, the average maturity of the assets of the fund in the case of bonds, net asset value and other fundamental factors of the fund.

Like open-end mutual funds, the net asset value is important in the valuation of the share price. However, unlike open-end funds, share prices of closed-end funds can sell above or below their net asset values. For example, when market rates of interest decline, there may be heavy demand for closed-end funds which could push up their share prices above their net asset values. Hence, these funds would trade at a premium. Similarly, when market rates of interest go up, shares of closed-end bond funds could trade at significant discounts to their net asset values. For example, a closed-end bond fund could have a net asset value of $9 per share and be selling at $7.50 per share (trading at a $1.50 discount per share). At times, the discounts to net asset values of closed-end funds can be as much as 20–30 percent.

The type of assets held in the fund will affect the share price. The more risky the assets, the greater the volatility in share price.

Like open-end funds, there are many different closed-end funds: stock funds, bond funds, international funds and specialized funds. Among the bond funds, there are corporate bond funds, municipal bond funds, government bond funds, international bond funds and balanced funds. Balanced funds invest in both stocks and bonds. There are also many different types of closed-end stock funds. There are diversified equity funds, specialized stock funds and convertible funds. Diversified stock funds hold the stocks of companies from different industries and, as the name suggests, provide the investor with a diversified portfolio of investments. Specialized funds concentrate on specific types of securities or industries such as ASA Limited, which focuses on South African gold mining shares. Other examples are country funds such as the Italy Fund, Turkey Fund and Chile Fund, which focus on that country's investments.

Depending on the investment objectives of the closed-end fund, the professional managers (of the funds) will invest in different financial assets to make up a diversified portfolio. Even though closed-end funds do not issue new shares to expand their capital structure, their portfolio assets can and do change. Existing stock and bond issues may be sold and new ones bought for the portfolio. Thus, when bond issues mature, the proceeds received are used to buy new issues. Closed-end funds, like open-end funds, never mature.

Net asset values for closed-end funds are calculated in much the same way as for open-end funds. The total assets minus any liabilities equals the net worth for the fund, which is divided by the fixed number of shares to give the net asset value per share.

Occasionally, closed-end funds become open-end mutual funds, and the net asset value becomes the price that the shares trade at through the mutual fund. That is if it becomes a no-load fund. For a load fund, an additional commission will be added to the net asset value.

There are other types of closed-end funds that individual investors should be aware of: unit investment trusts (UITs), real estate investment trusts (REITs) and dual funds.

■ Unit Investment Trusts

In the closed-end bond fund market, unit investment trusts have become very popular. More than $6 billion was invested in unit trusts in 1992, and roughly $11 billion of unit trusts were managed by three firms—Blackrock Financial Management, Hyperion Capital Management and Piper Jaffrey (Bary). Brokerage firms such as Merrill Lynch and Bear Stearns, as well as Nuveen and Van Kampen and Merritt, sponsor unit trusts.

Unit investment trusts have been seductively marketed as the investment that gives high current income as well as returning an investor's entire investment when the trust assets mature. Theoretically, this is possible, but in practice, it may not always be possible and we will see why. By examining how unit trusts work, the difficulties of living up to these lofty promises will become apparent.

A unit investment trust, like a closed-end fund, will sell a fixed number of shares. For instance, assume that the trust sells one million shares at $10 per share for a total of $10 million. Sales commissions of $500,000 would be deducted, leaving the unit trust (closed-end bond fund) $9.5 million to invest in different bond issues. The trust (closed-end fund) will then remit the earnings on the investments after management fees to the shareholders. When the different investments mature, the trust will pay back the proceeds from the investments to the shareholders. (Closed-end funds differ in that when issues mature, the proceeds are reinvested in other issues). This is how unit investment trusts and closed-end funds work.

However, before looking at the factors that could make it difficult for the trust to live up to its promise of high income and the full return of principal, it may be more useful to examine some of the differences between unit trusts and closed-end funds.

Generally, with unit investment trusts, the portfolio of investments stay the same once they have been bought. In other words, no new bonds are bought and no existing bonds are sold. Theoretically, as the bond issues approach maturity, the prices of the individual bonds will rise towards their par prices. Again theoretically, management fees should be lower on unit investment trusts than closed-end funds because the portfolio remains unmanaged. In fact, there should be no management fees on a unit investment trust because the portfolio is unmanaged, but in most instances this is not the case. With closed-end bond funds, the portfolio changes as issues are bought and sold.

Shares of unit investment trusts, like closed-end bond funds, trade on the secondary markets. However, in certain conditions, shares in unit investment trusts can be quite illiquid. This happens when interest rates are rising and new investors would not want to buy into a trust with bond investments that are locked into lower yields. Hence, existing unit trust shareholders may have difficulty selling their shares due to illiquidity.

The Risks of Closed-end Bond Funds and Unit Investment Trusts

Both closed-end bond funds and unit investment trusts are subject to *interest rate risk*. When market rates of interest increase, prices of the bond issues held in both the portfolios of unit trusts and closed-end bond funds will go down. This, of course, means that the share prices will fall. Moreover, there is a double-edged sword effect, in that, if there is selling pressure on the shares, the decline in share prices will be even greater than the decline in the net asset values. The opposite is true in that if interest rates fall, there will be appreciation in the assets and, of course, in the share price.

Interest rate risk has another effect on unit investment trusts. The yields of the fixed coupon bonds will theoretically remain the same despite changes in interest rates because the assets in the portfolio remain the same. Whereas, with closed-end bond funds when the assets mature or are sold, new issues with higher (or lower) coupons will be bought. Thus, yields on closed-end bond funds will fluctuate more than those on unit investment trusts. However, if unit investment trusts invest in mortgage securities and interest-only strips, a reduction in market rates of interest would cause a reduced return for shareholders. Interest-only strips fall in price when market rates of interest decline. This has happened to some of the Hyperion Trust funds which have had negative rates of return on some trusts and poor returns on others (Bary "In Whom Do You Trust?").

Many unit investment trusts have used leverage to increase their yields. Leverage is where the trusts use borrowed money to supplement amounts invested by shareholders to invest in portfolio assets. Currently, this has worked well for many trusts because of the yield curve, which is the relationship between long-term and short-term rates. Currently, short-term rates are lower than long-term rates of interest. Therefore, trusts have been borrowing on a short-term basis (3 1/2 percent) and investing the funds in long-term issues (7–8 percent). This strategy worked well for trusts during the 1992–1993 period because interest rates had been coming down and were at their lowest levels in 20 years.

However, this is a risky strategy because when interest rates bottom out and begin to rise, not only will borrowing costs climb but the increased costs will cut into the yields paid to shareholders. Moreover, prices of the different bond securities held in the portfolio will decline, which of course translates into lower share prices. Thus, the use of leverage adds further risks when compounded with changes in market rates of interest.

There is the risk that share prices of both closed-end funds and unit investment trusts can fall way below net asset values due to excess selling pressure on the stock markets. Then of course there is always the danger of not being able to recoup the original price paid for the shares when selling.

For unit investment trust shareholders, there is the added risk of not getting back the full amount of their original investments. This could be due to a number of factors. Bond issues may be called before maturity with the call price being less than the face value. Other factors are the composition of the trust's assets: commissions and high management fees charged to the trust; the dividend yields; and, as mentioned earlier, the use of leverage.

The managers of unit investment trusts and closed-end bond funds charge in many cases very generous annual fees as well as upfront commissions for the original sale of the shares. This means that these funds will not only have to earn spectacular returns so that the managers of these funds (trusts) can collect their fees without eroding yields significantly, but they will also have to rake up some capital gains to be able to recoup the sales commissions in order to return to the shareholders their entire investments at maturity. This explains why many investment trusts use leverage and resort to derivative securities as ways to try and boost their returns.

When interest rates fall, there is the risk that bond issues will be called. This means that shareholders of unit trusts will get their money back which they will reinvest at lower rates of interest. This reduces overall returns. The types of investments that the fund or trust holds will have a marked effect on the net asset value and the volatility of the share price. Unfortunately for the original shareholders of closed-end bond funds and unit investment trusts, there is no way of knowing the composition of the portfolio investments when they originally subscribe to the shares of the fund/trust. The original shareholders will invest their money to buy the shares; only then will the managers of the fund/trust buy the investment assets. Thus, shareholders may not be able to anticipate the levels of risk of the assets until the portfolio has been constituted. The composition may include low-quality bonds in addition to complex derivative securities for the purpose of boosting the yields of the portfolio. This strategy could backfire in that low-quality securities could deteriorate and market rates of interest could face unanticipated changes in direction, which would send prices of these funds/trusts into a steep decline. Thus, investors trying to exit the fund/trust would experience losses through the decline in the share price.

What you see is not always what you get with advertised yields. Certain funds will include capital gains as well as returns of principal from mortgage-backed securities to boost their yield figures. The true yield on a closed-end fund is only the net investment income per share (after management fees) divided by the price per share. This is the current yield. For closed-end funds where there is no maturity, a yield-to-maturity calculation is not meaningful. The total return for closed-end funds depends on the yield of the investments and the fluctuations in share price.

With unit investment trusts, the selling feature is often a high yield, which means that in a climate of low interest rates many trusts will disregard the risks of picking high-yielding, lower quality securities for their portfolios. This happened to many unit investment trusts that loaded up on Washington Public Power Securities before they defaulted, resulting in losses that fell to the shareholders (Thau).

In summary, investors in unit investment trusts should look beyond the advertised yield and scrutinize the makeup of the portfolio of investments. In reality, shareholders of unit investment trusts have no protection against both the deterioration of the quality of the investments in the portfolio or interest rate risk (Thau). Similarly, if there is an exodus of shareholders from unit investment trusts and closed-end funds, shareholders may find it difficult to sell their shares without taking large losses.

Real Estate Investment Trusts (REITs)

Real estate investment trusts (REITs) offer individual investors the opportunity to invest in real estate without having to own and manage individual properties. A REIT is a form of closed-end mutual fund in that it invests the money received from the sale of shares to shareholders in real estate. REITs buy, develop and manage real estate properties and pass on the income from the rent and mortgages to shareholders in the form of dividends.

REITs do not pay corporate income taxes, but in return they must by law distribute 95 percent of their net income to their shareholders. What this also means is that there is not much income left to finance future real estate acquisitions.

There are three basic types of REITs:

- *Equity REITs* which buy, operate and sell real estate such as hotels, office buildings, apartments and shopping centers.

- *Mortgage REITs* which make construction and mortgage loans available to developers.

- *Hybrid REITs* which are a combination of the equity and mortgage REITs. In other words, they may buy, develop and manage real estate in addition to providing financing through mortgage loans.

These different types of REITs have different risks; they should be evaluated carefully before an investment in them is made. Generally, equity REITs tend to be less speculative than mortgage REITs, but the level of risk depends on the makeup of the assets in the trust. Mortgage REITs lend money to developers, which involves a greater risk of loss. Consequently, the shares of mortgage REITs tend to be more volatile than the shares of equity REITs.

Equity REITs have been the most popular type of REIT recently, and their performance of 5.31 percent (on average) has outpaced the S&P average of a negative 3.9 percent for the first six months of 1994 (Zuckerman, 35). Equity REITs derive their income from rents received from the properties in their portfolios and from increasing property values.

Mortgage REITS are more sensitive to interest rate moves in the economy than equity REITs. This is because the former holds mortgages whose prices move in the opposite direction to interest rates. While equity REITs may be less sensitive to changes in interest rates, they too suffer the consequences of rising interest rates.

In 1993, when interest rates were falling, mortgage REITs outpaced the S&P with a whopping 18 percent return versus 4.8 percent for the S&P in the first six months of 1993.

Due to the different assets that mortgage and equity REITs hold, mortgage REITs tend to be more income oriented in that the emphasis is on current yields, whereas equity REITs offer the potential of capital gains in addition to current income.

REITs can either have finite or perpetual lives. Finite life real estate investment trusts, also known as FREITs, are self-liquidating. In the case of equity REITs, the properties will be sold at the end of a time period; in mortgage REITs, when the mortgages are paid up, the profits are paid to the shareholders.

Guidelines for Selecting REITs

There are over 230 publicly listed REITs, making it difficult for investors to plow through them to find the better ones to invest in (Byrne, 32). These guidelines may be helpful:

∎ Investigate the REIT that you are interested in before you buy. Get an annual report from your broker or call the REIT directly and ask them to send you this information. Additional information can also be obtained from the National Association of Real Estate Investment Trusts, 1101 17th Street N.W., Washington D.C. 20036.

∎ Look to see how long the REIT has been in business. Directly related to this is how long the managers have been in the real estate business and how well they manage the assets. Select REITs whose managements have been in REITs for at least eight years (Dunnan, 181). Another question concerning management is, How large is their stake in the REIT? According to Byrne insiders should own at least 10 percent of the stock.

∎ Look at the level of debt of the REIT. The greater the level of debt the greater the risks because more of the revenues will be needed to service the debt, and if there is a downturn in revenues, the interest payments will become harder to service. Look for REITs with debt to equity ratios of less than 50 percent (Byrne, 32).

∎ Don't choose a REIT mainly because it has the highest yield. The higher the yield, the greater the risks. There have been cases where underwriters have raised the yield to hide poor fundamentals (Zuckerman, 35). On the other hand, too low a yield may mean the stock is overvalued.

■ Select REITs that have low price-to-book values (1 to 1 or less).

■ Check the dividend record of the REIT. There should be a history of dividends. Be wary of REITs that have recently cut their dividends. You should also check the source of cash for the payment of dividends. The source of cash for dividends should come from operations, not from the sale of properties.

■ Location is everything in real estate. Look at the locations of the properties in the trust. You may want to avoid REITs that have invested in overbuilt or depressed locations.

Caveats

■ Avoid REITs that are blind pools. These are set up generally by well-known management who raise funds to invest in unidentified properties. You want to see the makeup of the real estate assets and liabilities in any project before you invest.

■ Do not invest more than 10 percent of your total investment portfolio in real estate.

■ Dual Funds

A dual fund is a hybrid type of closed-end fund that has two classes of stock. One class receives the income/dividends from the investments, while the other class receives the capital gains/losses from the sale of the investments in the fund. The latter class is known as the common stockholders. There is generally an expiration date for dual funds whereby the common stockholders vote to determine whether to liquidate the fund or to continue it on an open-end basis. There are not many dual funds traded on the markets.

■ How to Buy and Sell Closed-End Funds

When closed-end funds and unit investment trusts are newly issued, the shares are underwritten by brokerage firms and sold by brokers. Brokerage fees can be as high as 8 percent, which means that the investor's investment is immediately reduced by 8 percent. For instance, if a fund or trust sells one million shares at $10 per share for $10 million, it will have only $9.2 million to invest after deducting $800,000 (8 percent) for brokerage commissions. This means that after shareholders have paid $10 per share to invest in the new fund or trust, the shares will drop in value and trade at a discount. This is known as a quick erosion in capital and is a well-documented phenomenon for closed-end funds and unit investment trusts. This will not be a topic of conversation brought up by brokers who stand to earn high commissions from the sale of these shares. Many brokers assert that closed-end funds are sold commission-free. This is a play on words because while it may be commission-free, in its place is a hefty underwriting charge that is absorbed by the shareholders. Investors would do better to wait until the funds or trusts are listed on the stock exchanges than to buy them at issue only to see the shares drop in price.

Another reason not to buy closed-end funds or unit investment trusts at issue is that the portfolio of assets has not been constituted so investors do not know what they are getting and they most certainly won't know what the yields will be. Unit investment trust sponsors do not like to see the shares of their trusts fall to discounts, and so they often advertise above-market yields to keep the shares from trading at discounts to their net asset values.

The advice from an expert, Thomas Herzfeld, who follows closed-end funds and unit investment trusts is to pay attention to the price of the funds you are interested in and the time to buy is when the discount is 3 percent wider than the normal discount for the fund (Thau).

Common sense suggests that besides the attractiveness of buying into a fund when its shares are selling below their net asset values, there are other factors to consider:

∎ The yield, particularly if investors are buying into the fund in order to get the income. Examine the yield, total return and expense ratios before investing.

∎ The frequency that dividends are paid: semi-annually, quarterly or monthly.

∎ The composition of the assets and the credit quality of the assets.

∎ The average length of time to maturity of the portfolio investments.

Information on closed-end funds can be found in Thomas J. Herzfeld Advisors annual *Encyclopedia of Closed-end Funds, Value Line Investment Survey, Standard & Poor's Record Sheets, Moody's Finance Manuals* and Wiesenberger's *Investment Companies* (in most public libraries).

Share prices of the listed closed-end funds, unit investment trusts and REITs can be found in the stock exchange sections of the daily newspapers. For example, the following is a quote of the Hyperion

Trust 97 listed on the New York Stock Exchange from the *New York Times*, August 10, 1994:

365 day				Yld		Sales				
Hi	Low	Stock	Div	%	P/E	100s	High	Low	Last	Chg
9 1/2	7 3/8	Hy Tst 97	.60	7.9	—	1376	7 5/8	7 1/2	7 5/8	+1/8

Reading from left to right:

■ The first two columns indicate the year's high of $9.50 per share and the low of $7 3/8 per share.

■ The name of the stock is the Hyperion Unit Trust, with a maturity in 1997.

■ The dividend is $0.60 per share.

■ The yield percentage is 7.9 percent, which is the dividend divided by the last price of the day (.60/7.625).

■ The sales volume indicates the number of shares traded that day, 137,600 shares.

■ The high, low and last indicate that the high price on the day quoted was $7.625, the low price for that day's trading was $7.50 and the last price was the closing price of $7.625.

■ The change column indicates that the share price closed up 1/8th of a point from the previous day's close.

Barron's, the weekly financial newspaper, publishes a comprehensive list of closed-end funds, including unit investment trusts. For example, the information provided on Hyperion Trust 1997 from *Barron's* closed-end bond funds for the week ending August 8, 1994, provides different information than that offered in the daily financial newspapers:

| Fund Name | Stock Exchange | NAV | Market Price | Prem/ Discount | 52 Week Market Return |
| Hyperion 1997 Tm | N | 8.16 | 7 5/8 | − 6.6 | 8.0 |

■ Hyperion 1997 Term Trust trades on the New York Stock Exchange.

■ The net asset value as of the week's close was $8.16 per share.

■ The closing market price for the week was $7.625 per share.

∎ The –6.6 indicates that the market price was trading at a 6.6 percent discount to its net asset value. A + would indicate that the fund/trust is trading at a premium to its net asset value.

∎ The 52-week return for Hyperion 1997 Term Trust is 8 percent.

By combining the information in the daily newspapers with that provided in *Barron's*, investors can better follow the closed-end funds they are interested in buying or selling. Shares listed on the exchanges are sold through brokers.

Before buying closed-end funds or trusts ask your broker or call the fund sponsor for the annual or quarterly report.

The Advantages of Closed-End Funds and Unit Investment Trusts

∎ Investors can buy into closed-end funds and trusts trading at discounts to their net asset values, which may offer the potential for capital gains and increased yields. The downside of this strategy could be capital losses if the discount to the net asset value widens.

∎ The shares of the larger, actively traded closed-end funds and trusts can easily be bought and sold on the stock exchanges. The less actively traded funds will not be as liquid.

∎ For income-seeking investors, most unit investment trusts pay dividends on a monthly basis.

∎ Unit investment trusts have maturities when investors will have all (or most) of their capital returned to them.

The Disadvantages of Closed-End Funds and Unit Investment Trusts

∎ Closed-end funds, unit investment trusts and REITs are subject to interest rate risk. Unit investment trusts have no protection against a rise in interest rates because their portfolio of investments is fixed.

∎ There is the risk that the prices of shares of funds and trusts can move independently to the value of the securities held in the fund's/trust's portfolios. More investors exiting the fund/trust than buying the fund/trust will have the effect of driving the price down despite the fact that the assets in the fund are doing well. This often represents a buying opportunity when the fund's (trust's) shares trade at a discount to its net asset value.

■ Brokerage commissions along with management fees can be high, which eats into the yields of closed-end funds and unit investment trusts.

■ Some of the shares of the smaller, less actively traded funds and trusts may be illiquid.

■ Buying into funds and trusts when they are first offered to shareholders means that these shareholders are investing in an unknown portfolio of assets. This is of particular significance for unit investment trusts in that investors cannot gauge the level of risk in the composition of the assets and whether the trust will use leverage to try and increase yields.

■ Unit investment trusts offer no protection against the credit deterioration of their assets because their portfolios are fixed.

Caveats

■ Investors should avoid investing in closed-end funds and unit investment trusts when they are first offered to the public because a percentage of their initial funds will go towards paying underwriting fees and selling commissions. For example, if investors pay $10 per share and $0.80 goes towards these expenses, net asset values will fall to $9.20 directly after issuance.

■ Compare the long-term performance of closed-end funds, unit investment trusts and REITs before investing. Some have not performed well and investors may want to avoid those with poor long-term track records.

■ Examine the fees charged before buying into closed-end funds and investment trusts. Fees can be quite high.

Are Closed-End Funds and Investment Trusts Suitable for Me?

Under certain conditions, closed-end funds, unit investment trusts and REITs have provided investors with profitable returns. When they are trading at premium prices, bargains in these types of investments are hard to find. For example, when a fund is trading at a premium of 2.5 percent to its net asset value, an investor would be paying $1.025 for every dollar of assets (not taking into account brokerage fees to buy the shares).

It is far more advantageous for investors to wait until they can buy into closed-end funds, unit investment trusts and REITs when they are trading at discounts to their net asset values. In fact, many investment advisors recommend buying closed-end funds and investment trusts when they are trading at large discounts by historical standards to their net asset values and selling them when they have small discounts or premiums.

You should also look for closed-end funds that are to be converted to open-end funds. If the shares of these funds are trading at discounts to their net asset values, they will rise to their net asset value price at the date of conversion. This also represents a buying opportunity.

Unit investment trusts need to be examined carefully before buying because of their inherent characteristics. They have maturity dates, which means that investors will have their principal returned to them at a specified time. Whether they will get all of their principal back is questionable. If interest rates continue to go down and the unit investment trust benefits from the use of leverage, shareholders should get close to all of, if not all of, their original principal back. However, if interest rates rise and borrowing costs climb, the return of their entire principal may be jeopardized.

With closed-end funds, unit investment trusts and REITs, share prices will fluctuate due to supply and demand for the shares on the stock market. Thus, if investors cannot find closed-end funds or investment trusts that are trading at discounts and they do not want the added risks of further fluctuations in price over net asset values, they should consider open-end mutual funds.

∎ References

Bary, Andrew. "Whom Do You Trust?," *Barron's* (February 8, 1993): M8–M9.

———. "Father Knows Best? How Lew Ranieri's Bond Funds Fared So Poorly," *Barron's* (May 17, 1993): 14–15.

Byrne, Thomas C. "Beyond Yield," *Individual Investor* (July, 1994): 32.

Dunnan, Nancy. *Guide to Your Investments 1990* New York: Harper & Row Publishers, 1990.

Faerber, Esmé. *All About Bonds*. Chicago: Probus Publishing Co., 1993.

Thau, Annette. *The Bond Book*. Chicago: Probus Publishing Co., 1992.

Zuckerman, Lawrence. "A Look Under the Hood at Realty Stocks," *New York Times* (July 16, 1994): 35.

Chapter 10

Stock Derivative Investments

Key Concepts

- Options and How They Work
- Call Options and How to Benefit from Them
- Put Options and How to Benefit from Them
- Combination of Put and Call Options
- Writing Put and Call Options
- Rights
- Warrants

This chapter focuses on some stock derivative investments even though bond derivatives feature much more prominently in the news. For information on bond derivatives, a bond book would be helpful.

The mutual fund industry has brought the attention of derivatives into the public eye. Stock funds use derivatives to hedge their risk or as a lower-cost method of investing in the market. For example, international stock funds use both foreign currency options and stock index futures to protect against adverse foreign currency fluctuations and adverse swings in stock market prices. Generally, the use of derivatives in stock funds has not been as worrisome and has not caused the losses that derivatives have with some bond and money market mutual funds. By hedging with currency options, international stock funds can in fact reduce the risks facing the funds.

Stock derivatives are securities that offer investors some of the benefits of stocks without having to own them, such as options and futures. The focus in this chapter is on options, rights and warrants, even though technically rights and warrants are not stock derivatives but are more like stock equivalents. Futures contracts are complex investments that should not feature in the portfolios of most investors due to the risks. Ninety percent of all futures trades lose money, despite the fact that a few people have turned small amounts into vast sums. Futures contracts will not be discussed in this book.

∎ Options   *Options ARE not Obligations.*

A stock option is a derivative security because its value depends on the underlying security, which is the common stock. Other underlying securities for option contracts besides common stock are stock indices, foreign currencies, U.S. government debt and commodities. This accounts for the large number of options traded.

Options are traded on the Chicago Board Options Exchange (CBOE) as well as on the New York Stock Exchange (NYSE), the American Stock Exchange (AMEX), the Philadelphia Exchange (PHLX) and the Pacific Exchange (PSE).

Options should be understood by investors because they provide an additional tool that can be used successfully in increasingly volatile markets. Options can be used to speculate on the movement of future stock prices and to reduce the impact of the volatility of stock prices.

In some respects, options are similar to futures contracts; one of these is that option holders with a small investment can control a large dollar amount of stock for a limited time. However, the risks of loss are much less for option holders than they are for futures holders. Options fall somewhere in the middle between trading stocks and trading futures.

Before pursuing an investment strategy using options, an investor should explore the different hypothetical pricing scenarios on paper to see the possible range of potential profits and losses.

What Is an Option and How Does It Work?

There are different types of options with many different characteristics, but only the most prominent types of options on common stocks will be discussed in this section. A stock option is a contract that gives the owner the right to buy or sell a specified number of common shares (generally 100) of a company at a specified price within a time period.

The two types of contracts to buy and sell stocks are *calls* and *puts*. The call stock option gives the owner the right to buy the shares, and the put option contract gives the owner the right to sell the shares. The option holder has the right to convert at their discretion. It is not an obligation. In other words, they can exercise the option when it is to their advantage.

There are four items of note in an options contract:

■ The name of the company whose shares can be bought or sold.

■ The number of shares that can be bought or sold.

■ The exercise or strike price, which is the purchase or sale price of the shares

■ The expiration date, which is the date when the option to buy or sell expires.

As in any contract, there are at least two parties: buyers and sellers. The option buyer is also referred to as the option holder, and the seller of the contract is also referred to as the option writer. *CALL*

A hypothetical example will explain how options work. Investor A wants to buy a call option contract for 100 shares of Exxon Corporation with a strike price (or exercise price) of $65 per share. At the same time, Investor W decides to write a contract to sell 100 shares of Exxon Corporation stock with a strike price of $65 per share. Exxon is currently trading at $62 per share. Both investors have different outlooks as to the direction of Exxon's share price. Investor A believes the share price will go up, whereas Investor W anticipates that the share price is headed southward in the near future.

Investor W bears the risk if the price of Exxon goes up instead of down. If Investor A exercises the option to call in the stock, Investor W will have to buy Exxon stock at a higher price and deliver it to Investor A. Investor W is compensated for this risk by charging the buyer of the contract an amount of money called a premium or option price. If the premium is $3 per share, Investor A will pay $300 to Investor W to buy the call option contract, which gives Investor A the right to buy 100 share of Exxon stock at $65 per share before the expiration of the contract.

If the price of Exxon stock rises above $65 per share within the time period before expiration, Investor A will profit by exercising the option. Assume that Exxon stock rises to $69 per share when Investor A decides to exercise the option. Under the call option terms, Investor A has the right to buy 100 shares of Exxon stock at $65 per share. Investor A pays Investor W $6,500 for 100 shares of Exxon. Investor W will buy the stock at $6,900 (100 shares at $69) and transfer it to Investor A.

Investor A has paid a total of $6,800: $300 for the option (premium price) plus $6,500 for the stock. The costs for Investor W result in a total loss of $100, composed as follows: an outlay of $6,900 which is partially offset by the receipts from Investor A of $6,500 for the stock and $300 for the option contract. This example is illustrated in Figure 10–1.

If, on the other hand, the price of Exxon stock stays at $62 through the duration of the contract, Investor A will have lost the amount of the contract premium ($300). Thus, the greatest amount that an investor can lose buying an option is the cost of the option. The advantage of a call option is that the investor has a high degree of leverage (a small amount of money, $3 per share, which controls a larger sum, $65 per share). The option buyer can also profit from selling the option if there is an increase in the premium price.

Investor W also has some alternatives. If Investor W wants to get out of this contract, he or she can sell the contract to someone else. The trading of options is greatly facilitated by the Options Clearing Corporation (OCC), which, besides maintaining a liquid marketplace, also keeps track of the options and the positions of each investor.

Buyers and writers of options do not deal directly with one another but instead deal with the Options Clearing Corporation. When an investor buys a contract, the OCC acts as an intermediary, guaranteeing that the provisions of the contract will be fulfilled. When the contract is exercised, the OCC guarantees that the option buyer will receive the stock even if the writer defaults on delivery.

Similarly, the OCC facilitates the process of buyers and writers closing out their positions. When a buyer of an option contract sells the contract, the OCC will cancel both entries in the investor's account. The same process is true for a writer of a contract. If a writer wants to get out of his or her position, he or she will buy a contract, which will then offset the original position.

Figure 10–1   How a Call Option Works

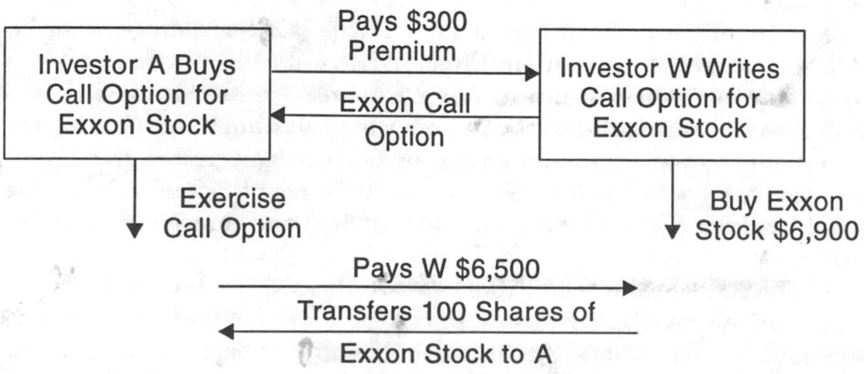

The astute reader will immediately realize that in order for the OCC to guarantee this process, they would have to have standardized contracts. Generally, two options on a stock are introduced to the market at the same time with identical terms except for the strike (exercise) price. Options have a maximum time of nine months before expiry, although options for actively traded stocks may be introduced to the market with only one to two months before expiring. A newer, longer-term option contract, called a LEAP, has been trading on the exchanges. LEAPs (long-term equity anticipation securities) may have a life span of up to three years before expiry.

After options on a stock have been introduced to the market, new options on the stock with the same terms but different strike prices may be introduced. Once an option is introduced and listed on the exchange, it will remain until it expires. Due to the standardization of listed options contracts, options on common stocks expire on the Saturday after the third Friday of the specified month of expiry.

■ Call Options and How to Benefit from Them

A call option gives the holder the right to buy 100 shares of the underlying stock at the exercise or strike price until the date of expiration of the option.

If we use the Exxon example cited in the previous section, we can see how buying a call option can be beneficial to an investor.

In return for paying the premium of $300 ($3 times 100 shares), Investor A has the right to buy Exxon shares at $65 per share anytime until the expiration of the option. The downside risk is that the option will not be exercised and the investor will lose the $300 plus the commission, which could be an additional $40. Buying a call means that the investor puts up a fraction of the cost of the stock in order to participate if the stock moves above the strike price of $65.

The basic problem is that the stock would have to move up in price above the strike price before the option expires because the option is worth nothing at expiration. It is a wasting asset. There is a time value to the price of an option. The more time before the option expires, the greater is the time value of the option. Similarly, as the option moves closer to its expiration, so the time value of the option decreases in value.

The links to the time value of the option is the underlying price of the stock and the call's strike price. This is referred to as the intrinsic value of the option. In the Exxon example, if the market price of

$$\text{Intrinsic value} = \text{mkt Price} - \text{Strike Price}$$

Exxon stock moves up to $67 per share, the intrinsic value of the option is $2:

$$\text{Intrinisic Value} = \text{Market Price of the Stock} - \text{Strike Price}$$

$$= \$67 - \$65$$

$$= \$2$$

The time value of the option can be computed as follows:

$$\text{Time Value} = \text{Option Premium} - \text{Intrinsic Value}$$

$$= \$3 - \$2$$

$$= \$1$$

The option premium price will fluctuate depending on two factors:

■ The underlying price of the stock.

■ The time left until the expiration of the option.

If Exxon's stock moves up to $70 per share, the intrinsic value of the option will now be $5. This will cause the option to trade for much more than the $3 premium price at the option was originally sold for.

Another course of action for the call buyer is to sell the option for a profit rather than exercising it. The leverage that can be obtained explains why so many investors prefer this course of action. See the example in Table 10–1 which illustrates the benefits of leverage.

Buying and selling the stock gives a return of 11.29 percent. This is not to be sneezed at; but compared to buying and selling the option, it comes in a poor second to 66.67 percent. At the price of $69 per share, it hardly becomes beneficial to exercise the option in the third alternative of Table 10–1. This alternative only becomes beneficial when the stock price moves well above the total costs of $68 per share (strike price of $65 per share and the $3 per share call premium). Moreover, this alternative also requires the greatest outlay of capital ($6,800 versus only $300 for the call option and $6,200 to buy the stock).

Buying and selling the option not only gives the greatest return on investment but also requires the lowest capital outlay. By buying a call option instead of the stock, the investor can invest a small fraction of the cost of the stock. If the stock price rises significantly above the strike price within the period before expiration, the investor can profit

The call holder can 1. exercise the option
2. let it expire
3. sell the option

Table 10–1   Leverage

Buying the Stock

Buy 100 shares of Exxon stock at $62 per share	$6,200
Sell 100 shares of Exxon at $69 per share	$6,900
Profit	$ 700
Return on Investment 700/6200	11.29%

Buying and Selling the Option

Buy Exxon option	$ 300
Sell Exxon option	$ 500
Profit	$ 200
Return on Investment 200/300	66.67%

Exercise Option

Buy Exxon option	$ 300
Cost to exercise option	6,500
Total cost	$6,800
Sell Exxon stock at $69 per share	$6,900
Profit	$ 100
Return on Investment 100/6800	1.47%

by selling or exercising the option. In the latter case, the investor can then sell the stock or hold it for long-term capital appreciation.

The most that an investor can lose buying call options is the cost of the option. Thus, the downside risk is limited, as opposed to the potential loss in the case of buying the stock. There are many examples of high-flying stocks that have risen to abnormally high prices only to fall back into oblivion resulting in tremendous losses for those investors who had invested when the stocks were trading at high multiples of earnings.

Situations Where Calls May Be Used

Call options benefit buyers when the price of the underlying stock is rising. The Exxon example shows that if an investor bought the call option instead of the stock, the greatest return would come from selling the option, due to the concept of leverage. If the market price of the stock declines below the strike price of the option, the most that the investor would lose is the option premium.

⚹ Call options may also be used to hedge against an upturn in the price of a stock on a short position. Assume that an investor had sold short 100 shares of Merck stock when it was $40 per share. When the price of Merck declines to $29 per share, the investor wants to protect the $11 profit per share against a rise in the price of Merck stock. The investor could buy a call option which a strike price of $30 per share. For every $1 increase in Merck stock above $30 per share, there is a profit on the call option that offsets the loss on the short sale. If, however, Merck continues to go down in price, the investor has lost only the amount paid to buy the option. This strategy allows an investor to protect profits without having to close out his or her position. This is often beneficial for tax planning to shift gains into the following year.

∎ Put Options and How to Benefit from Them

A put option gives the holder the right to sell 100 shares of the underlying company's stock at the strike price up until the expiration date of the option. This is the opposite of a call option. The put option buyer profits when the price of the underlying stock falls below the strike price. The put option holder has various alternatives:

∎ Buy the stock at the lower market price and exercise the option at the higher strike price.

∎ Sell the option at a profit.

∎ Let the option expire and lose the amount of the premium paid for the option.

When the price of the underlying stock declines, the value of the put increases. Investors buy puts when they are bearish about the stock. It is for this reason that the premiums on puts are generally smaller than those for calls on the same stock. Generally, more investors are bullish than bearish, and hence fewer puts options are traded than call options.

The put option holder also benefits from the leverage. For a small premium, the investor can control a large dollar amount of the stock.

As with calls, puts are wasting assets and have no value at expiration. The price of the put option has two parts:

∎ The intrinsic value.

∎ The time value.

The Intrinsic Value = Strike Price − Market Price of the Stock

for Puts

The intrinsic value cannot be less than zero (a negative number) by convention. If an option has no intrinsic value, it is said to be *out-of-the-money*. When it is profitable to exercise the put option, it is said to be *in-the-money* as it does have intrinsic value. If the strike price equals the market price of the stock, the option is said to be *at-the-money*.

The Time Value = Premium − Intrinsic Value

Generally, options are not normally exercised until they are close to expiry because an earlier exercise means throwing away the remaining time value. Another generalization with options (both calls and puts) is that most options are not bought with the intent of exercising them. Instead, they are bought with the intent of selling them.

When an option is *in-the-money*, the option holder may sell and receive an amount of money greater than the premium paid, whereas if the option is exercised, the put holder has to come up with the money to buy the stocks (if they are not already owned), so they can be sold at the strike price. Transaction costs are incurred in both of these transactions.

When to Buy Puts

Investors profit from buying puts when the price of the underlying stock declines and when they want to protect existing profits.

Declining Stock Price (*Almost like selling a stock short*)

Rather than selling a stock short when a decline in the stock's price is anticipated, an investor can buy a put option. For example, if an investor is bearish on the Mexican stock Telefonos de Mexico, which is currently trading at $66.50 per share on the New York Stock Exchange, a September put option with a strike price of $65 could be bought for $137.50 (contract for a 100 shares). If Telefonos de Mexico does go down in price, the investor can either exercise the option, by selling 100 shares of the stock at the strike price of $65 per share and buying them at the lower market price, or sell the put option at a profit.

The use of put options limits the risks of loss as compared with short selling where the risks of loss are open-ended. When selling short, the price of the stock may increase rather than decrease, thereby increasing the amount of money that can be lost. The greatest amount that can be lost with a put option is the premium paid to buy the option.

Hedging to Protect Existing Profits

Put options can also be used as a hedge to protect existing profits in a stock without having to sell the stocks. Assume that an investor bought 100 shares of Johnson & Johnson stock at $38 per share earlier in the year. The stock is currently trading at $49 3/8, which means that this investor has a profit of $11 3/8 per share. If the investor wants to protect this profit without having to sell the stock this year, the investor could buy a put option. A Johnson & Johnson put option with a strike price of $50 expiring in January of the next year can be bought for $275 plus commissions (for a put option contract for 100 shares).

This strategy locks in the existing profits if Johnson & Johnson stock declines back down to $38 per share. However, if Johnson & Johnson stock continues to rise in price, all that the investor has lost is the premium of $275 plus the commissions to buy the put option. This concept can be viewed as an insurance premium to protect profits against a decline in the price of the stock.

∎ The Use of a Combination of Puts and Calls

As investors get more sophisticated in their use of options, there are situations where a combination of puts and calls can be combined for profit opportunities. A _straddle_ is the use of a put and a call with the same strike price whereas a _spread_ is a combination of put and call options with different strike prices.

The following example illustrates how an investor can profit from using a straddle. Suppose an investor is interested in buying some oil stocks, but with the potential political problems in Nigeria and the possibility of Iraq being allowed back to supplying oil on the world markets, the investor is not sure whether the price of oil will go up or down.

Consequently, instead of buying oil stocks, the investor could buy a combination call and put option on an oil stock. Options on Exxon, whose stock is currently trading at $59 7/8 per share, can be bought as follows:

∎ $2 3/8 ($237.50 per contract) for a January call with a strike price of $60.

■ $2 3/8 ($237.50 per contract) for a January put with a strike price of $60.

The total cost of this straddle is $475.00 ($237.50 + $237.50) plus commissions, which means that the greatest potential loss is limited to this cost if Exxon stock does not rise above $64 3/4 or below $55 1/4 per share in the next six months before expiration.

If there is a Nigerian oil strike, the price of oil would likely be driven up and oil stocks could jump in price. Assume that Exxon stock goes up to $68 per share: the call option could be sold around $800 ($8 × 100 shares), resulting in a profit for the investor. If on the other hand a strike does not take place and Iraq comes back into the worldwide supply of oil, oil stock prices could fall. If Exxon stock falls to $53 per share, the put option could be sold for around $7 per share, resulting in a profit from selling this option.

If Exxon stock trades above $64.75 or below $55.25, the investor will profit from selling the call or put options, respectively. If Exxon trades within the $55.25 to $64.75 range, the investor will lose money on the straddle. The amount of the loss will depend on the price of Exxon stock. For example, if the investor sold the call option when Exxon stock was trading at $63.50, the option could be sold around $3.50, or $350 per contract. The loss would then be $125 (the cost of the straddle options, $475, minus the proceeds received from the sale of the option, $350). Commissions will increase the loss further.

This example illustrates the use of a straddle. To profit from this combination, the price of the underlying stock has to move considerably in either direction, upwards or downwards.

■ Writing Options

Investors may also write or sell options, which provide additional income through the premiums received from the buyers. However, the upside potential is limited for option writers because the most they can make is the option premium.

Options may be written two ways. The more conservative method is to write covered options. A _covered option_ is when the writer of the option owns the stock against which the options are sold. The second method is called _naked option writing_ and this entails selling an option on a stock that is not owned by the writer/seller.

Writing Covered Calls

The writing of covered calls is used by investors who seek ways to increase their income on stocks they already own. This works the same way as a call except that the writer owns the stock. An example illustrates how writing covered calls work.

Suppose an investor has 1,000 shares of Citicorp stock that was purchased some time back at $30 per share. Citicorp is currently selling around $44.50 per share. Instead of selling the stock outright, the investor can write call options on Citicorp. If the investor writes 10 call contracts of 100 shares per contract with a strike price of $45 at a premium of $3 ($3,000 for 10 contracts) with an April expiration, he or she will receive $3,000 minus commissions.

If Citicorp stock never reaches $45 per share before expiration, the buyer will not exercise the call and the writer will come away with an additional $3,000 minus commissions.

If the stock price rises above $45 per share, the buyer exercises the call and buys the stock for $45 per share. The writer makes a profit of $18 per share ($45 minus the $30 cost of the shares plus the $3 per share premium). This is the maximum profit that the writer will get from the covered call option, even if Citicorp rises to $100 per share. This additional appreciation will be lost because the writer must surrender the stock at the strike price of $45.

Summing up, a covered call limits the appreciation the writer can realize. Therefore, it is a good idea to write covered calls on stocks you think will not rise or fall very much in price. The other side of the coin is that if the stock falls significantly in price during the option period, the writer will lose money if the writer eventually sells the stock at the low price. The call buyer will not exercise the call because the market price of the stock will be cheaper than the strike price.

Writing Naked Calls

Writing a naked call on a stock is more risky than writing a covered call because of the potential for unlimited losses. A naked call is when the writer does not own the underlying stock, which would limit the losses if the stock rocketed up in price. For example, assume that a writer writes a naked call on Citicorp stock for which the writer receives a premium of $3 per share with a strike price of $45 per share. If Citicorp rises dramatically to $60 per share and the option buyer exercises the call, the writer will be left with a large loss. The writer will receive $45 per share (the strike price) plus the premium price of $3 per share, but he or she will also have to pay $60 per share to buy the stock to deliver to the buyer. Of course, if the writer had anticipated the rise in price, he or she could have bought Citicorp earlier at a lower price or bought back the option to close out his or her position.

Writers of naked (or uncovered) options, calls and puts must deposit the required margins with their brokerage firms, whereas writers of covered options need not deposit any money with their brokerage firms.

Investors can profit from writing naked calls on stocks whose prices either decline or remain relatively flat. Writers of covered calls will benefit by receiving the premium without the call ever being exercised in the period before expiry.

Writing Covered Puts

A put is the opposite of a call. The writer of a covered put receives a premium in return for having to possibly buy back the shares of the underlying company at the strike price. The writer can also close out the contract by buying back the put.

For example, assume that an investor owns Citicorp stock that is trading at $44.50 per share—well above the purchase price. The investor thinks the stock will continue to rise and writes a covered put option at $40 for a premium of $1.50 ($150 for a 100 share contract). If Citicorp stock stays above $40 per share, the put will not be exercised and the writer gains from the premium income of $150 for the contract. If the stock falls below $40 per share, the writer must either buy the stock back from the buyer if exercised or buy back the put to close out the contract. The latter action will reduce the writer's profit or result in a loss, depending on the premium price paid to buy back the put.

Writing Naked Puts

If the put writer does not own the underlying stock, the contract is a naked or uncovered put, which necessitates that the writer deposit an amount of money with the brokerage firm for the required margin. Thus, without owning the underlying stocks the potential loss is not cushioned if the price of the stock falls rapidly.

For example, if an investor writes a naked put on Citicorp with a strike price of $40 and Citicorp falls to $30 per share, the writer would have to buy Citicorp at $40 at exercise. If the writer is bearish on the stock or needs the money, he or she would sell the stock at the market price of $30, resulting in an immediate loss of $10 per share.

What Are the Advantages of Options?

∎ Options allow investors to speculate on the future direction of the price of a stock by investing a relatively small amount of money.

∎ Investors can use options as insurance to hedge against large losses from adverse changes in stock prices.

∎ Writing options provides a source of income for investors.

∎ The losses from buying options are limited to the amount of the premium.

What Are the Disadvantages of Options?

∎ Options are wasting assets in that they have short lives (up to nine months). LEAPs have longer lives.

∎ If the price of the stock does not reach or go beyond the strike price, the option investor will lose money.

Caveats

Although options may be used to produce relatively large percentage profits from the small amounts invested, investors need to be aware that commissions tend to be high on a percentage basis. Therefore, these should always be considered before money is committed to options.

It is a good idea to test various pricing possibilities on paper to see the potential gains or losses before taking a position using options. The use of options is not without risks, and should not be used as a tool for investing by beginning investors.

∎ Rights

Rights have some similar features to stock options, particularly call options. Stock rights are issued to existing shareholders on a stated date. A stock right allows current shareholders to buy more common stock of the company in advance of the public at a discounted price (subscription price). It is also known as a preemptive right.

If a corporation has a preemptive rights clause in its charter, it must give its existing shareholders the opportunity to maintain their proportionate ownership percentages in the company when new shares are sold.

Generally, each share of stock receives one right. Thus, if an existing shareholder owned 10,000 shares of common stock, that shareholder would receive 10,000 rights during a rights offering. The board of directors determine the number of rights needed to buy each new share.

For instance, if a company has 200,000 shares outstanding and it plans a new issue of 50,000 shares, the number of rights needed to buy each new share of common stock is four, calculated as follows:

$$\text{Number of Rights to Buy a New Share} = \frac{\text{Number of Shares Outstanding}}{\text{Number of New Shares Offered}}$$

$$= \frac{200,000}{50,000}$$

$$= 4$$

This gives existing shareholders the opportunity to maintain their same proportionate ownership in the company after the new issue of common stock. If a shareholder has 20,000 shares before the new issue with a 10 percent ownership of the company (20,000/200,000), the rights offering of the new shares will entitle this shareholder the right to buy 5,000 new shares (20,000 rights /4 rights per share). After the new share issue, this shareholder will have the opportunity to retain his or her 10 percent share of ownership in the company (25,000/250,000).

To be eligible to buy these additional shares at the subscription price, the common stock of the company must be owned as of the record date set by the board of directors. Most rights offerings have a short period of time (between two and six weeks) for existing shareholders to either subscribe to the new shares or sell the rights. It is during this period that the stock is said to be trading *cum rights,* where the value of the right is included in the market price of the stock. After a specified date, known as the *ex-rights date,* stock transactions do not include the rights. Theoretically, the stock price goes down after this date when the rights trade separately.

Rights of the larger companies trade on the stock exchanges, same as their stocks; those of the smaller companies are traded on the over-the-counter markets where those companies' stocks trade.

Like an option, the value of a right depends on the market price of the stock; the subscription price of the right; and the number of rights necessary to buy each new share. There is a formula to determine the value of the rights before they trade independently of the stock.

$$\text{Cum Rights Value} = \frac{\text{Market Price of Stock} - \text{Subscription Price}}{\text{Number of Rights to Buy a Share} + 1}$$

Suppose a stock whose market price is $20 is offered at a subscription price of $14 and five rights are needed to purchase each new share; the cum right value is $1.00 ($20 - 14)/6.

After the stock goes ex-rights, its price declines by the value of the right, as the rights trade separately from the stock. In this example, the market price of the stock would decline from $20 to $19 per share. Investors who want to buy the rights can purchase them on the market in the same way that they can purchase the stock. The ex-rights value is calculated as follows:

$$\text{Ex–rights Value} = \frac{\text{Market Price of Stock} - \text{Subscription Price}}{\text{Number of Rights Needed to Buy a Share}}$$

$$= \frac{\$19 - 14}{5}$$

$$= \$1.00$$

This happens to be the same price as the cum rights value. In reality, the market value of the right will fluctuate as the market price of the stock changes, but it will not deviate very far from its theoretical value (calculated with the formula above).

When the price of the stock rises, the value of the right will also increase but at a larger percentage rate due to the leverage factor. A two-point increase in the stock will cause the right to increase by $0.40, which is a 40 percent increase. Leverage also works in reverse when the price of the stock falls. A small decrease in the price of the stock would result in a greater percentage decline in the value of the right.

Rights, like options, may be bought for one of two reasons: either to exercise their rights or to speculate on their rights. This then leads to the question many rights owners ask, When should you sell your rights?

The value of the right is linked to the price of the stock, but owners are also acutely aware of the short period of time before their rights expire. This almost implies that prices of rights may be higher earlier in the subscription period. Theoretically, the closer the expiration date, the greater will be the decline to the value of the right.

Rights offer their holders distinct advantages:

■ The ability to buy more common stock at a discounted price.

■ The ability to maintain their same ownership position in the company when more shares are sold.

■ The opportunity to profit from trading the rights.

The disadvantage is that with the short life of the right, the investor needs to act before the right expires.

Bearing this in mind, beginning investors should not plunge into the speculative aspects of trading rights. This should be left for more experienced investors.

■ Warrants

A warrant is like an option in that it gives the owner the right to buy a stated number of shares of the underlying company's stock at a specific price within a specific period of time. There are some differences from options, in that with warrants the specified price may be fixed or it may rise at certain intervals, such as every five years, and the expiration date may also be extended by the company.

Warrants have longer lives than options. An option may have a life of nine months; warrants extend for years, and some companies have issued perpetual warrants. Generally, there is a waiting period before warrants can be exercised.

Warrants are issued by companies as a sweetener with other securities of the company. They may be attached to bonds or preferred stocks. In some cases, warrants have been distributed to shareholders in place of stock or cash dividends.

Attaching warrants to a new bond issue or preferred stock issue may make the issue more marketable to potential investors. If the warrants are not detachable, they can be exercised or sold along with the bond or preferred stock (almost like convertible bonds or convertible preferred stock).

If the warrant is detachable, it will trade separately on the markets or over-the-counter. Stock warrants are quoted along with the stocks in the stock markets where their respective company's stocks trade. Investors can follow the prices of the warrants in the stock market sections of the newspapers. With detachable warrants, investors may sell the warrants for a profit and still retain the underlying security (bond or preferred stock). However, in order to profit from the sale of the warrants, they will need to have some value.

When warrants are issued by the company, the purchase price of the stock is generally fixed at a higher price than the market price of the stock at issue. For instance, if a company floats a new bond issue with detachable warrants that gives the holders the rights to buy the common stock of the company at $25 per share when the market price of the stock is only $15 per share, the warrants will have no intrinsic value. However, if the market price of the stock rises to $32 per share, the warrant will have an intrinsic value of $7 ($32 – $25).

If the market price of the stock never rises to the strike price of the warrant during its life, it will never be exercised and will expire.

The major advantage of warrants over options is that warrants have a longer life. Warrants do well when stock prices are rising, but investors should still be selective about the warrants that they buy. If the stock never goes up in price, there is little to no opportunity to profit from buying the warrants. Generally, as with options, warrants should be bought to trade and not to exercise. All brokerage firms have lists of the warrants trading on the markets.

∎ Conclusion

Investors can use stock derivatives and stock equivalents to take advantage of their positions in the market. Investors who are bullish in their perspectives on individual stocks and the markets have long positions. Options, rights and warrants offer greater leverage than most other investments. These derivative securities are additional tools, which, if used carefully and at the right time, can help investors to not only increase their profits but to protect existing profits and limit their losses.

Chapter 11

Investing in Foreign Stocks

Key Concepts
- Why Invest in Foreign Stocks?
- The Risks of Foreign Stocks
- How to Invest in Foreign Stocks
- Is International Investing Good for Me?

Investing in international stocks has become very much easier and more popular with many investors. European, Asian and Latin American stock markets have provided investors with tremendous growth opportunities not matched by the American markets in recent years. This process of investing abroad has been facilitated by technology. With computerization, there is an almost instantaneous flow of information about financial events. A precipitous decline in the Hang Sen Index on the Hong Kong Stock Exchange will impact not only the other Asian stock markets but also the European and American stock markets. Similarly, an early morning rally on Wall Street can spur stock markets in Europe to close at higher levels.

Thus, while economic and financial events around the world may be interconnected and move stock markets in the same direction at several points over time, there is a low correlation to this movement over a longer period.

▌ Why Invest in Foreign Stocks?

There are several compelling reasons why investors should consider adding foreign stocks to their portfolios. Foreign stocks as a group have outperformed U.S. stocks during the period 1988 through 1993 (as measured by the Morgan Stanley Capital International EAFE

[Europe, Australia, Far East] Index versus the Standard & Poor's 500 Stock Index). Moreover, there will always be some equity markets abroad that will outperform U.S. stocks in any particular year. Because economic cycles in different countries move separately from each other, investors can take advantage of the different stock market situations. This is indeed confirmed by the fact that the majority of the stocks traded in the world originate outside of the United States.

Investing in foreign stocks gives investors the opportunity to diversify their portfolios, which reduces the overall risks and volatility of the portfolio. If the stocks in one country go down, there is a good chance the stocks in another country will go up to even out the variability in stock prices.

Investing in foreign stocks provides a hedge against a slump in the U.S. stock market or any other economic woes such as inflation or rising interest rates. The same factors apply to foreign stock prices as they do to American stock prices. The earnings and economic health of the company is reflected in the stock price as well as the economic and political conditions of the country.

∎ The Risks of Foreign Stocks

Investors need to understand the additional risks they face from investing in foreign stocks. As mentioned earlier, all companies face business and financial risks, but additional risks pertain to foreign stocks.

Currency fluctuations can adversely affect the value of the stock for U.S. investors. If the value of the foreign currency moves sharply relative to the U.S. dollar, the value of the stock will either produce spectacular gains or very large losses, even if the stock price remains unchanged.

Initially when buying foreign stocks, dollars are converted into the foreign currency of the stock. When the stock is sold, the proceeds in that currency are converted back into dollars. For example, the dollar has recently fallen against the Japanese yen, which has provided rather large gains for U.S. investors in Japanese stocks. However, if the dollar strengthens against the yen, these gains could be reversed.

Political risk is another important factor. The Sao Paulo stock market in Brazil plunged over 50 percent during the early part of 1994 when the socialist presidential candidate showed an initial lead in the polls. Thereafter, when the conservative candidate took the lead, the Brazilian stock market soared. The Mexican Bolsa was also badly shaken not only by the assassination of the leading presidential candidate before the elections, but also by the peasant uprising.

Many foreign countries tend to be less stable politically than the United States, and any political upheavals in these countries can erode foreign investments.

Another factor facing foreign investors is the information gap. Foreign companies whose shares are not traded on the U.S. stock exchanges do not have to follow U.S. accounting and reporting standards. For these foreign companies, information may be scarce, and even if there are reports in the financial newspapers interested investors can miss them because they may not be feature news items.

Foreign companies whose stocks trade as ADRs (American Depository Receipts, explained in the next section of this chapter) on the U.S. exchanges are required to recast their financial statements using U.S. accounting standards. This can explain some of the differences in the reporting of accounting standards of foreign countries. When Daimler Benz, the German auto company, requested a listing on the U.S. exchange, it reported profits of $294 million in Germany. When their financial statements were converted to the U.S. generally accepted accounting principles, the profit was reduced by $60 million (Glasgall and Lindorff, 102). With less information available on foreign companies and different accounting procedures, investment decision making on foreign stocks becomes more complex than investing in American stocks.

Quotes on some of the thinly traded foreign stocks (and the pink sheet ADRs) may be difficult to get, which may make it difficult to buy and sell at predetermined prices. However, this is changing as more of the computer on-line services go global.

These risks need to be weighed against the advantages of investing in foreign stocks. Despite the foreign exchange risks, over the long term foreign stocks can balance a portfolio in terms of safety and can increase overall returns.

■ How to Invest in Foreign Stocks

American investors have been scrambling to invest globally at a time when the U.S. stock market has stagnated and foreign stock markets have been flourishing. There are a number of different ways for U.S. investors to invest abroad:

   ■ Buy foreign stocks listed on foreign exchanges.

∎ Buy foreign stocks trading in dollars as ADRs (American Depository Receipts).

∎ Invest in international and global mutual funds.

∎ Invest in country funds, run mostly by closed-end mutual funds.

Foreign Stocks on Foreign Exchanges

Investors can buy shares of foreign companies that list on foreign exchanges, which is the riskiest of the four methods to invest internationally. The additional risks, over and above those mentioned in the previous section, include the differences in trading regulations of foreign brokers and their exchanges. There is very little recourse open to U.S. investors as to the protection of their investments from unscrupulous practices in these countries. High fees (transaction costs and other additional fees such as foreign withholdings taxes) may be imposed, which could erode potential profits. In addition, lags in time and information may make it difficult for investors to determine when to buy and sell. Without the benefits of obtaining daily information about these foreign companies and industries, investors may not be able to make timely transaction decisions. This pertains particularly to those companies whose stocks are not quoted in the U.S. newspapers in the Foreign Stock Quotes section.

For example, some of the smaller South African mining companies that are quoted on the Johannesburg Stock Exchange in rands (the local currency) are not reported in the U.S. financial newspapers. With the lack of daily information (unless a call is placed on a daily basis to the foreign broker), an investor may miss out on selling the stock at the high price. For example, the lack of information about South African mine strikes and the daily ups and downs in the price of a mining stock resulted in an investor selling at a low price after the stock had plummeted from its highs of the year.

Buying foreign stocks listed on foreign exchanges should be left for the more experienced investors who are knowledgeable not only about these foreign companies and their industries, but who also have access to daily information about them and are familiar with the different trading practices. Japanese stocks, for instance, trade at very much higher Price/Earnings multiples than American stocks, and industry statistics in foreign countries are not easy to come by. It is difficult enough for most investors to select stocks trading on the American exchanges; direct investment in foreign stocks can be like navigating a mine field in the dark riding on the back of an elephant.

Investors should be aware that on some foreign exchanges, manipulation of share prices may be quite common by the brokerage firms.

Buying Foreign Stocks Trading as ADRs

An easier way to invest in foreign stocks is to buy American depository receipts (ADRs) or shares of foreign companies traded in U.S. dollars. ADRs are negotiable receipts that represent ownership of the shares of foreign companies traded on the American securities markets. The ADRs are issued by American banks who hold in trust the shares representing the ADRs. Each ADR certificate represents a percentage ownership of the securities held in trust. For example, a Glaxo Holdings ADR share traded on the NYSE represents two shares of Glaxo common stock traded on the London Stock Exchange. In this case, one ADR represents two shares of Glaxo common stock. The terms of ADRs are negotiated by the banks when they are originally issued.

ADRs work in the following way: when a broker gets an order to buy 100 shares of an ADR such as Glaxo Holdings, the British pharmaceutical company, the broker will pass this order on to either the brokerage firm's London trading desk or another British firm's trading desk. The foreign firm will buy the stock, which is then deposited with the custodian bank. The custodian bank authorizes the American depository bank to issue an ADR certificate, which is then sent to the brokerage firm. The broker sends the certificate to the investor, in the same way as it would be done for the purchase of a domestic stock.

For actively traded ADRs, brokers don't need to fill the orders from abroad, as there are so many ADR certificates in circulation in the United States. Large brokerage firms can often match the buy and sell orders of the large, actively traded ADRs from their own inventories. When selling ADRs, the process described above is completed in reverse.

ADRs give U.S. investors the opportunity of buying and selling foreign companies' stocks with the same ease as the stocks of U.S. companies. ADR buy and sell transactions are completed in the same period of time (five days) as it takes for American stocks. The settlement period will be three days after June 1, 1995.

ADR holders have voting rights and may participate in the rights offerings if the company registers with the SEC. If the company does not register with the SEC, the ADR bank will sell the rights and remit the value to the ADR shareholders.

There are two forms of ADRs: sponsored and unsponsored. Sponsored ADRs are those issued through banks by the foreign companies that have registered with the SEC. Unsponsored ADRs are of those companies that have not fully registered with the SEC; their shares trade on the over-the-counter markets.

Even though investors can trade ADRs on the markets as easily as they can domestic stocks, they are still exposed to many of the risks outlined earlier. ADRs trade in dollars on the U.S. markets, which eliminates the need to exchange dollars for a foreign currency. However, the value of the ADR is influenced by exchange rates. When the dollar declines relative to a foreign currency, that company's stock is worth more when converted to dollars. Conversely, when the value of the dollar increases, the foreign currency is worth less. When dividends are paid, the issuing bank will receive them and distribute them to the ADR holders, minus their fees.

Information on the companies issuing ADRs is increasing due to the increasing demands of U.S. investors to diversify their portfolios (see Table 11–1 for a list of some of the ADR stocks). However, information on these companies is still not as readily available as it is for domestic companies.

International Mutual Funds

An even easier way to invest internationally is through mutual funds that specialize in foreign investments. Investors invest in international mutual funds in the same way as they choose domestic stock and bond funds. International mutual funds invest in the stocks of foreign countries.

Some funds have a mixture of countries, including the shares of U.S. companies. Depending on their mix of foreign holdings, mutual funds may be classified as follows: international, global, regional and country.

International funds invest in the securities of companies whose stocks trade on foreign exchanges. *Global funds,* as the name implies, invest in securities around the world, including those of U.S. companies. *Regional funds* specialize in the securities of companies located in a specified geographic area of the world. For example, there are funds that specialize in the Pacific Rim area, Latin America, Europe and the emerging economies. Many of these may be closed-end funds that trade on the exchanges as opposed to the open-end mutual funds that are bought and sold through the investment companies or through brokers, in the case of load funds. Only *country funds* invest in the securities of a specified country. Examples of these are Japan funds,

Table 11–1   Some Selected ADRS

Company	Country	Industry	Symbol	Exchange
American Barrick	Canada	Gold Mining	ABX	NYSE
Buffelsfontein	South Africa	Gold Mining	BFELY	OTC
Coca-Cola Femsa	Mexico	Beverage	KOF	NYSE
Ericsson Telephone	Sweden	Telecommunications	ERICY	OTC
Fuji Photo Film	Japan	Photographic	FUJIY	OTC
Gambro	Switzerland	Drugs	GAMBY	OTC
Glaxo Holdings	Britain	Drugs	GLX	NYSE
Royal Dutch Petrol	Netherlands	Oil	RD	NYSE
St. Helena Gold	South Africa	Gold Mining	SGOLY	OTC

Spain funds, Portugal funds, Switzerland funds, Chile funds and India funds. As with regional funds, there are open-end and closed-end funds.

Open-end mutual funds and closed-end funds are discussed in detail in Chapters 8 and 9, respectively. Investors should be aware of the nuances, risks, advantages and disadvantages between these types of funds before they invest.

One of the advantages of choosing mutual funds over investing in individual foreign stocks is that with a mutual fund, the investor owns a part of a broadly diversified portfolio. To obtain such diversity with individual stocks would require enormous amounts of money. International funds offer more diversity of investments than sector and country funds. However, when the markets of sector and country funds are "hot," they can easily outperform the more broadly diversified international funds. The converse is true when these markets slump. For instance, in 1993 investments in funds specializing in the Pacific Rim region outperformed the international funds, as the stock markets in Hong Kong, Singapore and Malaysia reached their peaks. With the downturn in these markets in the early part of 1994, there were large declines in the Pacific Rim funds, whereas many of the more broadly diversified international funds posted more stable results.

The results of the international, global, regional and country funds will depend on the holdings of the fund. If the bulk of an international fund's holdings are concentrated in the European countries, that fund may not experience the benefits of worldwide diversification. European economies are somewhat connected and may have similar economic cycles. However, many international and global funds concentrate on certain sectors of the globe.

Investors should request a prospectus from the fund with a list of the fund's country holdings. By identifying the mix of stocks in the different countries, an investor can allocate investments on a geographical basis. For example, an investor who wants a broadly diversified portfolio might have to invest in a few different international mutual funds to get this broad diversification.

Investing in international mutual funds is advantageous for investors who do not have the time or the inclination to research individual foreign stocks. The portfolio managers of these funds will select the foreign stocks after researching the companies and economic climates of the countries.

Another advantage of investing in funds over individual foreign stocks is that portfolio managers of international funds may be able to reduce the risks of unfavorable currency fluctuations by using hedging strategies. These involve the use of foreign currency options and futures contracts.

Not all international funds use these strategies, while some use them only on an occasional basis. The objective of international investing is to invest in not only those foreign stocks that will go up in price but also to take advantage of the devaluation of the dollar relative to these currencies. Thus, due to the costs of these contracts to hedge currency positions, these strategies can also limit the potential gains in a portfolio as well as limit the potential losses.

For long-term investors in foreign stocks and/or funds, the currency effects tend to even out over long periods of time.

Investors need to be aware of the objectives of the fund, the stated returns and risks, and the fees charged. These all need to be in conformity with the investor's overall objectives.

Country Funds

Country funds specialize in the securities of a particular country. Country funds can be open-end or closed-end, but the majority of country funds offered are closed-end. Examples of these are the Korea fund; Italy fund; Thai fund; Japan fund; and ASA Limited which specializes in the South African gold mining companies.

Many of the securities in these portfolios are thinly traded stocks, which points to an advantage of choosing a closed-end fund over an open-end country fund. With closed-end funds, portfolio managers do not have to sell stocks in their portfolios to meet the redemption needs of their shareholders. The number of shares is fixed at the initial offering, and they subsequently trade on the exchanges or the over-the-counter markets. Open-end portfolio managers have to sell some of their portfolio holdings to raise the cash to buy back the shares of the shareholders at the net asset value.

Closed-end funds may trade at large discounts or premiums to their net asset values, depending on the supply and demand for their stocks and other factors. Potential investors in closed-end funds should be aware of the net asset values so that they do not end up buying a fund that is trading at a healthy premium over the net asset value.

Country funds make it very easy for investors to invest in markets about which they have very little knowledge and information. For instance, stock markets in Turkey, India, New Zealand, South Africa and Singapore have recently outperformed many other markets. For investors who do not have the time or inclination to research these markets for promising stocks, there is the convenience of a county fund. However, in selecting country funds, investors still need to be aware of the country's potential economic outlook, political stability and the exchange rates. Country funds are specialized to those countries and as a result may be quite volatile.

When the Japanese stock market rose to its 10-year high, Japanese country funds were trading at large premiums to their net asset values. Currently, the Japanese stock market has fallen, and Japanese country funds are trading at more realistic values. When the prime minister of India was assassinated in 1991, India funds took a nosedive.

To achieve adequate international diversification and even out the risks of loss, investors should consider investing in several country funds in different countries or regions of the world.

■ Is International Investing Good for Me?

Foreign investments involve additional risks to those facing domestic investments. The risks of loss from political turmoil and/or currency exchange rates can wipe out any profits and produce losses on foreign investments that were carefully selected using the most up-to-date information available.

The difficulty in obtaining information about individual foreign securities may prompt many American investors to use mutual funds to make their foreign investments. Global and international mutual funds minimize some of the business, financial, economic, and political risks by investing in a broadly diversified portfolio of investments around the world. An investment in the more specialized regional and country funds has increased risks and rewards.

Investors need to weigh the risks against the potential returns. Overseas stock markets have over various periods of time outperformed the American stock markets. Thus, over long periods of time, investors should be rewarded, assuming that worldwide growth and trade continues. By diversifying your investments to cover many different economies, you are helping to even out the fluctuations in your overall portfolio and participating in the larger returns of the faster-growing foreign economies.

Investors who do not want to take the added risks of foreign investments might consider diversifying their portfolios to include the common stocks of U.S. multinational corporations. Corporations such as Pepsi Cola, Coca Cola, McDonalds, Exxon and General Motors achieve a large percentage of their sales and earnings outside the United States. Thus, if the American economy slumps, their financial results may be cushioned by their foreign operations.

Investors who can tolerate the additional risks of foreign investments should invest directly in foreign stocks or indirectly through international mutual funds.

∎ References

Glasgall, William and Dave Lindorff. "The Global Investor," *Business Week* (September 19, 1994): 96–104.

Chapter 12

Portfolio Management*

Key Concepts:

▌ Investor's Objectives

▌ Characteristics of the Investor

▌ Asset Allocation

▌ Selection of Individual Investments

▌ Portfolio Management

Managing a portfolio can mean different things to different people. For some people, it means buying the most conservative investments and holding them through maturity or indefinitely. At the other extreme are those investors who are busy changing their investments on a regular basis.

Managing a portfolio has some analogies to managing your health. Eating healthy foods and exercising regularly works well for people who are in good health. However, for a person who has a major illness or something chronically wrong, healthy foods, exercise and good health alone won't rectify the overall problem.

Similarly, managing a portfolio of investments means assembling those investment securities that together will perform to achieve the investor's overall objectives. When this has been accomplished, the investor can sit back and eat an apple a day while monitoring the securities in the portfolio. However, in another scenario, if the investment assets are haphazardly chosen and the investor has not set objectives

---

* Portions of this chapter have been previously published by Esmé Faerber in *All About Bonds*, published by Probus Publishing Company, 1993.

229

or goals for the portfolio, there is no way of telling how well or badly this portfolio is doing. It can be likened to a walk in space and you don't know where you are drifting to, which means that you will not have a clue where you will end up.

Knowing what you want to accomplish from your investments allows you to manage your portfolio effectively. Buying and selling investments is relatively easy, but knowing what to buy and sell is more difficult. In essence, the choice of assets to hold is determined by the investor's objectives and personal characteristics.

∎ Investor's Objectives

The investor's objectives will determine the purpose and time period for the investments. For instance, one investor may be saving for retirement in 5 years time and another investor may be saving for retirement in 30 years time. Although their objectives may be the same (saving for retirement) the time period and elements of risk tolerance are very different.

Thus, the first step in any plan is to determine long-range, medium-range and short-range objectives. For example, a young family with small children may have the following objectives:

Short-Range:
— Capacity to meet financial emergencies.
— Need for additional income.
— Save for a vacation.

Medium-Range:
— Save for a down payment on a house.
— Buy a new car.

Long-Range:
— Save for children's education.
— Save for retirement.

Once objectives have been developed, it becomes easier to see what the investor can aim for from the portfolio. Before setting a strategy to achieve these objectives, investors should examine their personal circumstances, which will serve as a guide in the selection of the portfolio assets.

■ Characteristics of the Investor

The characteristics of the investor are important because they will define the level of risk the investor can absorb.

Marital Status:	single, married, widower
Family:	no children, young children, teenage children, empty nest
Age:	under 25, 25–39, 40–60, over 60
Education:	high school graduate, college degree, graduate degree
Income:	stable and level, future growth prospects
Job/Profession:	skills and expertise, ability to improve level of earnings
Net Worth/Size of Portfolio:	level of income, assets, and net worth will determine the size of the portfolio.

These variables will determine the types of investments and the level of risk that can be absorbed in the development and management of the portfolio. For example, a nonworking widow who depends entirely on income generated from her investments will not be able to tolerate the high risks of investments in junk bonds, small company growth stocks or newly issued public offerings of common stocks. This portfolio of assets would need to generate income but not at the expense of capital preservation.

Likewise, the sole breadwinner of a young family may be risk-averse, but the circumstances may allow for more emphasis on growth assets. A prosperous litigation lawyer can withstand more risk aimed at expanding capital (net worth) rather than generating current income.

Thus, depending on the investor's characteristics, there will be a trade-off between assets generating current income and assets seeking capital appreciation. If investors opt for capital appreciation assets, they may sacrifice on current income.

▮ Asset Allocation

Asset allocation is a plan to invest in different types of securities so that the capital invested is protected against adverse factors in the marketplace. This, in essence, is the opposite of putting all your eggs in one basket. Imagine an investor with $200,000 to invest who had invested it all in IBM stock bought at $100 per share a few years ago. The value of the portfolio currently would have been cut in half to $100,000, as IBM was trading at $50 per share. Currently, IBM has risen to $69 per share, which is still a hefty loss.

Developing a portfolio is generally based on the idea of holding a variety of investments rather than concentrating on a single investment. This is to reduce the risks of loss and even out the returns of the different investments. The latter point can be illustrated with the following hypothetical example of a portfolio.

	Total Investment
Assume the investor buys:	
1,000 shares of XYZ Co. at $50 per share	$50,000
and 100 convertible bonds of ABC Co. at $1,000 per bond	100,000
	$150,000

A year later, the portfolio is valued as follows:

1,000 shares of XYZ Co. at $70 per share	$ 70,000
and 100 convertible bonds of ABC Co. at $800 per bond	80,000
	$150,000

The investor has spread the risks of loss by owning two different types of securities as well as averaging the returns of the two types of investments. Certainly the investor would have done very much better had he invested totally in XYZ shares, but hindsight always produces the highest returns. The fact that we are not clairvoyant points to the benefits of diversifying across a broad segment of investments. In other words, diversification seeks a balance between the risk-return trade-off (discussed in Chapter 2).

Diversification is achieved by selecting a portfolio of investments of different types of securities in different industries. For example, investing in the stocks and bonds of General Motors, Ford and Chrysler hardly achieves any diversification. By carefully selecting at least the stocks of 6–10 different companies in different industries and/or investing in equity mutual funds, some of the risks of loss on any one security (or fund) will be evened out.

Classifying some of the types of investments on a continuum of risk, we see that common stocks are considered the most risky (in terms of variability in share price), followed by long-term bonds, with the shorter maturities on the low-risk end. Bear in mind that there are many other types of investments that are riskier than common stocks, such as commodities, futures contracts and options. Similarly, there is a great variation of quality among common stocks. The common stocks of the well-established, blue-chip companies are considered less risky than the bonds of highly leveraged companies with suspect balance sheets.

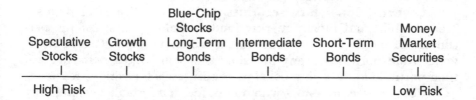

Common stocks are considered the most risky due to the volatility of stock prices. However, over long periods of time where the ups and downs of the stock market can be waited out, stocks have provided higher returns (see Chapter 2). Common stocks provide the growth in a portfolio and should be included among the investments. The percentage allocated to common stocks will depend on the investor's objectives and personal characteristics. As mentioned earlier, a retired widow who is dependent on the income generated from the investments in the portfolio may have a small percentage allocated to common stocks. However, if the portfolio generates more than a sufficient level of income for the widow's current needs, a larger portion of the portfolio could be invested in common stocks to provide more growth in the portfolio for later years.

Bonds are sought by investors primarily for their ability to generate a steady stream of income. However, what is often overlooked is that long-term bonds (15- to 30-year maturities) can also be quite risky. Although 30-year U.S. Treasury bonds are safe investments in that the U.S. Government is not liable to default on the interest and principal payments, they can be quite volatile in price due to changes in interest rates. Corporate and other types of long-term bonds will be more volatile than Treasuries due to the increased risks of default.

Investors have to weigh the advantages of taking on the greater risks of investing in other types of long-term bonds over Treasuries by examining their coupon yields. If the yields are significantly greater than those of long-term Treasuries, investors may want to contemplate purchasing these other types of long-term bonds.

Some of the volatility in the price of bonds is reduced by shortening the maturities to intermediate-term bonds. Even though returns are reduced by shortening the length of time to maturity, intermediate-term bonds offer investors greater flexibility. For instance, if an investor's characteristics change and that investor no longer is dependent on current income from investments, intermediate-term securities are generally much more liquid than longer term bonds and can be more easily changed to more growth-oriented investments.

Low-risk, low-return securities such as certificates of deposit, Treasury bills and money market funds should account for the percentage of the investor's portfolio that will serve liquidity and emergency fund purposes. Many investors keep too large a percentage of their portfolio in these low-risk, low-return assets for various reasons.

Conservative investors who do not feel comfortable keeping only an amount equal to liquidity and emergency needs should increase the percentage. Often, however, the returns from these low-yielding investments over the years do not even keep pace with inflation without taking into account the effects of taxation on the interest.

There isn't a rigid formula for asset allocation. Rather, it is a good idea to think about the concept as a guideline when investing money. The percentage allocated to the different types of assets can always be changed, depending on circumstances. As individual circumstances change, so will the investor's objectives. If the emphasis shifts, for example, to greater income generation and preservation of capital from capital growth, the percentage of the investments in the portfolio can be changed accordingly.

An example of asset allocation for a young, childless couple, both of whom are working professionals, may look like this:

20%	Foreign stocks or international mutual funds
55%	Common stocks with emphasis on growth
15%	Intermediate term municipal bonds
10%	Money market securities
100%	

See Figure 12–1 for a further breakdown of the types of stocks in this portfolio.

However, when the wife decides to give up her career to stay home to care for an infant, the allocation of assets may change to provide for greater income generation. The portfolio might be altered to look like this:

15%	Foreign stocks/ mutual funds
30%	Common stocks with half invested in blue-chip companies and the rest in growth stocks
10%	Long-term bonds
30%	Intermediate term municipal bonds
15%	Money market securities
100%	

What may work for one couple may not work for another couple. Asset allocation depends very much on the investment objectives, the

Figure 12–1   Portfolio Allocation for a Couple Seeking Long-Term Growth

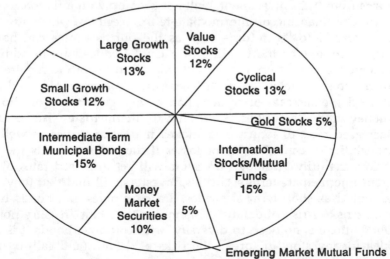

personal and financial situation of each investor and the total amount of the portfolio.

The most important aspect of investing is having an asset allocation plan that signifies the broad mix of assets to strive for. Once these broad categories are determined, the individual assets may be purchased.

▌ Selection of Individual Investments

In order to match your objectives with specific investments, you need to identify the characteristics of the different investments and their risks. Funds for immediate needs and emergency purposes should be liquid; in other words, able to be converted easily into cash without a loss in principal. These would be money market mutual funds, checking accounts and savings accounts. These are readily convertible into cash. By increasing the time horizon from immediate needs to short-term needs, investors can marginally increase their rates of return by investing in certificates of deposit, Treasury bills and commercial paper. However, of these only Treasury bills are marketable, which means that they can be sold on the secondary market before maturity.

These individual investments (savings accounts, certificates of deposit, money market mutual funds, Treasury bills, commercial paper) provide some taxable income, are liquid but not marketable (except for Treasury bills) and do not offer the possibilities of capital gains or losses. Although investors will not lose any of their principal by investing in this group of investments, there is a risk that the returns from these investments will not keep up with inflation.

The financing of intermediate-term objectives, which stretch several years into the future—such as the purchase of a car, house, or appliance and/or the funding of a child's education—in addition to emergency uses of funds that will crop up in the future require investments that are relatively safe. These investments would need to produce a greater rate of return than a savings account or short-term money market securities. Short-term to intermediate term bonds offer increased rates of return over money market securities as well as the possibility of capital gains or losses if the investor needs the money before maturity. Although investors will get increased rates of return from intermediate-term securities, investors will find that they are not as liquid as short-term securities. Treasury notes and bonds have no credit risk or risk of default. This means that with Treasury notes and bonds there is no need to diversify; with corporate bonds it is a good idea for investors to spread the risks of default (and call) by buying the bonds of different issuers. Similarly, it is a good idea to diversify when investing in municipal bonds and some of the smaller agency bonds.

Financing a child's education in five years requires a relatively safe investment. Most people would not gamble with the money earmarked for their children's education. Thus, the credit quality of the issuer is important. Similarly, if the yield differential between Treasuries and other types of intermediate bonds is not significant, it may be advantageous to stick with Treasury securities. This is not only because they are free of default risk, but their interest payments are tax-free at the state and local levels. However, if the yield differential of other types of bonds (agency bonds, corporate bonds and municipals) over Treasuries is large, investors should invest in these other bonds. Then again, it is important to choose a diversified portfolio rather than invest all the intermediate-term funds in the securities of one issuer. Federal taxes and changes in the individual tax rates may steer the investor towards municipal bonds.

Long-term objectives such as saving for retirement or an infant's college education in 18 years require investments that offer long-term growth prospects as well as greater returns. The level of risk that can be withstood on these investments will depend on the individual investor's circumstances.

A more conservative long-term portfolio would consist of long-term bonds, blue-chip stocks and conservative-growth stocks. The emphasis of this strategy is to invest in good quality bonds and the stocks of established companies that pay dividends and offer the prospect of steady growth over a long period of time. Securities offering capital growth are important even in conservative portfolios to provide some cover against any possible erosion in future purchasing power due to inflation.

A growth-oriented part of a portfolio would seek to generate long-term capital gains and growth in the value of the stocks. Investors would look for stocks in growth industries and identify the more dominant stocks in those industries.

A more speculative portfolio, where the investor can absorb greater levels of risk to strive for greater growth and returns, would include growth stocks; stocks of small, emerging companies; convertible bonds; junk bonds; real estate; options; commodities; and futures. By including the last three types of investments—options, commodities and futures—I am not advocating that these should play a major role in a portfolio. For a speculative investor who understands the nuances of these investments, these securities should account for no more than 5 percent of the total portfolio. Gambling in a casino is not included as an investment option! The other assets mentioned offer the investor the opportunity for large gains, but the risks of loss are also greater. Foreign bonds and stocks should also be considered, but investors should do their homework first so that they understand the risks fully. International mutual funds may be more helpful to spread some of the risks; although in the short-term there will always be currency risks when investing in off-shore investments. Over the long term, the exchange fluctuations tend to even out and would not be a significant factor.

Some investors may not feel comfortable buying individual bonds and stocks; they should stick with mutual funds. Investors willing to make their own investment decisions on individual securities can eliminate the fees and expenses charged by mutual funds. However, they would need to make sure that the brokerage commissions charged are discounted and competitive. Many full-service brokers will discount their commissions if they know that the investors have done their homework, and they will lose them to discount brokers if the commissions are not matched.

When considering the different types of securities to choose for a portfolio, investors should weigh the characteristics of the type of investment along with the risks. (See Table 12–1 for a summary of the strategies to reduce the different types of risks.)

∎ Portfolio Management

Investors need to be continually aware that not only do their objectives and individual characteristics change over time, but their investments need to be monitored due to changing financial conditions and markets. Companies change, and their securities may no longer fulfill the criteria they were purchased for. For example, IBM, which recently posted its largest loss in its history, is not the same company it was 10 years ago. IBM's securities (stocks and bonds), which were once considered as solid as a rock, might not be perceived in that light today in certain portfolios, despite the fact that the company seems to be on the rebound. Not all investments in the portfolio will realize their projected returns, so investors managing their portfolios will need to sell these and replace them with other investments. This does not mean that all or most of the investments in the portfolio should be continuously turned over. Only those investments that are not likely to achieve the goals specified should be liquidated.

The management of bond portfolios does not generally require as much attention as stock portfolios. In fact, bonds are much more con-

Table 12–1	Summary of Strategies to Manage Risk	
Investment	**Risk**	**Strategy**
Common Stock	Market Risk	Invest for a long period of time.
	Financial Risk	Diversification: Invest in companies with low leverage.
	Interest Rate Risk of Interest	Active or passive strategy, depending on the investor's time horizon.
	Declining Market Rates of Interest	Increase the percentage of the portfolio allocated to stocks.
	Increasing Market Rates	Decrease the percentage of the portfolio allocated to stocks.
	Credit Risk	Invest in good-quality stocks.
	Purchasing Power Risk (when inflation increases)	Requires active portfolio management. Invest in stocks that will weather the effects of inflation better, such as gold stocks and oil stocks

ducive to a passive management style because they pay a fixed stream of income and mature at a specified date. By selecting a convenient maturity date for the issue, the investor can wait until the issue matures to get back the principal. Not only does this strategy minimize transaction costs, it also makes fluctuations in the value of the issue before maturity meaningless. However, if the investor needs the money for any reason before maturity, the current market value would be important.

Many investors follow a more active management style than the buy-and-hold strategy, and they will continue to react to changing economic and financial conditions. Anticipating changes in interest rates could prompt investors to reallocate the types of investments in their portfolios. If higher rates of interest are anticipated, the investor has a number of different options. Profits may be taken by selling stocks that have appreciated, or the investor may decide to sell stocks in the interest-sensitive industries, such as financial stocks, cyclical sector stocks in the automotive and home building industries and utility stocks. Some investors may buy stocks in the pharmaceutical and food industries, which tend to weather the effects of higher market interest rates better than other sectors of the economy.

Other investors may decide to hold their existing stocks but not invest any new money in the stock market until interest rates start to level off. True market timers may liquidate their entire stock positions and wait on the sidelines for more favorable conditions.

Purchasing power risk or inflation hurts all financial investments to some degree or another. However, traditionally, returns on stocks tend to outperform those of bonds and money market securities during low to moderate rates of inflation. Mining stocks, such as gold and platinum, and aluminum stocks have been good hedges against inflation.

Even a passively managed portfolio should be examined at various intervals with regard to the returns on the different investments as well as the changing economic conditions. Not all investments will achieve their anticipated returns and if they turn out to be poor performers, they may need to be liquidated.

Investors who do not have the knowledge and skills to manage their portfolios may turn to professional advisors. Financial planners and accountants offer advice on the planning and management of portfolios. For investors who do not wish to be involved in the management of their assets, there are professional money managers and trust departments of various institutions. Their fees are often a stated percentage of the total dollar amount of the portfolio, which often requires that the portfolio be substantial in dollar terms.

∎ Conclusion

Portfolio management begins with clear objectives. With careful analysis of personal and financial characteristics, an asset allocation plan of the categories of investments for the portfolio is made. The next step is the choice of the individual investments and the extent of the diversification among these investments. Finally, the management of the portfolio will be guided by the investment objectives. Managing a successful portfolio is more than selecting good investments.

Investors should invest only in those investments they fully understand. If the investor does not follow or fully understand the nuances of investing in individual stocks or bonds, the investor should stick with mutual funds. Besides the investments mentioned in this book there are many others that were not discussed. This does not mean that they are not important or that they do not have a place in your portfolio. Investing in stocks provides growth to a portfolio and, historically over long periods of time, stocks have outperformed other financial instruments.

■ References

Faerber, Esmé. *All About Bonds.* Chicago: Probus Publishing Co., 1993.

Glossary

Active strategy. An investment strategy designed to earn positive risk-adjusted returns through buying and selling securities to exploit market inefficiencies.

Adjustable-rate preferred stock. A preferred stock whose dividends are adjusted to reflect market rates of interest, thereby eliminating interest rate risk.

Aggressive stocks. Stocks that have beta coefficients greater than one.

American Depository Receipts (ADRs). Certificate issued by a U.S. bank representing ownership of a certain number of shares of a foreign company.

American Stock Exchange (AMEX). A national, organized security exchange which is the second largest in the U.S.A.

Annual report. A published report that corporations with at least 500 shareholders must distribute to its shareholders. It contains audited financial statements, performance reviews of the year and a discussion of the company's future prospects.

Arbitrage. The simultaneous purchase and sale of the same (or essentially similar) security in different markets to profit from pricing discrepancies.

Arbitrageur. A person who engages in arbitrage.

Ask (asked) price. The price at which the market maker is willing to sell a security to a buyer.

Asset allocation. Dividing investment funds among different types of investment assets.

At-the-money. An option whose strike price is the same as the market price of the underlying security.

Auction market. A phrase used to describe trading on the stock exchange.

Auditor's opinion. The opinion of a certified public accountant concerning the financial statements of a company with regard to their conformity with generally accepted accounting principles.

Averaging down. A strategy whereby an investor purchases more stock when the price declines to lower the average price of each of the shares.

Back-end load (or redemption fee). A fee charged by a mutual fund company when the investor sells shares back to the mutual fund.

Balance sheet. A financial statement that indicates the wealth of a company at a particular point in time.

Balanced funds. A mutual fund that invests in stocks, bonds and preferred stock to provide income and some capital appreciation.

Barron's **Confidence Index.** A ratio that shows the yield spread between high-grade bonds and more speculative bonds. This indicator is used by technical analysts to identify investors' confidence in the economy and the direction of the stock markets.

Bear market. A period during which stock prices are falling.

Beta coefficient. A measure of the systematic risk of a stock relative to the rest of the market.

Bid-and-asked price. The prices at which a security dealer offers to buy and sell a stock.

Bid price. The highest price at which a market maker is willing to purchase a stock from a seller.

Big board stocks. Stocks that trade on the New York Stock Exchange.

Blue-chip stock. The common stock of a large, well-established corporation that has a history of steady earnings and paying regular dividends.

Block trade. A trade of 10,000 shares or more.

Board of directors. Individuals elected by the shareholders to set the policies of the company.

Bond. A security issued by the borrower of funds who promises to repay the funds in addition to a stated rate of interest.

Book value. The net worth of a company (total assets minus the total liabilities).

Breadth of the market. The total number of shares traded on the market relative to the total issues listed in the market.

Breakout. When the price of a stock rises significantly above a resistance level or declines significantly below a support level.

Broker. An intermediary or agent who facilitates the trading of securities for investors.

Bull market. A period during which stock prices are rising.

Business cycle. A swing in economic activity over a period of time.

Business risk. The risk associated with the nature of the company's business.

Call feature. A provision in a bond or preferred stock issue that allows the issuer to call the issue at a call price (generally a premium price).

Call option. A contract that gives the right to buy 100 shares of the underlying common stock at a specified price within a specified period of time.

Capital appreciation. An increase in the value of the security over the acquisition value.

Capital Asset Pricing Model (CAPM). A model whereby stocks are valued according to their risk characteristics, and their returns are related to their beta coefficients.

Capital gain. The amount by which the proceeds from the sale of a security exceed the purchase price or cost basis.

Capital loss. The amount by which the proceeds from the sale of a security fall short of the purchase price or cost basis.

Cash account. A brokerage account that requires a cash payment for all security purchases.

Cash dividends. Dividends paid to shareholders in the form of cash.

Cash equivalents. Short-term securities that are highly liquid and carry little risk of capital loss.

CBOE. Chicago Board Options Exchange, the first organized exchange for put and call options.

Charting. The plotting of price and volume data of stocks to predict future price movements.

Chartist. A technical analyst who uses charts of price and volume movements of stocks to evaluate securities.

Churning. Excessive trading of customer accounts to generate commissions for the broker or brokerage firm.

Clearinghouse. An intermediary between the buyers and sellers of fu-tures and options contracts that guarantees the performance of the contracts by all the parties in the market.

Close. The last price that a security trades at during the trading session.

Closed-end fund. An investment company that offers a fixed number of shares in a one-time offering to the public. After the offering, these shares trade on the exchanges or the over-the-counter markets.

Commissions. Fees charged by agents or brokers to execute orders for their clients.

Common stock. Equity capital contributed by shareholders that gives them the right to vote on company policies and to receive dividends (if declared).

Common stock equivalent. Options, rights and warrants that can be used to purchase the underlying common stock of a company.

Confirmation. Written confirmation of the execution of an order.

Consolidated tape. A system that electronically reports the trades on all the exchanges and over-the-counter markets.

Constant dollar plan. A formula plan for investing in which the investor maintains a fixed dollar amount in the portion of the portfolio allocated to stocks or bonds. This requires buying or selling securities to maintain the fixed dollar amount on a periodic basis.

Constant ratio plan. A formula plan for investing whereby the investor maintains a fixed ratio among the types of securities in the portfolio. This requires buying or selling different types of securities to restore the constant ratio of the assets within the portfolio.

Contrarian. An investor with opposing views to the majority about the market. A contrarian would be buying when others are selling, and would be selling when the majority in the market are buying.

Convertible preferred stock. A preferred stock that may at the holder's option be converted into a fixed number of common shares of that company.

Country fund. A fund that invests in the securities of the named country.

Coupon payment. The periodic interest payments on a bond.

Coupon rate. The fixed rate of interest paid on a bond. The dollar amount of the interest payment is expressed as a percentage of the par value of the bond.

Covered option. The process of writing an option on an asset owned by the option writer.

Cum-rights. The period during which the preemptive rights accompany the purchase or sale of the underlying common stock.

Cumulative preferred. A preferred stock for which unpaid dividends accumulate in arrears and must be paid before any common dividends are paid.

Cumulative voting. A method of voting for corporate directors that allows shareholders to place their votes in any combination they choose.

Currency options. Options for which the underlying asset is a foreign currency.

Currency risk. The risk that a particular currency may depreciate in value relative to another currency.

Current asset. An asset that will be converted into cash within one year.

Current liability. An obligation that will be paid within one year.

Current ratio. A measure of a company's liquidity. The ability to pay off its current obligations from the turnover of its current assets into cash.

Cyclical industry. An industry whose financial health is tied to the economy.

Date of record. The date on which the shareholder must be a registered owner of the shares in order to receive a dividend.

Day order. An order that is canceled if it is not executed on the day it was entered.

Dealer. A person who makes a market in a particular security. Also referred to as a market maker or principal.

Debt-to-equity ratio. The ratio of total debt to total equity.

Declaration date. The date on which the board of directors announces the amount and date of the next dividend, rights offering or stock split.

Defensive stocks. Stocks whose prices remain stable or go up when the general economy is in recession. These stocks have beta coefficients of less than one.

Delisting. The process whereby a security is removed from trading on a particular exchange.

Diversification. A portfolio of different securities in different industries to minimize the risks of loss.

Dividend. A payment from profits made to shareholders by a corporation.

Dividend reinvestment plan (DRIP). A plan in which shareholders elect to have the company reinvest their cash dividends to purchase additional shares of stock of the company.

Dollar-cost averaging. Investing the same amount of money at regular intervals over a long period of time.

Dow Theory. A technical measure of the market based on the idea that the movement of prices as determined by the primary trend will determine the behavior of the market.

Dual fund. A closed-end fund that divides its returns between shareholders who receive the capital appreciation and those who receive the current income.

Dual listing. A security that trades on more than one exchange.

Earnings per share. A corporation's earnings divided by the number of its common shares outstanding.

Efficient market hypothesis. The theory that market prices of securities reflect all information and that consequently it is difficult to outperform the markets because securities are priced at their intrinsic values.

Equity fund. A mutual fund that invests the major part of its funds in common stocks and/or preferred stocks.

Ex-dividend date. The date on which the stock trades without the right to receive the dividend.

Ex-rights. The stock does not trade with the preemptive right.

Exercise price. For options, the price at which the buyer or seller may trade the stock with the option writer.

Expiration date. For an option contract, the date on which the right to buy or sell a security ceases.

Family of funds. Different funds with different investment objectives and portfolios managed by the same investment company.

Floor broker. A member of an organized security exchange who assists commission brokers in the handling of orders when they (commission brokers) have too many to fill.

Floor trader. A member of an exchange who trades solely for his or her own account.

Formula plans. Systematic methods of investing to take advantage of changing prices of securities.

Fourth market. A secondary market where institutional or large investors trade directly with one another, bypassing the brokers and dealers on the exchanges and over-the-counter markets.

Front-end load. A sales charge applied when an investor buys shares in a mutual fund that assesses a front-end load.

Fundamental analysis. The evaluation of companies as to their investment potential based on their financial, competitive and earnings position.

Global fund. A mutual fund that invests in the securities of companies located in the United States and abroad.

Good 'til canceled (GTC) order. An order to buy or sell securities that remains in effect until executed or canceled.

Growth and income fund. A mutual fund whose objectives are to earn both long-term growth and income.

Growth fund. A mutual fund whose objectives are long-term growth and capital gains.

Growth stocks. Common stocks of companies that are expected to experience high levels of growth in sales and profits.

Hedge fund. A mutual fund that seeks to offset some of its long positions with short positions.

Hedging. An attempt by an investor to eliminate risk by undertaking different investment positions whereby the gain on one investment offsets the loss on another.

Income fund. A common stock mutual fund that invests in stocks that have large dividends.

Income statement. A financial statement that shows earnings and profits over a period of time.

Income stock. A common stock of a company that pays large, regular dividends.

Index fund. A mutual fund that seeks to match the portfolio composition of a particular index.

Industry analysis. An evaluation of the investment attractiveness of an industry.

Inflation. The increases in the prices of goods and services in an economy.

Inflation hedge. An asset whose value varies in direct relationship with the level of prices.

Initial margin requirement. The minimum percentage of the margin purchase or short sale price of a stock that an investor must deposit with the brokerage firm.

Initial public offering (IPO). The initial offering of shares to the public.

Insider trading. Trading by investors who have access to unpublished information about the company.

Interest rate risk. The uncertainty of returns on investments due to changes in market rates of interest.

International fund. A mutual fund that invests in non-U.S. securities.

In-the-money option. An option whose strike price is more favorable than the market price of the underlying security.

Intrinsic value. Value of an option; equal to the market price minus the strike price.

Inverse floater. A derivative security that reflects the changes in price of the underlying bonds sold with them.

Investment companies. Companies that sell shares in diversified portfolios of investments to investors.

Investment objective. The desire of the investor to increase his or her wealth.

Investment plan. A written plan describing how the investor's funds will be invested to achieve the investor's objectives.

January effect. A study that showed stock returns to be higher in the month of January than in other months.

Junk bonds. Speculative bonds with ratings below investment grade.

Leverage. The use of debt or securities such as options and warrants to increase potential returns.

Limit order. An order to buy or sell a security at a specific price.

Liquidity. The ability to convert a security into cash with a minimum capital loss.

Listed security. A security traded on an organized security exchange.

Load charge. A sales commission or fee charged by load mutual funds when investors buy or sell shares in the fund.

Load fund. A mutual fund that charges a load fee.

Long position. The ownership of securities, as opposed to a short position where the investor has sold securities that are not owned.

Majority voting system. The most common corporate voting method in which each shareholder has one vote per share of stock and may vote that number of votes for each position on the board or for each policy issue.

Management fee. A fee charged for the management of mutual funds.

Margin account. An account with a brokerage firm in which the investor borrows a part of the purchase price from the brokerage firm to buy securities, or borrows the securities from the brokerage firm when securities are sold short.

Margin call. A demand by the brokerage firm for the investor to increase the equity in his or her margin account to the required level (set by the Fed).

Markdown. The difference in price between what a brokerage firm receives and what the investor receives for a stock sold in the over-the-counter market.

Market maker. See **Dealer**.

Market order. An order to buy or sell a security at the best available price.

Market risk. Uncertainty over the movement of market prices of securities.

Market timing. Active management of stocks that entails shifting funds between stocks and money market securities as economic conditions change.

Marketability. The ability to sell an investment quickly.

Markup. The difference between what an investor pays and the brokerage firm pays for a security purchased on the over-the-counter market.

Monetary policy. The regulation of the supply of money and credit to affect a country's economic growth, inflation, unemployment and financial markets.

Money market. The financial market where assets with maturities of one year or less are traded.

Money market funds. Mutual funds that invest in high-quality money market securities.

Municipal bond. A debt security issued by state, county, city and local governments to finance public needs.

Mutual fund. An investment company that manages the funds for shareholders who buy shares in the fund.

Naked option. An option on a security that is not owned by the writer.

NASD (National Association of Securities Dealers). The self-regulatory organization that monitors the activities of brokers and dealers in the over-the-counter market and establishes the rules and regulations.

NASDAQ (National Association of Securities Dealers Automated Quotation System). A computerized communications system that provides brokers, traders and market makers with the current bid and asked quotes for stocks on the over-the-counter market.

NASDAQ National Market System. A segment of the over-the-counter market that consists of the best capitalized, most actively traded stocks.

Net Asset Value (NAV). The total market value of the securities in a fund, less any liabilities, divided by the number of shares outstanding.

No-load fund. A mutual fund that does not charge a sales commission to buy shares in the fund.

NYSE (New York Stock Exchange). The largest U.S. stock exchange.

OCC (Option Clearing Corporation. Issues all options contracts and guarantees the terms of the contracts.

Odd lot. Less than 100 shares of stock.

Open-end fund. A mutual fund that has no limit on the number of shares that it can issue.

Open order. An order that remains in effect until it is either executed or canceled by the investor.

Opening price. The first trade price of the day for a security.

Option. A contract whereby one party has the right to buy or sell a specific security at a specified price within a time period from another party.

Out-of-the-money. An option with no intrinsic value.

Over-the-counter market (OTC). Consists of dealers, linked by a computer system, that make a market in many securities.

Overbought. A technical term pertaining to securities that have risen significantly in price and are likely to decline in price in the near future.

Oversold. A technical term pertaining to securities that have fallen significantly in price and are likely to rise in price in the near future.

Par value. A value that is assigned to a stock when it is issued. Does not mean much for common stock from an investment point of view.

Participating preferred stock. A preferred stock that pays a fixed dividend and participates in any additional earnings that may be distributed to common shareholders.

Passive investment strategy. A strategy of buying and holding a well diversified portfolio of securities.

Payment date. Date on which dividends are paid to investors on record.

Payout ratio. The percentage of the company's earnings paid in dividends to shareholders.

Penny stocks. Low-priced stocks that usually sell for less than a dollar.

Pink sheets. The daily published listing of some of the thinly traded over-the-counter stocks.

Poison pill. A phrase used to describe a security that has features to defend against a hostile takeover.

Preemptive right. The right of common shareholders to buy new shares before they are offered to other investors.

Preferred stock. A hybrid security that carries a fixed dividend and allows preferred shareholders preference over common shareholders for claims to assets in the event of liquidation.

Price/Earnings Ratio (P/E). A measure of the number of times that a stock's price exceeds its earnings.

Primary market. The market for the sale of securities by the issuer to the public for the first time.

Prospectus. A condensed version of the registration statement filed with the SEC for a new issue; designed to provide information to prospective investors.

Proxy. A form that allows a shareholder to vote in absentia by transferring the vote to a designated party.

Purchasing power risk. The uncertainty associated with inflation.

Put option. A contract that gives the owner the right to sell a security at a specified price within a time period.

Random walk theory. The theory that stock price movements are unpredictable and independent of previous price movements.

Record date. The date on which a shareholder must be a registered owner in order to receive dividends declared by the company.

Red herring. A preliminary prospectus that does not show the security's price or the date of the offering.

Redemption fee (back-end load). A fee charged by some mutual funds when shareholders sell shares in the fund.

Reinvestment risk. The uncertainty related to the rate at which dividends paid from one investment will be reinvested.

Resistance level. A price level to which a security (or market) cannot rise above.

Retained earnings. The past and current earnings of a company that have not been paid out in dividends.

Right. An option issued to shareholders that allows them to buy a specified number of the company's new shares at a subscription price.

Round lot. One hundred shares of stock or multiples of 100.

Rule 12b-1. A SEC rule that allows mutual funds to charge their marketing and distribution expenses directly or indirectly to the net asset value.

Secondary market. The market in which the securities that are traded have been issued at some previous point.

Sector fund. A mutual fund that specializes in a segment of the economy, such as technology, energy or gold.

Security analysis. The process of gathering information to determine the intrinsic value of a stock for investment purposes.

Settlement date. The date on which the securities and cash are exchanged after the purchase and sale.

Short interest. The number of a company's shares that are sold short and have not been covered or bought back.

Short position. To sell an asset that is not owned in the hopes of buying it back in the future at a lower price.

SIPC (Securities Investors Protection Corporation). A government agency that guarantees the safety of brokerage accounts up to $500,000, of which no more than $100,000 may be for cash.

S&P 500 Index. A value-weighted index based on the share prices of 500 large companies.

Specialist. An exchange member who makes a market in listed securities.

Spread. The difference between the bid and asked price of a security.

Stock dividend. Dividends paid to shareholders in the form of additional shares of the company's stock.

Stock split. When a company increases the number of shares outstanding by exchanging a specified number of new shares for each existing share.

Stop limit order. A trading order that specifies both a limit price and a stop price. When the price of a security reaches the stop price, a limit order is created at the limit price.

Stop order. A trading order that specifies a stop price. When the security reaches the stop price, a market order is created.

Straddle. A combination of a put and call option on the same security with the same strike price and expiration date.

Street name. Registration of the investor's securities in the brokerage firm's name.

Strike price. For options, the price at which the buyer or seller may trade the stock with the option writer.

SuperDOT. A NYSE system that automatically routes small, routine orders to the specialists.

Support level. A price level to which a security falls and then rises above.

Technical analysis. A method of evaluating securities using past price and volume data.

Thin market. A market with few buyers or sellers for a security.

Third market. A secondary security market where exchange listed stocks trade on the over-the-counter.

Ticker tape. A tape device that displays stock market trades.

Trading post. The location on the floor of the exchange where a specialist for a particular stock is located.

Transfer agent. A designated agent of a corporation that administers the transfer of shares between old and new owners.

Transfer tax. A New York State tax on the transfer of common stock.

Treasury stock. Outstanding stock that is repurchased by the issuing company.

Trend. A technical term describing the price movements of a security or of the market over a period of time.

Uncovered option (naked option). An option on a security that is not owned by the writer.

Underwriter. A brokerage firm that acts as an intermediary between the company and the purchasers of the securities in the primary market.

Unit investment trust. An unmanaged investment company that has a finite life and raises funds from investors to purchase a portfolio of investments.

Unlisted stock. Stocks not listed on the exchanges.

Unsystematic risk. The risk of a security that does not relate to the market and can be diversified away.

Uptick. A trade in a security that is made at a higher price than the previous trade.

Volatility. The amount by which the price of a security rises or falls during a period of time.

Volume. The number of shares of stock traded over a period of time.

Warrant. A contract issued by a corporation, allowing the holder the right to purchase that corporation's common stock at a stated price within a specific time period.

Wash sale. The Internal Revenue Service regulation prohibiting the realization of a capital loss on a security and then immediately buying back that security.

Writer. An individual who writes or sells an options contract.

Yield. The percentage rate of return on an investment.

Index

About the Author

Esmé Faerber is an assistant professor of business and accounting at Rosemont College. She is a licensed CPA in Pennsylvania, and is also a consultant in accounting and finance.

Professor Faerber is the author of *Managing Your Investments, Savings and Credit* (Probus, 1992), and *All About Bonds* (Probus, 1993).